BENTHAM'S
POLITICAL
THOUGHT

BENTHAM'S POLITICAL THOUGHT

EDITED BY

BHIKHU PAREKH

BOOKS
10 East 53d St., New York 10022
(a division of Harper & Row Publishers, Inc.)

PUBLISHED IN THE U.S.A. 1973 BY
HARPER & ROW PUBLISHERS, INC.
BARNES & NOBLE IMPORT DIVISION

ISBN-06-495379-3 HARDBACK
ISBN-06-495380-7 PAPERBACK

PRINTED IN GREAT BRITAIN

Contents

CONTENTS

Preface

Although Bentham wrote voluminously in the field of political philosophy, he did not write any one single work that, like Hobbes's *Leviathan* or Hegel's *Philosophy of Right* or even like Rousseau's *Social Contract*, comprises the essential outlines of his political philosophy. A good deal of interesting material lies scattered in his various published works; what is worse, much of it still lies buried in his manuscripts in University College, London, the British Museum and the University of Geneva.[1] The present work is an attempt to construct a coherent statement of Bentham's political philosophy from these writings.

As the book is designed to offer a statement of Bentham's political philosophy, its contents and structure are naturally determined by the editor's conception of what is expected in a work on political philosophy. However much we may disagree on the nature and scope of political philosophy, we would at least agree, first, that politics, irrespective of how it is defined, has an inescapable moral dimension and cannot be understood without some general conception of the type of creature man is, and second, that whatever else it is, philosophy is an attempt to provide a co-ordinated framework of general categories in terms of which to comprehend human experience. In other words, most of us would agree that an author's political philosophy cannot be dissociated from his moral philosophy, his theory of man and his general philosophy. It will be agreed, further, that philosophical analysis of political activity involves discussion of the nature of the state, law and sovereignty, the way the state operates and cannot but operate, how the state should ideally be organized, and the way political issues should properly be discussed and debated. Although the administratively and pedagogically convenient separation between 'political philosophy' and 'political institutions' in our universities has tended to inspire a rather narrow view of political philosophy that places consideration of the details of political organization outside its scope, many of us would agree that this is unfortunate. At any rate, like nearly all past

7

political philosophers, Bentham took the view that, since it was part of a political philosopher's concern to explore the type of political society that best accords with human nature and most effectively copes with problems thrown up by human predicament, he cannot avoid discussing the structure and composition of government and the proper relationship between its various parts.

The book therefore begins with two chapters on Bentham's ontology; the first outlines his theory of general and political reality, and the second his logical procedure for explaining and analysing different types and levels of what he calls fictions. The next two chapters outline his theory of man. Chapter 5 contains Bentham's exposition and defence of the principle of utility, and Chapter 6 includes his analysis of the nature of virtue. Since pleasure and pain are central to Bentham's account of human life, Chapter 7 outlines what he means by them and how he proposes to measure them. The rest of the book deals with Bentham's political thought proper. Chapters 8 to 13 are concerned with his analysis of the nature and structure of the state and of certain key concepts like right, power and law. Chapters 14 to 18 outline his ideal political society. The last three chapters are concerned with the nature of political argument. Chapter 19 expounds and exposes the fallacies which Bentham thinks are commonly employed by 'sinister interests', while Chapter 20 deals with the fallacious mode of reasoning that, in his view, was characteristic of the radicals of his time. Chapter 21 outlines what Benthem considers to be the only valid mode of political discourse, and Chapter 22 sums up his political thought in the form of a catechism. The Appendices are statements of Bentham's views on problems intimated, but not pursued, in the text.

For the composition of the book I have relied either on the works Bentham himself published in his lifetime or on his manuscripts. This is so because nearly all Bentham's editors have tampered with his manuscripts. Dumont, who popularised his works on the Continent, was the worst of them all, but Peregrine Bingham and Richard Doane, who edited Bentham's *Book of Fallacies* and *Constitutional Code* respectively, were not much better. Compared to them, much-maligned Bowring is an exemplary editor. Although he unwisely interspersed Bentham's texts with passages translated from Dumont or selected from other manuscripts, and although he occasionally rewrote or omitted Bentham's sentences, he at least transcribed the texts fairly accurately and, what is most important in an editor, did not use them as a vehicle to propound his own philosophy. However, as Bowring did not always follow the order of and sometimes recast Bentham's manuscripts in the way indicated, I have ignored his collected works completely and relied entirely on the originals. Except when absolutely essential, I have not indicated Bowring's deviations. That would have involved scores of footnotes. As for Chapters 11, 12 and 13, which are included in Professor H. L. A. Hart's edition of *Of Laws in General*, it will be seen that my reading of Bentham's manuscripts differs from his in several places. Since Professor Hart's work is widely used by Bentham scholars, I have indicated in appropriate places where our readings differ. All the manuscripts used in the book are in University College, London, and are identified by the box and the folder or page number.

Bentham is a very difficult man to edit. Some of his manuscripts are more like a first draft and, in some cases, are mere sketches, and therefore not ready for publication. Even those clearly prepared for publication pose difficulties. They are studded with brackets, leaving one wondering whether Bentham wanted entries in the brackets to be omitted. In a few cases, again, there are phrases and sentences in the margin with no clear indication as to where they are to be inserted. Furthermore, in several cases, Bentham offers an alternative version of a word, a phrase and even a sentence on top of the original version, leaving it to the editor to make a choice. What is worse, some interlinear insertions are incomplete, leaving out a verb, a subject or a preposition. Again, Bentham sometimes remarks that a sentence or a paragraph on another page is to be inserted in a certain place, but there may be nothing on that page that could be related to the original reference. Bentham's punctuation marks are notorious. He often uses hyphens where we would use a comma, and a colon where we would use a semi-colon; and sometimes a very long sentence has no punctuation marks at all. There are also cases where Bentham repeats whole or parts of sentences and even illustrative examples.

In all these cases, it seemed sensible to be guided by the twin considerations of clarity and consistency. Following the lead of the Bentham Committee I have used my judgment and omitted brackets and/or their contents when they seemed superfluous or when contextual evidence showed that Bentham wished them to be omitted. As for Bentham's alternative formulations, a slightly different policy had to be followed. As several interlinear insertions are incomplete, to have given both the original and the alternative version, as Professor Baumgardt does, would have made the text totally unintelligible. At the same time, however, there are a few places where alternative versions make a slightly new point, and not to give them would have meant sacrificing part of Bentham's meaning. It seemed best therefore to follow the general policy of giving only one version, but mentioning the alternative formulation whenever it seemed to clarify or add to the meaning of the text. As to the choice between the original and the alternative version, it seemed wrong to choose only the one or the other in all cases. Sometimes it is the original entry, but usually, it is the interlinear insertion that is incomplete or unclear. It seemed best therefore to choose whatever gave greater clarity and consistency to the text. As for Bentham's punctuation marks, they have been altered whenever necessary in the interest of clarity. When Bentham misses out a word, it has been supplied and placed in a square bracket. Brackets occurring in the manuscript are printed as round brackets. When there are entries in the margin that Bentham wished to insert in the text, they have been inserted into what seemed to be their proper places and indicated thus in the footnote. Bentham's footnotes are indicated by suprascript letters, and the editor's by suprascript numerals. In the interest of uniformity, both Bentham's and the editor's notes have a continuous sequence for each chapter of the text. Bentham's notes appear at the foot of the page, and the editor's at the end of the book. Where the manuscript has a title, I have used it for the corresponding chapter. In other cases I have made one up and put it in a square bracket. In the interest of clarity a large number of words that Bentham italicises or puts in capital letters have been de-italicised or put in small letters.

My concern in the book is not to edit a definitive text of one or more of Bentham's works but to produce a coherent statement of his political philosophy within clearly defined limits of space. While complete chapters have been given wherever possible, there have been places, especially in chapters 15 to 20, where this was clearly impossible. Even here, however, an attempt has been made to include a complete discussion of one point rather than to give a few lines on a number of topics. If the book gives a reasonably coherent account of Bentham's political philosophy and inspires students of Bentham to go to original works, the labour will not have been undertaken in vain.

I am grateful to Dr John Micklewight of the Bentham Project for his help in deciphering parts of the manuscript and for checking chapters 1, 2, 6 and 18 against relevant manuscripts. Dr Michael Woodstock and Mr M. R. A. Harris of the Bentham Project were also helpful in deciphering parts of Bentham's writings. I am also grateful to the staff of University College, London, for access to the manuscripts and for other assistance, and to the Librarian for his permission to publish them. Miss England, Miss Hallam and Mrs Percival were expecially helpful in photocopying bundles of Bentham manuscripts. My thanks are due to Mrs Josephine Naylor, Miss Susan Davies, Mrs Susan McRobert and to Miss Charmian Hall for typing the mss. Mrs Naylor's expertise in deciphering Bentham's writing was especially valuable. My thanks are also due to David Croom for encouraging me to compose this work and for bearing with its slow progress. Dr Gordon Hutton kindly read the Introduction and made useful stylistic changes. I would like to thank Pramila and Raj for their help in checking the final text against the manuscript. My more general debt is to Professors Michael Oakeshott, Maurice Cranston and Elie Kedourie who guided my work on Bentham in its early years. To them I am deeply grateful for their help and many acts of kindness over the years.

Introduction

Jeremy Bentham was born in 1748 and died in 1832. A clue to his long and uneventful life is perhaps provided by a dream he had in 1780. 'I dreamt the other night that I was a founder of a sect; of course, a personage of great sanctity and importance. It was the sect of the utilitarians.'[1] Historically speaking the dream was truly prophetic. Bentham did spend the rest of his life spelling out the implications of the 'sacred' principle of utility and gathered around him a band of devoted disciples. There was hardly a subject on which he did not write; he wrote on ontology, logic, methodology, psychology, ethics, law, politics, economics and education, to name but a few. It is impossible to discuss all these in a short introduction, it would be best to concentrate on three aspects of his thought that are likely to be of greatest interest to students of political philosophy. They are Bentham's psychological and moral theory, his analysis of the nature of political society, and his theory of the nature and functions of government. Of these, the first has received a great deal of attention in recent discussions of Bentham, and therefore a few words should suffice.[2] The other two have not been given the amount of attention they deserve,[3] and therefore we shall concentrate on them.

I

Bentham's psychological and moral theory is relatively simple. He is a psychological and ethical hedonist, and expresses his basic position fairly clearly in the opening paragraph of his *Introduction to the Principles of Morals and Legislation*:

Nature has placed mankind under the governance of two sovereign masters, pain and pleasure. It is for them alone to point out what we ought to do, as well as to determine what we shall do. On the one hand the standard of right and wrong, on the other chain of causes and effects, are fastened to their throne. They

13

govern us in all we do, in all we say, in all we think: every effort we can make to throw off our subjection, will serve but to demonstrate and confirm it. In words a man may pretend to abjure their empire: but in reality he will remain subject to it all the while'.[4]

In Bentham's[5] view there can be no action without a cause, and what causes human action is a motive. Since the pursuit of pleasure and avoidance of pain are the only motives a man has, all human actions are and cannot but be caused by the desire for pleasure or aversion to pain. As Bentham puts it, 'take away all pleasure and all pain, and you have no desire', and without a desire, there can be no action.[6] If we took any human desire and analysed it into its basic components, we would see, says Bentham, that it is at bottom a desire for pleasure. A politician seeks office because he finds pleasure in exercising power; a businessman seeks wealth because he finds pleasure in owning and spending money; a martyr dies for his cause because he finds more pleasure in it than in anything else. Again, take any of the moral virtues like temperance and justice or moral vices like cruelty. What makes them virtues, Bentham argues, is the fact that they promote human happiness. Cruelty is bad because it causes pain; temperance is a virtue because it avoids the pains of excesses, and justice is a desirable quality because it 'prevents the pain of disappointment'. Or take, again, the ideas of duty and obligation. A man discharges a legal obligation because he fears the punishment that would otherwise follow, and he fulfils a moral duty because he loathes the pains of social disapproval and those arising from 'pangs' of conscience. On the basis of this primitive analysis Bentham concludes that man by the very constitution of his nature desires pleasure and loathes pain.

Bentham goes on to offer an equally unsatisfactory account of why he thinks pleasure alone is good. He says that by good we mean likeable or enjoyable. Now he has already shown that man likes pleasure. He thinks it therefore follows that pleasure is *a good*. Since Bentham thinks he has already shown how all good things are pursued only because of their hedonistic content, it also follows that pleasure is *the good*, the only good there is. He goes even further. By good we mean whatever we enjoy; but this is also how pleasure itself is defined, pleasure being the sensation we enjoy. Thus pleasure and good are conceptually identical and represent two different ways of describing the same thing. Pleasure, in other words, is not just *a* good, or *the* good, but *goodness itself*. To say that X is good but not pleasant, or that Y is pleasant though not good, is, in Bentham's view, to make a self-contradictory statement.

Since pleasure alone is good, Bentham argues, it is only rational to have as much of it as possible. To pursue less of it when more is available, or to forego opportunities of pursuing it, is patently irrational.[7] It is an action without a reason. Further, since pleasure alone is good, Bentham argues, it is good irrespective of whether it is your pleasure or mine. If an action of mine gives you two units of happiness and me only one, it is irrational of me to prefer my own happiness to yours. Bentham therefore concludes that a moral agent should aim to promote the greatest happiness in the aggregate, this being the only rational and right end of human action.[8]

When formulated so widely the principle of utility makes demands that Bentham knows are impossible to meet. It requires a moral agent to ask himself continually how best he can maximise the total quantity of happiness in the universe. It implies, for example, that when a man is deliberating whether or not to visit a friend in hospital, he should ask himself if he cannot increase the overall quantity of happiness by, say, writing letters to the victims of an Iranian earthquake or Indian famine, or by going from house to house raising money for a charity. Since the possibilities of increasing happiness are myriad, and no individual can be expected to know about them all, Bentham knows that if his standard is not to founder on the rock of practicability, he must draw a line somewhere. For the most part therefore he formulates the principle of utility as a 'principle which approves or disapproves of every action whatsoever according to the tendency which it appears to have to augment or diminish the happiness of the party whose interest is in question'. The last phrase 'the party whose interest is in question' is crucial.

Although Bentham does not spell it out in any detail, he seems to want to say that every action takes place within a definite context, which delimits the class of men whose interests constitute the moral agent's primary concern. Since different individuals occupy different positions in society,[9] the range of persons whose interests are affected by their actions naturally varies. An ordinary man in ordinary circumstances undertakes actions that affect a relatively small number of people, and therefore he can only be expected to take account of the interests of these men. Thus in deciding whether or not to visit a friend in hospital, I do not need to think of the starving millions in the Third World or of countless old age pensioners I could cheer up, but only of those likely to be affected by whatever decision I take in this particular case and context. If I had promised to look after my neighbour's children who would be upset if I were to leave them alone and whose misery might cause a great deal of pain to their paralysed mother, I should weigh up the total pain likely to be caused to all these individuals against the amount of pleasure my visit might give to my friend, and decide accordingly. The government is in a different position. It is the custodian of the interests of the community as a whole and its actions affect all its members. Its context of action, and its moral constituency, are much wider than those of a private individual. It should therefore promote the happiness of the entire community.

Characteristically Bentham looked for a simple formula that could neatly encapsulate his moral theory. He thought Priestley's expression, 'the greatest happiness of the greatest number', served this purpose well and accordingly used it in the Preface to his *Fragment on Government*, published in 1776.[10] But he soon began to have doubts. In his next work, *Introduction to Principles of Morals and Legislation*, he drops the phrase altogether. It does not appear in any of his subsequent writings either. The expressions which Bentham generally uses are 'universal interest', 'interest of all' and 'happiness of the community as a whole'.[11] A diligent but by no means exhaustive examination of the Mss reveals that after an absence of nearly forty years the phrase makes a sudden reappearance in 1816.[12] Thereafter it keeps appearing in nearly all his subsequent writings. In 1829, however, Bentham began to have second thoughts. In his *Article on Utilitarian*ism written during that year he remarked that he had now come to see that the phrase, the greatest happiness of the greatest number, was self-contradictory.[13] He argues that distributing a minority of 2000 men as slaves among the majority of 2001 promotes the happiness of the greatest number, but not the greatest happiness in aggregate. He therefore decides to drop the appendage of the 'greatest number' and to use the shorter phrase, the greatest happiness. Why Bentham dropped the longer phrase after 1776 and revived it around 1816 are questions we cannot pursue at length here, and can only observe that the explanation probably lies in the change in Bentham's political attitude.[14] Bentham probably felt that in referring to the happiness of the *greatest number*, the phrase excluded the happiness of the rich and privileged few, and therefore implied political radicalism to which he was unsympathetic for a long time. As he became a radical around 1816 and realised that the democratic cause could be pursued only by attacking the interest of the few, he probably felt that he had to drop the phrases 'universal interest' and 'happiness of the community as a whole', and accordingly revived the more accurate phrase, the greatest happiness of the greatest number.

II

Bentham's account of political life is based on his psychological and ethical hedonism. If man is, and cannot but be, as he has described him, Bentham argues, political life can be fully explained only in terms of man's desire for pleasure and aversion to pain. All other explanations, in his view, rest on false psychological foundations and must remain unsatisfactory. In what follows we shall outline Bentham's hedonistic account of how political societies come into being and are held together.

Bentham defines political society as follows. 'When a number of persons (whom we may style subjects) are supposed to be in the *habit* of paying *obedience* to a person, or an assemblage of persons, of a known and certain description (whom we may call *governor* or *governors*) such persons altogether (subjects and governors) are said to be in a state of political society'.[15] When a number of persons, however, are 'in the habit of conversing with each other, at the same time that they are not in any such habit as mentioned above, they are said to be in a state of *natural* society'. A natural society, which Bentham also calls a state of nature, is a society because men in it are mutually related, but it is a natural not a political society because they do not have a common superior whom they habitually obey. Bentham believes that men have always lived in some kind of society and that therefore there can never be a state of nature which is not some kind of society.

A political society is a society in which some person or body of persons is acknowledged as a common superior. The common superior himself may or may not be in the habit of obeying anyone outside his community. If he is not, he is sovereign, 'a person or assemblage of persons to whose will a whole political community are (no matter on what account) supposed to be in a disposition to pay obedience, and that in preference to the will of any other person', and his is an independent political society. If the supreme authority in a political society is in the habit of obeying an outsider, it is not sovereign, and the political society concerned is not an independent political society. Inasmuch as its members obey a government, it is a political society, although not an independent political society.[16] A sovereign may from time to time bow to the authority of another, for example, when it is militarily weak; but as long he does not acknowledge another sovereign as his *superior* and render him *habitual* obedience, his sovereignty remains unaffected.

The habit of obedience in a political society, Bentham maintains, is a matter of degree and can take a number of forms. There is no known society in which it is totally absent; and 'as long as man remains man' there will always be occasions when he will disobey his ruler. 'Perfectly' natural and perfectly political societies are therefore never to be found in practice. They represent logical extremes, and all societies fall somewhere between them. As the habit of obedience in a society increases, that is, as more and more of its members engage in more and more acts of obedience, the society in question moves away from the state of nature and becomes more political. Bentham argues that the habit of obedience in Britain, for example, was 'more perfect' in the time of Saxons than in that of Britons, and is 'more perfect' now than in the time of Saxons. In other words Britain today is a 'more perfect' political society than in former days. It is this increase in the degree of a society's political character, that is, it is the increase in the habit of obedience and the consequent moving away from the state of nature, that in Bentham's view constitutes political 'progress'.

He insists that unless the habit of obedience in a society has reached a certain degree, it cannot be said to be a political society proper; but what such a degree is, he does not explain. It is essential that a *large* number of its members should *generally* be in a *habit* of obeying a common authority, but Bentham does not examine how large a number it should be, and how often and how long they should render obedience in order for it to count as a habit.[17] Except in certain clear cut cases, a judgement as to whether a society is natural or political must therefore remain somewhat arbitrary.

The habit of obedience, as we remarked earlier, can also take a number of forms. There may be societies in which subjects obey their sovereign in all matters; but there may also be societies in which they obey him in some respects and another man in others. In one society, for example, subjects may accept their sovereign's jurisdiction in religious matters as well, while in another they might accept someone else, say, the Pope as their religious 'sovereign'. Again, (and this is a point to which we shall later return) the highest political power in one society might be vested in one man, while in another it might be shared by several men. Again, as we saw earlier, the civil sovereign in one society might be subject to someone outside it, while in another society he might not be so subject. In the latter case, although not independent, the society in question is a political society. A political society, Bentham goes on, may be one in which people obey a common superior on all occasions; or it may be in an intermittently political society in which they obey him only on some, and remain in a natural condition on other, occasions, as is the case with American Indians who subordinate themselves to a common chief in times of war but return to their customary natural condition upon the return of peace. Theirs is, in his view, a society which is 'alternately in a state of nature and a state of government'.[18] Bentham cannot see why a habit of obedience should not 'suffer interruptions'.

To say that a sovereign is supreme over a given body of men is to say that he is able to make these men comply with his will. In Bentham's view he can do so in one of two ways. First, he can so influence their *will* that they will want to do what he commands them to do. Will is created by motives; motives, in turn, are only desires looked at from a certain point of view; and all human desires are either desires to seek pleasure or to avoid pain. The sovereign can therefore influence his subjects' will either by offering them pleasure or reward in case of their compliance, or by threatening them with painful consequences in the event of their non-compliance. For a variety of obvious reasons Bentham thinks that the threat of inflicting pain is the most potent. But the threat might not work, and then the sovereign will need to resort to the second way of ensuring compliance, which consists in affecting his subjects' *body* by inflicting physical pain on them or by restricting their movements. The power exercised over the subjects' will, Bentham calls the *power of imperation*; and that exercised over their body, he calls the *power of contrectation*. The former power is 'ultimately based on' and derived from the latter, which therefore is the foundation of the sovereign's sovereignty.

The power of contrectation or, simply, the power to punish is ultimately a physical power, and is derived from 'muscular strength'. A sovereign's own physical power is clearly never enough to subdue all his subjects, and therefore he has to rely on the physical power of his subjects. He can only hope that for the most part his subjects will be disposed to obey his commands, and that when some do not, the rest, at least the army, will offer him physical assistance in punishing them. In other words the sovereign's power, his sovereignty, is ultimately derived from his subject's disposition to obey him. If they, or a large majority of them, are not disposed to obey him, he clearly has no power. And a sovereign without power, a sovereign who is not obeyed, is by definition not a sovereign. It is because all political power is ultimately derived from subjects obedience that Bentham defines political society in terms of disposition to obedience rather than the sovereign's *right* or *authority* to command, in terms of what *subjects* do rather than what the *sovereign* demands.

The amount of the sovereign's power then is 'but the sum of the physical powers of all those who in point of fact are disposed to lend their hands' to him.[19] At its maximum his power is equal to the 'muscular strength' of all his subjects. In practice however it is always less, and varies 'in proportion to the popularity' of the sovereign in general and of the law in question in particular.[20] His subjects will be more disposed to obey him, the more they think he is promoting their interests. But even a popular sovereign occasionally makes unpopular laws which his subjects might not be inclined to support. He will therefore find it easier to execute one law rather than another, and he might even find that he is completely powerless with respect to some particular law. In other words, the sovereign's power 'is liable to much diversity and continual fluctuation'. It admits of degrees and varies from law to law, 'from day to day', from individual to individual and from occasion to occasion. Although subjects' fear of the sovereign gives him the *minimum* power he needs to sustain a general disposition to obedience, it is their approval of his actions that gives him the *maximum* power. In Bentham's view fear operates only when there is a chance of detection, and therefore does not guarantee obedience and support when a subject thinks his disobedience will not be noticed. Bentham also argues that men generally offer far more of their strength when they agree with what is required of them than when they do not. He maintains that, although it may seem surprising, a democratic government is generally far more powerful than a despotic one.

Like David Hume, Bentham argues that the subjects' disposition to obey their sovereign is ultimately a product of habit and considerations of pain and pleasure. He speculates that people must have originally obeyed their sovereign because of their fear of what he might do to them,[21] but that gradually the perception of the advantages of civil society would have led them to continue their obedience and so converted it into a habit and later into a disposition. He allows[22] that there might even have been 'a convention' where people consciously resolved to continue to obey their sovereign. But he thinks that this is historically rare and that, inasmuch as what people will at one moment they can just as easily revoke at another, such a contract cannot provide a lasting foundation for the disposition to obedience. By contrast habit, being 'the result of a system of conduct of which commencement is lost in the abyss of time', is much more reliable and durable. However, even a long-established habit of obedience can break down if a subject finds it in his interest to disobey a law, and therefore the fear of the sovereign is necessary to reinforce his habit of obedience. No doubt, a subject will be punished only if most others support the sovereign; and it may be that on some particular occasion they are not disposed to support him, so that a subject who refused to obey the sovereign will go unpunished. However the fact is that no subject can predict precisely how the vast majority of his fellow-subjects will react. This ignorance of each other's intention further reinforces their habit of obedience. Once a disposition to obedience is generated by fear, self-interest and habit,[23] it acquires its own momentum and reinforces the three factors responsible for creating it. The more the people obey their sovereign, the more powerful he becomes and the greater the protection he is able to offer to life, liberty and property; and the stronger he is and the greater the protection he gives, the stronger is the influence of fear, self-interest and habit, and the firmer and more widespread becomes the disposition to obey him.

Bentham argues that from the fact that it is the subjects' disposition to obey the sovereign that constitutes the 'efficient cause' of his sovereignty, two conclusions follow. First, the sovereign's power is always limited in practice, and second, there is no reason why sovereignty cannot be shared or divided.

The sovereign's subjects are not things or animals but men who have definite moral, social and religious beliefs, who follow definite moral, social and religious rules, and who have fairly firm ideas on what the sovereign should and should not do. The sovereign might be able to and, indeed, should try to change the beliefs and practices that appear to him harmful to public well-being, but until he has actually succeeded in doing so, they impose limits on what he can do. Taking a few historical examples, Bentham argues that the Jews were willing to do everything for Antiochus except eat pork, the exiled Protestants were prepared to do everything for their French king except go to the Mass, and the Catholics in Britain today are willing to obey every law save one requiring them to stay away from the Mass. It is perfectly natural and indeed a common experience, says Bentham, for a people to 'be disposed to obey the commands of one man against the world in relation to one sort of act and those of another man in relation to another sort of act', or those of one man at one time ('for instance the dictator of Rome') and those of another man or set of men at another time ('for instance, the assembly of the governing part of the Roman People'). In religious matters Catholics recognise the authority of the Pope and not that of their civil sovereign, and similarly Jews acknowledge the authority of Moses. A sovereign who tried to assert his power over their religious practices will only provoke a rebellion that might expose his powerlessness.

Indeed Bentham seems to think that a civil sovereign cannot help recognising the authority of other men and bodies within and outside his society. The Pope, for example, holds considerable power over Catholics, and threatens them with powerful religious sanctions in case of disobedience. If the civil sovereign did not recognise the power of the Pope, he would have to punish him for committing the offence of inflicting 'mental injuries'[24] on his subjects, and this no civil sovereign can do. In the ultimate analysis the sovereign's subjects obey him because they think it more advantageous to do so. If they felt that obeying someone else's commands was more to their advantage, they would do so, irrespective of the harm their civil sovereign might cause them. Power, in Bentham's view, is ultimately created by peoples' fears, and therefore there are as many centres of power in a society as there are men whom they fear. Each centre limits and is limited by the rest. Paradoxical though it may seem, it is the very nature of power, and therefore of sovereignty, that the more it ignores the limits set by the nature and habits of those over whom it is exercised, the less effective it becomes. Bentham argues that the theory of absolute sovereignty which insists on the sovereign's power to regulate all areas of life and asserts that limited sovereignty is a contradiction in terms is therefore false. What is more, it is 'dangerous'. By creating the illusion that he is not really sovereign unless he decides all matters in his society, the theory of absolute sovereignty encourages the sovereign to throw his weight around in all areas of life. This overstrains his subjects' disposition to obey him and cannot but provoke a rebellion which must ultimately destroy his power.

Bentham thinks that not only is the sovereign's power limited, it can also be divided and shared. If sovereignty was indivisible, we would have to say 'that there is no such thing as government in the German empire; nor in the Dutch provinces; nor in the Swiss Cantons; nor was of old in the Achaean league'[25]; and that, in Bentham's view, is absurd. Bentham repeats this argument at another place. 'In the United Provinces, in the Helvetic, or even in the Germanic body, where is that one assembly in which an absolute power over the whole resides? where was there in the Roman Commonwealth?'[26] Although he does not discuss the point explicitly, Bentham seems to wish to say that in a federal state each unit is sovereign in areas clearly recognised to be within its sphere of jurisdiction, and that all of them are 'conjunctively' sovereign in areas of collective and common jurisdiction.

Bentham also examines other cases of divided sovereignty. He suggests that under a system of judicial review where courts have the power to annul laws, 'a portion of the supreme power'[27] is transferred from the legislature to the judges and that therefore the former's sovereignty is limited. However, since the power to annul laws is only a 'negative power' and therefore 'much inferior' to the positive power to make laws, Bentham thinks it would be going 'too far' to say that supreme authority is here transferred from legislative to the judicial power or that this is a case of divided or shared sovereignty. But taking the case of a political society in which one person or body has 'every power of the state', except that in case of a public accusation another has the power to pronounce and execute judgment on him, Bentham argues that, although the latter's authority is only occasionally exercised, it still includes the right to judge and punish the former, and that therefore it is 'plain' that neither of them alone but both 'conjunctively' must be considered sovereign. Bentham finds it difficult to believe how anyone can maintain that sovereignty is *both* unlimited and indivisible. In the cases above cited, one either says that both the legislature and the judiciary, or both the federal and the state governments, are 'conjunctively' sovereign, in which case one must admit that sovereignty is divisible; or else one says that only one of them is sovereign in which case its sovereignty, although not shared, is clearly limited.[28]

Not only can sovereignty be shared and divided; Bentham even hints at the possibility of a plurality of sovereigns in a single political society. He points to the Roman Commonwealth as an example of a political society without a single absolute sovereign. Although Bentham does not mention it, Professor Hart is right that Bentham was probably aware of Hume's famous essay, *Of*

Some Remarkable Customs.[29] Hume observed that in the Roman Republic the *comitia centuriata* and the *comitia tributa* established two distinct legislatures, 'each of which possesses full and absolute authority within itself, and stands in no need of the other's assistance in order to give validity to its acts'. This, he went one, 'may appear beforehand altogether impracticable . . . but there is no need for searching long in order to prove the reality of the foregoing supposition; for this was actually the case with the Roman Republic'. Bentham remarks that situations of dual sovereignty lead to conflict only when the bodies involved wield the same type of power, or wield it over the same body of men, or when the laws distinguishing them are 'ambiguous or obscure'. Where these difficulties are avoided sovereign power, he seems to think, can easily be assigned to different bodies.[30]

Bentham has said so far that the sovereign's power is limited in practice by his subjects' habit of obedience. Now one might admit this, but contend that the limits on the sovereign's power that Bentham has emphasised are only limits *de facto* and not *de jure*, and that while Bentham is perhaps right to suggest that a sovereign *should* not try to regulate all areas of life, he is wrong not to see that there is no power to stop him from doing so if he wanted to; in other words, one might argue that Bentham is confusing what a sovereign *should* or *should not* do with what he *can* or *cannot* do. Bentham was aware of this objection, but did not think much of it. If one man says that a sovereign *can* pass a certain law, and another that he *cannot*, there is no way to resolve this scholastic controversy. The two could keep arguing until the end of time and be none the wiser for it. Abstractly both positions are 'alike conceivable'[31] and therefore the only proper questions to ask are as to which of them it is 'expedient' to adopt[32] and whether in *actual fact* a sovereign ever does what it is asserted a determined sovereign can do.

Although Bentham does not put it this way, he seems to wish to argue that when we maintain that a determined sovereign *can* do something, we mean either that he has a *right* to do it or that he has a *power* to do it. As we shall see fully later,[33] Bentham gives a positivist account of rights and obligations. Rights, in his view, are created by obligations, and not the other way around. It is because X has an obligation to do Y that Z has a right to require X to do Y.

Further, to have an obligation to do Y is no more than to be liable to punishment for failing to do it. Obligations, in other words, are not merely enforced but *created* by sanctions, by power, which is the ability to impose sanctions. A right, in Bentham's view, is therefore ultimately based on and derived from power. A sovereign has a right to command his subjects if he has power to punish them for non-compliance. As Bentham puts it, 'whatever persons do actually exercise Supreme power, these persons have the right to exercise it'.[34]

It follows therefore that whether or not a sovereign has a *right* to do X ultimately depends on whether or not he has a *power* to do it. Bentham has already shown that the sovereign's power is ultimately derived from his subjects' obedience. Whether or not the sovereign has a power to do X therefore depends on whether his subjects assist him in enforcing X. If they will not, he has no power and therefore no right to do X. In other words what a sovereign can do—using 'can' in either of its two senses—depends on what his subjects think he *may* do, or rather on what they will *let* him do. Although the controversy concerning whether a sovereign can or cannot do X appears *prima facia* to be a philosophical controversy concerning the logical nature of the sovereign's rights, it is, in Bentham's view, an empirical controversy concerning the actual habits and dispositions of his subjects. It is a controversy, as we will put it today, not in the philosophy but sociology of law.

While Bentham's answer is interesting and meets the objection at least partially, a difficulty still remains. Part of what we mean when we say that a sovereign *can* do X is that it is within his *legal* power to do it. He may not have the *physical* power to enforce it, but the point is that he will not be acting *illegally* in doing it. The question which Bentham therefore needs to answer is whether the sovereign's power can be *legally* limited, that is, whether it ever makes sense to describe the sovereign's act as *illegal*. Bentham is clearly aware of this question, as can be seen in his reference to the sovereign having 'assignable bounds' and in his description of the system of judicial review as allegedly providing a 'legal' restraint upon the sovereign's will. His answer, however, is muddled, and after some vacillations he comes down on the side of the view that the sovereign's power cannot be *legally* limited.

Bentham considers three types of situation in which a sovereign is said to be legally bound. One, where a sovereign enters into 'compacts and engagements';[35] two, where he is limited by an 'express convention';[36] and three, where there are clearly established constitutional laws.[37] Bentham does not explain how compacts and engagements differ from express conventions, but it is clear that he wished to distinguish them. As the following discussion shows Bentham considers an express convention but not a compact or an engagement binding. It is likely that he thought the convention to be a significant historical event, and compacts and engagements 'every day' occurrences.[38] It is more likely that he intended to use the term convention to describe a covenant in which a sovereign *submits* himself to another and a new political authority is created.

The first type of situation obtains when a sovereign enters into a treaty with another sovereign. Here, Bentham argues, a sovereign chooses to limit his power voluntarily. Since there is no higher power to punish him in the event of his disregarding it, the treaty clearly cannot impose a *legal* obligation and limit on him. His violation of the treaty may affect the other sovereign's disposition to be friendly to him; but this is a moral and not a legal sanction and therefore imposes only a moral limit on his power.[39] As is well known Bentham uses the term moral to refer to the power of public opinion, to the control exercised by the community at large, and uses it synonymously with the term 'popular'; when a sovereign is likely to be 'punished' by his subjects for doing something, in Bentham's view he has a *moral* obligation to do it. As is only to be expected, Bentham does not always manage to stick to this usage, and from time to time uses the term 'moral' in its ordinary and conventional sense.

When a sovereign *submits* himself to another, or when a number of independent states enter into a federal union, set up a common body 'that is distinct from all of them'[40] and invest it with power over the constituent states, in Bentham's view they can be said to have entered into an express convention. Although he never discussed them explicitly, federal states interested Bentham greatly, and almost all the examples that he gives of a sovereign being limited by an express convention—examples of German Empire, Switzerland, United Provinces and Achaean League—are examples of federal union. Bentham is convinced that the power of the sovereign who enters into a convention is *morally* limited. The convention, in his view, is an indication, a 'signal', of the extent of the subjects' disposition to obey their sovereign. All laws in accord with it, they are prepared to obey; and those in violation of it, they are disposed to resist. The sovereign therefore should observe the convention, as otherwise his subject will rebel.

Bentham goes further, and asserts unequivocally at several places that a convention imposes a *legal* limit on the sovereign's power. He does not explain why or how an express convention binds the sovereign *legally*. He seems to think that this is so because it sets 'assignable' and 'certain' bounds to his power.[41] But this is odd, since the same is true of treaties, and also, as we shall see, of constitutional laws whose violation Bentham does not consider illegal. Bentham's real reason, as we said earlier, seems to be different. He seems to think that an express convention legally limits the sovereign's power because it creates a *new* political society and/or a *new* political authority, to which the participants are now *subject*. This is why the legal status of a convention is different from that of a treaty; the latter does not create a new authority. This may also explain why Bentham thinks that a sovereign's power is legally limited when he has 'submitted' himself to another by some engagement, but not when he has signed a treaty.

As for constitutional laws, which Bentham also calls laws *in principem* or the 'transcendent class of laws', his discussion is a little more detailed but no more satisfactory. Realising that there are certain areas of life in which they will not obey their sovereign, Bentham argues, his subjects might lay down by an original contract or covenant, 'where any such thing has taken place',[42] or by some other method, that he cannot make laws affecting these areas or that he cannot alter specific existing laws. Bentham is muddled as to how to describe such constitutional laws, and, as was to be expected, the basic limitation of his legal theory is exposed in his discussion of them. He is convinced that constitutional laws and positive laws are 'two distinct sorts of laws, very different from each other in their nature and effect'.[43] But if they are so different in their nature, the crucial question arises if they are both laws in the same sense. Bentham's answer is ambiguous. At times he says that they are both laws because they both originate from the sovereign, and differ only in the fact that one is addressed to the sovereign himself and imposes 'an obligation' on him, whilst the other is addressed to his subjects and imposes an obligation on them. But this is strange, since Bentham has argued that a law, properly so called, should not only be willed by the sovereign but should also have a sanction attached to it, and therefore only a law which satisfies *both* these conditions can be called a law in the strict sense of the term. Now positive law satisfies these conditions, and is therefore law. Constitutional law is different. No man can punish himself as Bentham has constantly reminded us, and there is by definition no higher authority than the sovereign that can enforce the constitutional law on him. Since constitutional law satisfies only one of the two conditions required of a law it is not a law in the sense in which Bentham has defined the term, and cannot impose a legal limit on the sovereign. Bentham is torn between conflicting sympathies and cannot see his way out. He sometimes asserts that sanction is necessary only to make a law 'effectual' but not make it a law proper; but at other times he takes the opposite view that law, being a command, must be *both* willed and sanctioned by the sovereign. In the end he opts for the latter view, and concludes that constitutional laws are not 'commands' but 'concessions of privileges', 'only promises from the sovereign to the people' that he will not make certain sorts of laws. A constitutional law, not being a law, cannot by definition impose a legal limit on the sovereign, and therefore Bentham remarks that a sovereign's act, even when 'unconstitutional', 'cannot be illegal'.[44]

Although constitutional laws have no legal sanction and therefore are not legally binding on the sovereign, they are almost invariably backed up by moral and at times religious sanctions. If his subjects think that he should observe them and are willing to punish him by 'various manifestations' of their 'ill-will', the sovereign has a clear *moral* obligation to observe constitutional laws. If the sovereign believes that God wants him to observe them and will punish him for failing to do so, he has a clear *religious* obligation to observe them. It is essential, says Bentham, to ascertain empirically what his subjects think and/or what he himself believes before ascribing to the sovereign a moral and/or religious obligation. If his subjects did not care, or if he thought that God does not care, whether or not he observed constitutional laws, the sovereign cannot be said to have an obligation to do so. One might, of course, say that the sovereign *ought* to observe them, but inasmuch there is no sanction behind them, he cannot be said to have an *obligation* to do so.

While religious sanction is not generally common, Bentham thinks it inconceivable that moral sanction should not be universally operative. Constitutional laws are intended to check the sovereign's despotism and to protect his subjects' life, liberty and property, and therefore it is unimaginable that his subjects should want to put up with his violation of them. The sovereign knows this and would therefore generally be afraid to violate them. What begins in fear and self-interest gradually becomes a habit and acquires a new momentum. As successive sovereigns observe constitutional laws, subjects begin to expect their sovereigns to do so 'as a thing of course';[45] and they might even come to believe that to accept the office of the sovereign is necessarily to undertake to abide by constitutional laws. Like Austin, Bentham concludes that constitutional laws are basically principles of morality and that it is an act of 'immorality' on the part of the sovereign to violate them.

III

As we saw earlier every government is required by the principle of utility to maximise the happiness of its subjects. Unlike the private individual, the government's actions affect the entire community whose well-being must therefore be its supreme concern. This raises two questions. First how can we ensure that the government will always pursue its subjects' happiness? And second, and far more important, what does their happiness consist in, and what does promoting it precisely involve?

Bentham's answer to the first question is fairly straightforward. Like everyone else the government is guided by its own interest,[46] and will harm public interest when it finds it in its interest to do so. If therefore we could somehow identify its interest with that of the community, we can be reasonably certain that it will always pursue public interest. This identification can be achieved in two ways. We could either reward it for pursuing public interest, or punish it for ignoring it. Now reward is expensive, and its effectiveness is never certain. Punishment therefore is the only reliable method. Bentham thought that election provided the most effective punitive weapon. If the government was popularly elected, it would know that it will not be re-elected if it ignored public interest. By the same token, Bentham reasoned, the government will only pursue the interests of those who had a right to vote. Since the government ideally should pursue the happiness of all its subjects, every adult should have a right to vote. The more frequent the election the greater the popular check on the government; Bentham therefore advocates annual election. Elections, however frequent, have no sanction on the government if people lacked full information on its activities. Bentham therefore advocates fullest possible publicity, which includes free press, unlimited access to government offices, and the right to attend legislative sessions. Once annual election, universal franchise, and fullest publicity are established, no government, Bentham thinks, would ever 'dream' of pursuing its interest at the cost of that of the community.

Bentham's answer to the second question is philosophically far more interesting and important. It contains many powerful and original insights into the nature of government and reveals some of the crucial assumptions underlying his political thought. It therefore deserves to be considered in detail.

Surprising as it may seem, the concept of service is central to Bentham's theory of government. Man in his view is a creature so dependent on others for his well-being that human life would be extremely miserable and even impossible if men did not render various types of services to one another. No child would survive if its parents did not look after him; no political society would last if its members did not render their rulers the service of obedience; and no society would be prosperous if its members did not render each other the service of refraining from interfering with their property. Indeed, society is ultimately only a system of services men render to one another.

It would have been noticed that Bentham uses the term service far more widely than is common in ordinary discourse. As befits an utilitarian he uses it to describe an action whereby one man benefits another, that is, gives him pleasure or removes or reduces his pain.[47]

Thus in Bentham's view a priest who tells me how 'to avoid' eternal damnation renders me a service; and so does a priest 'who would draw me out of purgatory by his masses'.[48] Heaven and hell may not in fact exist, but as long as I believe that they do and feel tormented by them, the priest, says Bentham, must be considered to render me the service of relieving my 'agony' and 'pain'. In the same way, in going to bed with me my wife, Bentham continues, renders me the service of satisfying my sexual desire.[49] A service in his view need not be rendered consciously. A criminal who undergoes punishment imposed by the judge also renders a service to society. Indeed all punishments 'are services imposed upon those who undergo them for the good of society'. To Bentham even a dead man can render a service. A law that requires bodies of executed criminals to be handed over to surgeons for dissection is in effect requiring that murderers should render this medical 'service' to their community. And similarly when bodies of dead soldiers are used to fill up a ditch which their colleagues wish to cross, the former are said to render their colleagues a service.

Human happiness, we remarked earlier, depends on services men render to each other. They usually render some of these services freely and without any compulsion from the government. Parents look after their children without any payment and have done so since the human race began. Many other services like those of mutual forebearance, kindness and politeness are also rendered free and will continue to be so rendered, Bentham believes, as long as the 'principle of sociality' from which they originate remains an important part of human nature.[50] There are some services, however, that are so vital to social existence that they cannot be left to the precarious good will of our fellow men, who must therefore be compelled, even on pain of punishment, to render them.

Services so compelled generate obligations and rights. It is the concept of service, Bentham argues, that explains and indeed constitutes what are called obligations and rights. To have an obligation is to be required to act in a certain way on pain of punishment. Central to the concept of obligation are two basic notions. First, it consists in rendering a specific service to a specific person. To say that X has an obligation not to interfere with Y's property or to return his money is to say that X should render Y the negative service of refraining from interfering with his use of his property, or that he should render him the positive service of giving him a certain sum of money. Second, what makes rendering this service an obligation is the fact that X will be punished if he failed to render it. Punishment, however, is nothing but a service the government promises to render to Y in the case of X's delinquency, a service that consists in activating the entire machinery of the state in Y's favour.[51] An obligation, in short, is a mixture of two types of service, one rendered by the individuals concerned and the other rendered or promised by the government.

What is true of obligation is also true of right, Bentham argues. While there can be obligations that do not create rights, for example, those self-regarding obligations that are imposed on an individual in his own interest, there can be no rights that do not entail obligations. If I am said to have a right to the coat I am wearing, it would be very odd if you were to be left free to take it away from me whenever you wished. For me to be said to have a right to my coat, Bentham maintains, certain basic conditions must be satisfied. First, a commonly recognised authority should declare that this coat is mine and not anybody else's. Second, the rest of the community should be required not to interfere with my use of it. Third, I should be able to invoke the sanctions at the disposal of the authority to stop or punish anyone who does interfere with my use of my coat. Each of these conditions, Bentham believes, can be expressed in the language of service. For me to have a right to my coat the law should render me the service of announcing that it is mine; others should render me the negative service of not interfering with my use of it; and law should render me the positive service of protecting me in my use of it against others' interference. Rights, like obligations, are thus constituted by the services of private individuals and the government.

It is the idea of service that for Bentham explains the rationale of the institution of government. The government as Bentham understands it is a service institution, an institution designed to guarantee a cluster of services. Its first and most important job is to determine what services men should be compelled to render to one another, in other words, to set up a 'vast edifice' of rights and obligations. While Bentham agrees with his liberal predecessors that

2

this is the most important task of the government, he cannot see how a government, having a duty to maximise the happiness of the community, can rest content with this. He thinks it should also constantly explore ways and means by which the happiness of its subjects can be maximised. As we shall see later this involves creating economic prosperity, securing better distribution of wealth, and generating a social climate in which its subjects will be encouraged to render services to one another. Since enforcing rights and obligations is its *primary* and basic duty, Bentham thinks that the government should render these additional services only in a way consistent with, and within the limits of, the established system of rights and obligations.

The government's basic task then is to determine its subjects' rights and obligations; in other words, to lay down a compulsory system of services. But before we can determine what rights and obligations it should enforce, we must be clear, says Bentham, as to what precisely enforcing them involves. We have already seen that human happiness depends on men rendering services to one another, and that therefore the more the services rendered to a man the greater is his happiness. This would seem to suggest that government should compel its subjects to render more and more services to each other. This is, however, true, says Bentham, only so long as we look at services from the standpoint of the beneficiary. If we turn our attention to those rendering them, a very different picture emerges. Every service involves sacrifice on the part of the person rendering it. To be asked to help you when you are in difficulty involves a sacrifice of time and energy on my part. To be asked not to interfere with your property requires me to sacrifice my happiness which may be promoted by appropriating and using your property. A service, in other words, is a mixed blessing and is at once a source of both pleasure and pain, at once both desirable and undesirable.

If this is true of services rendered voluntarily it is all the more true of those that are obligatory. To have an obligation is to be required to render a specific service on pain of punishment. Every obligation thus restricts liberty; it restricts the individual concerned from doing what he wants to do, and requires him to do what he might not want to do. To be under an obligation is therefore to be in a state of servitude. After all, what is servitude but a condition in which one man is compelled to render specific services to another?[52] Further, since there can be no rights without corresponding obligations, and since all obligations restrict liberty, Bentham argues, all rights are purchased at the expense of liberty. In other words all rights involve servitude on the part of those burdened with corresponding obligations. Since rights are legally guaranteed liberties— liberties endowed with power and effectiveness, Bentham thinks we can say that one man's liberty is another man's servitude.

Given this peculiar and paradoxical logic of the concepts of right and obligation the government must be very careful, says Bentham, in establishing rights and obligations. My rights may or may not be a source of pleasure to me, but the corresponding obligations they impose on others are certain sources of pain to them.[53] The government therefore should never create rights, 'instruments of felicity' though they are, unless it can be absolutely certain that their probable advantages would more than compensate for their certain disadvantages. Besides, the government is an institution which by 'the incxorable law of nature'[54] deals in evil. For the effectiveness of everything it does it relies on commands and punishment which are certain sources of pain. It can do nothing, achieve no pleasure and relieve no pain, without producing at least some pain in the process. Its actions therefore should be subjected to most careful examination, and its gifts scrutinised with the greatest care. The question, then, is to determine what rights and obligations the government should enforce, so that the end result is a net surplus of pleasure.

The question can only be answered, Bentham believes, by identifying the types of pain that are so acute that they should be prevented at all cost. On the basis of empirical observation and, what he calls, axioms of corporal and mental pathology, he concludes that physical harm, loss of reputation, frustration of expectation, damage to status, and starvation and death are some of the acutest sources of pain. Because man suffers acute pain when physically harmed, the government must guarantee its subjects physical security and protection; that is, it should give them a right to the security of their person. Men suffer acute pain at the loss of reputation and therefore the government should grant them a right to the protection of their 'name' against abuses like blackmail, libel and slander. Since the frustration of expectations is a source of most acute pain, and since expectations are ultimately based on what one already has, the government should grant its subjects a right to the security of their possessions. No man, Bentham goes on, ever stands alone; he is involved in a complex pattern of relationships with other men, whether as a father, or a son, husband, wife, doctor, professor, civil servant, priest or a servant. This relationship Bentham calls status or, more commonly, a 'condition in life'.[55] Since an individual suffers great pain when his established relations with other men are interfered with, he should be secured in his condition in life: that is, in the exercise of the rights, powers and obligations implicit in his social status. The government, in other words, should give its subjects a right to security—security of person, name, possession and condition in life.[56]

We notice above that starvation and death are sources of great pain. The government should therefore ensure that all its subjects have subsistence, the term that Bentham uses rather widely to include 'everything the non-possession of which would be productive of positive physical suffering.'[57] Ideally, says Bentham, each individual should be able to provide for his own subsistence; but when he cannot or will not, the government should intervene, as otherwise it will be deemed to be 'the author' of his misery and death.[58] The government should encourage industrialisation and thereby create jobs for its subjects. It could also collect a 'regular contribution' from the rich and set up a common fund to be used for the well-being of the poor. It could also set up pauper establishments on the model of the Panopticon. Bentham is convinced that wherever poverty coexists with wealth, the onus always lies on the rich to show why they should not be taxed to provide for the poor.[59] It is worth observing that while Bentham insists that individuals have a *right* to security, he seems to believe that they do not have a *right* to subsistence; it is only a *duty* on the part of the government and society at large.

In addition to the services necessary for the achievement of security and subsistence, there are also several other types of services that in Bentham's view the government should require its subjects to render one another. These services are as essential to human happiness as those mentioned above. Bentham lays down three general principles on the basis of which to determine the content of these services. They are superior need, former service, and contract.[60]

As we observed earlier every service is at once a source of pleasure and pain, pleasure to its beneficiary and pain to the person required to render it. When therefore it can be shown that the pain likely to be caused to the latter is outweighed by the pain likely to be caused to the former in the event of a service not being rendered, the individual concerned should be required to render that service. Thus, for example, the services a father has to render to his children are burdensome to him; 'but this evil is nothing in comparison of the evil which would result from their neglect'. The duty of having to fight for his country is highly painful to a soldier, but the evil likely to be caused to the community from its possible loss of freedom is even greater. This is also true of the duty to pay taxes to the government. The principle of superior need therefore requires, argues Bentham, that several types of services at present left to individual discretion should be made obligatory. Thus if a drunkard has fallen into a puddle and is in danger of suffocation, a passerby who notices this should be required to drag him out or inform others. Or if a woman's dress catches fire a passer-by should be required to put it out and help her in all ways that he can.[61] It is, of course, crucial, says Bentham, that the person required to render the service should not be put to too much inconvenience, since otherwise the balance of pleasure will shift, rendering the principle of superior need inoperative.

By the principle of former service Bentham means that services already rendered should be required to be returned or reciprocated in some appropriate manner. Thus if a surgeon has given assistance to a sick man who was in no state to call for him, the latter should be required to indemnify him on his recovery. Likewise a man who has endangered his life to rescue another man should be duly rewarded. It is on the basis of former services, Bentham argues, that children can be required to maintain their old parents, and husbands to look after their wives 'when time has effaced the(ir) attractions'.[62] The reason for requiring former services to be requited, Bentham maintains, is not so much that those rendering them should be compensated for their hardship and pain as that this is the only way individual and public interest, or rather self-interest and benevolence, can be harmonised, and a constant supply of services guaranteed in the future. Bentham is, however, worried lest the legal recognition of the principle of former services should lead to the multiplication of unnecessary services and the consequent imposition of enormous hardship on the beneficiary. He therefore lays down three limits upon its application. First, in order that the beneficiary is not 'tyrannised' into paying for services he could have done without had he known that they were not rendered free, the person rendering them must be required to make it clear that his service is not disinterested. Second, the beneficiary should have the option to decline the service or to obtain it 'at a less expense'. Third, wherever possible, the law should assign the duty to render the service, especially where the beneficiary is a minor or incapacitated, to a specific person in the first instance, his parents or friends for example, so that the beneficiary is not 'overwhelmed by a crowd of assistants' in search of cheap praise or money.[63]

Contract or previous agreement is the third source of obligatory services. A contract, in Bentham's view, represents a mutually agreed alienation of benefits and services. In it each party parts with what it values in return for what it values more. A contract signifies that two rational men have come to the conclusion that a particular transaction will promote their happiness most. Since each individual knows his interest best, there can be no reason why a government should sit in judgement on the content of the contract. Its only duty is to enforce it. Not that contracts are inherently binding, but rather that only by keeping them can the greatest happiness be promoted. If they were not kept, one or both parties would suffer the acute pain of disappointment. What is more, people will be seriously discouraged from entering into contracts; and since no society can exist without mutual alienation of services, such a situation will create enormous pain.

Bentham gets into an interesting difficulty here which might briefly be noted. Contracts are binding because they promote the community's happiness. But this also means that while the institution of contract is generally binding, there may be specific cases where a contract does not promote general happiness and should not therefore be kept. Bentham lays down nine different situations such as fraud, coercion and genuine error in which contracts are not binding. In each case his reason is that a net balance of pain will result if contracts are not invalidated. Thus, for example, if you deliberately sell me an inferior article to the one you had originally shown, you no doubt derive pleasure from our transaction; but since 'the pleasure of gaining is not equal to the evil of losing',[64] your pleasure can *never* be greater than my pain. The contract should therefore be declared invalid. Now the axiom on which this reasoning is based is obviously rather dubious, and it is not difficult to imagine that invalidating the contract might result in a net balance of pain. Realising this Bentham changes his line of reasoning and argues that in selling me an inferior article you have cheated me and therefore not to invalidate the contract 'would be to reward a crime'. But this is to beg the question, since why should cheating be a crime in the first instance? And even if it could be shown that it should be, why should it not be 'rewarded' in this particular case where it clearly shows a balance of pleasure?

The government's *basic* task then is the following: to secure its subjects' rights to their person, reputation, possession and condition in life; to ensure them subsistence; and to make laws requiring that men in acute need of help should be helped, that former services should be requited, and that valid contracts be kept. The government secures these services by declaring that a failure to render them constitutes an offence and will be visited with punishment. Offences, in other words, are correlative of rights. Rights presuppose obligations; and nothing can be called an obligation the failure to discharge wihch is not declared an offence. Rights, obligations, services and offences, Bentham maintains, are 'born together, . . . exist together and are inseparably connected'.[65] By its very nature, law creates them all together. The law that prohibits me from killing you imposes on me the *obligation* not to kill you, grants you the *right* not to be killed by me, requires of me the negative *service* of not killing you and the positive service of helping you when your life is in danger, and makes it an *offence* to try to kill you. These four 'are so simultaneous that each of these words may be substituted the one for the other'; indeed, they are 'only the law considered under different aspects'.[66] To create rights is to create offences, and to create offences is to provide for their punishment. Defining rights is the concern of the civil law; prescribing punishment is the concern of the penal law, which thus is only 'the consequence, the continuation, the termination of a civil law'.[67] The government's basic task, to put it differently, is to maintain a system of civil and penal law.

Within the limits set by this general framework of civil and penal law which it is its *primary* and essential task to provide, the government, we noted earlier, is also to provide an *additional* cluster of services designed to increase the quantity of happiness in the community. Although Bentham's discussion here is somewhat muddled and inchoate he seems to want the government to do three things: first, to create prosperity; second, to reduce inequality; and third, to cultivate sympathy and benevolence in its subjects in order that they might promote each other's well-being in several small ways.

Although it is the duty of the government to maximise the total quantity of happiness available to its subjects, it is hindered by the fact that it can have no knowledge of the infinitely varied objects and activities in which its subjects find their pleasures and pains. However, Bentham thinks there is a way out of this difficulty. We know that most pleasures can be bought and most pains avoided with the help of money. The government can therefore increase the sum of happiness in the community by increasing the amount of money available to each of its subjects. In other words it should increase 'abundance', a term which Bentham uses to mean surplus wealth left in individual hands after their basic needs are met.[68] Bentham thinks that abundance, or what we today would call prosperity or affluence, can best be increased by guaranteeing to each man the due reward of his work and security of his possessions. As this is already covered by the government's initial and far more important task of creating a framework of civil and penal law, the government for the most part needs to do no more than to leave economic life alone. However, individual efforts may prove inadequate and then the government needs to intervene. It should establish institutions devoted to inventing new tools and gadgets, and should offer rewards for socially useful inventions. It should also deploy appropriate fiscal measures designed to encourage saving or the transfer of capital to socially useful industries. It should also pursue educational and other policies designed to produce technical manpower and to encourage habits of thrift and hard work. Above all it should fight those aspects of religious thought that encourage men to despise comforts and luxuries.

Reduction of inequality is the second object that the government in Bentham's view should aim at. 'All inequality,' he asserts, 'is a source of evil, for by the inferior more is lost in the account of happiness than is gained by the superior.'[69] Bentham does not give any evidence in support of this view, and simply asserts it as one of the basic truths about human nature. Although inequality is evil, it is a necessary evil. Without inequality of power, without someone having the right to command, there can be no political society. Inequality of wealth is a necessary consequence of the right to property which is essential if men are to be encouraged to work and save. Similarly, moral inequality, by which Bentham means inequality of moral virtues and attainments, is necessary both because it is an inevitable result of the socially worthwhile principle of open competition and because it encourages men to promote their society's well-being. Although intellectual inequality, that is, inequality in intellectual abilities and attainments, is a source of considerable pain to the intellectually inferior, it too is necessary for the same reasons that moral inequality is.

Inequality, a source of both pleasure and pain, is then a mixed blessing. The government should therefore endeavour selectively to reduce it as much as possible. Bentham has no proposals for reducing intellectual and moral inequalities and does not pursue the discussion any further, beyond saying that if intellectual and moral superiorities are used in the public interest and are not flaunted in a way that arouses jealousy, there is no cause for worry. As to inequality of power, he thinks it can be minimised by reducing the amount of power attached to public offices to the barest minimum, by declaring every sane adult eligible for them, and by making their incumbents accountable to those subject to their power. As for economic inequality, it can be reduced by a judicious system of death duty.[70] Although the law of diminishing utility, to which wealth is subject, requires that economic inequality should be reduced to the point when this law becomes operative, Bentham believes that such a drastic equalisation will come into conflict with security of property and should be eschewed.[71]

As we saw earlier, human happiness depends on countless small services that men render to one another, and therefore it is the duty of the government dedicated to the maximisation of general happiness to cultivate the spirit of benevolence among its subjects and to create a climate in which they feel encouraged to render mutual services on a much greater scale than at present. The government could do this in a variety of ways.[72] It could fight religious and sectarian prejudices which limit men's sympathies and incline them to treat outsiders as less than fully human. It could discourage artists and men of letters from ridiculing or making derogatory references to a section of their community.[73] It could prohibit cruel sports like fox-hunting, cock-fighting and fishing and thereby create a climate of gentleness and mutual concern. By encouraging the formation of charity organisations and such other methods designed to appeal to pity and compassion, it could constantly reinforce its subjects' desire to help one another.[74] It could also compose a code and a catechism of political morality which could be taught in schools and colleges and preached in churches.

IV

We sketched above the outlines of some aspects of Bentham's political thought. There is much in his thought, more particularly in his discussion of the nature of sovereignty, rights, obligations and liberty that is open to serious objections. But his ideas, especially his discussion of the nature and functions of government, also contain many insights that are capable of providing the basis of a worthwhile theory of government. However, since it is not possible to undertake here a detailed critical appreciation of Bentham, we shall only briefly comment on the way his thought marks an interesting and fruitful departure from the classical liberalism of Hobbes and, especially, of Locke.

Deriving his political theory from the doctrine of natural rights, Locke argued that the job of the government was to protect certain basic rights of its subjects. What he did not realise was that human self-interest, differences in men's ability to manipulate their environment, and the 'forces' of the market could create a situation in which many members of a community might be reduced to possessing these rights only in name, so that the government, devoted to safeguarding its subjects' rights impartially would in practice protect only those whose effective exercise of their rights has enabled them to carve out a comfortable place for themselves in the life of the community. In other words, a formally impartial government could in practice turn out to be a partial and partisan institution, not because it is corrupt but because of the social context in which it operates. This hiatus between what the government is in theory and what it is in practice, between its formal impartiality and practical partiality, creates a tension: either the government lives up to its ideal and rectifies the injustices and iniquities of social life, in which case the non-interventionist theory of government needs to be drastically revised; or it holds fast to its formal impartiality, in which case it is for all practical purposes a patently partisan institution. For a variety of reasons too complex to disentangle here, Locke generally chose the second alternative. He saw the dangers but not the benefits of positive government action.

Bentham saw the difficulties in Locke's position and criticised him for not grasping the full implications of the role of the government as a trustee of the community's well-being.[75] He argued that the government represented and held in its charge the happiness of the entire community and not merely of one section of it. He argued further that, since happiness was not simply a matter of formal right but of concrete experience, the government should not merely grant its subjects a formal right to happiness but effectively assist them to attain it. Bentham was thus able to assign the government a positive and creative role in the life of the community. In so doing he took the first step, tentative and indecisive as it was, towards emancipating liberalism from the shackles of atomic and negative individualism.

What is more, Bentham reorientated Lockean liberalism without rejecting what was, surely, its valid insight into the role of the government in the life of the community. A political theory that is dedicated to the realisation of a single ideal, be it virtue (Rousseau) or happiness (Bentham) or perfection (Mill), is exposed to the danger that it will pursue its ideal without pausing to consider what other ideals it sacrifices in the process. Indeed, if virtue or happiness *alone* is good, then, by definition nothing else is valuable and therefore its sacrifice is not worth worrying about. For the most part Bentham managed to avoid sliding down this slippery slope to collectivism by holding fast to the Lockean belief that the *primary* duty of the government was to create and maintain a framework of rights and liberties, and that its *additional* duty to maximise happiness must be discharged only in a way consistent with these rights and liberties. While one may criticise the specific rights that Bentham considered crucial to human well-being, it is difficult to see how total government control of social life can be avoided if government were not required to create and maintain a relatively inviolable framework of individual rights and liberties.

One could criticise Bentham on a number of grounds. His view of man is extremely crude; his moral theory is naive and as subjective as those he rejects; his ontology is primitive; his analysis of basic legal and political concepts is muddled and superficial; and his so-called science of happiness remains nothing more than a boring system of classification based on a crude bipartitionist method. Despite all this he remains an important historical figure for two main reasons. First, as will be seen in the text, he brilliantly knocked down, or at least threw serious doubts on the validity of, a number of currently dominant moral and political doctrines like moral intuitionism, social contract, state of nature and 'self-evident' natural rights. In so doing he opened up a wide range of problems that were to haunt generations of moral and political philosophers after him. Second, in tackling these problems he offered countless new insights into the nature of legal and political life, which collectively amount to nothing less than giving classical liberalism a new foundation. He freed it from its negative and formalistic individualism and taught it to appreciate the full magnitude of the creative role the government might play in creating a good society, however defined. In other words he gave liberalism a radical dimension—no mean achievement.

CHAPTER 1

Ontology[1]

[Although, for reasons of space, I have omitted a few passages, those selected present a balanced picture of Bentham's ontology, especially of his theory of reality and fiction which he considered to be the basis of his moral and political theory. Bentham has drawn a thin line over the first few sentences (from 'An entity . . . ' to ' . . . really meant to be ascribed'), but he had not crossed them out. Strictly speaking, perhaps, these few sentences should have been omitted. However, as they form a necessary introduction to his ontology and express his basic ideas crisply and accurately, they have been included here. Incidentally, Bowring retains them as well.]

An entity is a denomination, in the import of which every subject matter of discourse, for the designation of which the grammatical part of speech called a noun-substantive is employed, may be comprised.

Entities may be distinguished into perceptible and inferential.

A perceptible entity is every entity the existence of which is made known to human and other beings by the immediate testimony of one or more of senses.

An inferential entity is an entity which, at this time of day at least, is not made known to human beings in general, by the testimony of sense, but is inferred from a chain of reasoning.

An entity, whether perceptible or inferential, is either real or fictitious.

A real entity is an entity to which, on the occasion and for the purpose of discourse, existence is really meant to be ascribed.

A fictitious entity is an entity to which, though by the grammatical form of the discourse employed in speaking of it, existence be ascribed, yet in truth and reality existence is not meant to be ascribed.

Every noun-substantive which is not the name of a real entity, perceptible or inferential, is the name of a fictitious entity.

Every fictitious entity bears some relation to some real entity, and can not otherwise be understood than in so far as that relation is perceived—a conception of that relation is obtained.

Reckoning from the real entity to which it bears relation, a fictitious entity may be styled a fictitious entity of the first remove, a fictitious entity of the second remove, and so on.

A fictitious entity of the first remove is a fictitious entity, a conception of which may be obtained by the consideration of the relation borne by it to a real entity, without need of considering the relation borne by it to any other fictitious entity.

A fictitious entity of the second remove is a fictitious entity, for obtaining a conception of which it is necessary to take into consideration some fictitious entity of the first remove.

Considered at any two contiguous points of time, every real entity is either in motion or at rest.

Now when a real entity is said to be at rest, it is said to be so with reference to some other particular real entity or aggregate of real entities; for so far as any part of the system of the universe is perceived by us, we at all times perceive it not to be at rest. Such, at least, is the case not only with the bodies called planets, but with one or more of the bodies called fixed stars; and, by analogy, we infer this to be the case with all the rest.

This premised, considered with reference to any two contiguous points of time past, every perceptible real entity was, during that time, either in motion or not in motion; if not in motion, it was at rest.

Here, then, we have two correspondent and opposite fictitious entities of the first remove, *viz.* a motion and a rest.

A motion is a mode of speech commonly employed; *a rest* is a mode of speech not so commonly employed.

To be spoken of at all, every fictitious entity must be spoken of as if it were real. This, it will be seen, is the case with the above-mentioned pair of fictitious entities of the first remove.

A body is said to be in motion. This, taken in the literal sense, is as much as to say, here is a larger body called a motion; *in* this larger body, the other body, namely, the real existing body, is contained.

So in regard to rest. To say this body is at rest is as much as to say, here is a body, and it will naturally be supposed a fixed body, and here is another body, meaning the real existing body, which is *at* that first-mentioned body, *i.e.* attached to it, as if the fictitious body were a stake, and the real body a beast tied to it.

To language, then—to language alone—it is that fictitious entities owe their existence; their impossible, yet indispensable, existence.

In language, the words which present themselves, and are employed in the character of *names*, are, some of them, names of real entities; others, names of fictitious entities: and to one or other of these classes may all words which are employed in the character of *names* be referred.

What will, moreover, be seen, is that the fiction—the mode of representation by which the fictitious entities thus created, in so far as fictitious entities can be created, are dressed up in the garb, and placed upon the level, of real ones—is a contrivance but for which language, or, at any rate, language in any form superior to that of the language, of the brute creation, could not have existence.

Of fictitious entities, whatsoever is predicated is not, consistently with strict truth, predicated (it then appears) of anything but their respective names.

But for as much as by reason of its length and compoundedness, the use of the compound denomination, name of a fictitious entity, would frequently be found attended with inconvenience; for the avoidance of this inconvenience, instead of this long denomination the less long, though, unhappily, still compound denomination, fictitious entity, will commonly, after the above warning, be employed.

Of nothing that has place, or passes, in our minds can we give any account, any otherwise than by speaking of it as if it were a portion of space, with portions of matter, some of them at rest, others moving in it. Of nothing, therefore, that has place, or passes in our mind, can we speak (or so much as think) otherwise than in the way of fiction. To this word fiction we must not attach either those sentiments of pleasure, or those sentiments of displeasure which, with so much propriety, attach themselves to it on the occasion in which it is most commonly in use. Very different in respect of purpose and necessity, very different is the fiction of logic from the poetical and political; very different the fiction of the Logician from the fictions of poets, and those of priests, and lawyers.

For their object and effect, the fictions with which the Logician is conversant, without having been the author of them, have had neither more nor less than the carrying on of human converse; such communication and interchange of thought as is capable of having place between man and man. For this object and effect the fictions of the poet, whether in his character of historic fabulist or dramatic fabulist, putting or not putting the words of his discourse in metrical form, are pure of insincerity, and, neither for their object nor for their effect have anything but to amuse, unless it be in some cases to excite to action—to action in this or that particular direction for this or that particular purpose. By the priest and the lawyer, in whatsoever shape fiction has been employed, it has had for its object or effect, or both, to deceive, and, by deceipt, to govern, and, by governing, to promote the interest, real or supposed, of the party addressing, at the expense of the party addressed. In the mind of all, fiction, in the logical sense, has been the coin of necessity—in that of poets, of amusement—in that of the priest and the lawyer, of mischievous immorality in the shape of mischievous ambition; and too often both priest and lawyer have framed or made in part this instrument.

CLASSIFICATION OF FICTITIOUS ENTITIES

A. *Names of Physical Fictitious Entities*

To this class belong all those entities which will be found included in Aristotle's list—included in his *Ten Predicaments*, the first excepted.

1. *Quantity*. Quantity cannot exist without some substance of which it is the quantity. Of substance, no species, no individual can exist, without existing in some certain quantity.

2. *Quality*. Quality cannot exist without some substance of which it is the quality. Of substance, no species can exist without being of some quality; of a multitude of qualities, of which the number is, in every instance, indeterminate, capable of receiving

increase, and that to an indefinite degree, according to the purposes for which, and the occasions on which the several substances of which they are qualities, may come to be considered.

3. *Place.* Of place, the notion cannot be entertained without the notion of some substance considered as *placed*, or capable of existing, or, as we say, being *placed* in it.

Expressive of the notion of place, taken in their original, physical, archetypal signification, are the several words termed prepositions of place and adverbs of place. These are—*In; on,* or *upon; at; above; below; round; around; out, out of; from above; from under; from.*

4. *Time.* Time is, as it were, on an ulterior and double account, a fictitious entity; its denominations so many names of fictitious entities.

To be capable of being spoken of, time itself must be, cannot but be, spoken of as a modification of space. Witness the prepositions *in* and *at*: *in* such a portion of time—*at* such a portion of time; *in* an hour—*at* 12 o'clock; *in* such a year, month, day, *at* such an hour, *at* so many minutes after such an hour, *at* so many seconds after such a minute in such an hour.

Witness again, the common expressions, 'a short time', 'a long time', 'a space of time'.

By a line it is that every portion of time, every particular time, is conceived, represented, and spoken of;—by a line, *i.e.* a body, of which the length alone, without breadth or depth, is considered.

5. *Motion.* 6. *Rest.* 7. *Action.* 8. *Passion.* 9. *Relation.*

B. *Political and Quasi-Political Fictitious Entities*

I. EFFECTS. 1. Obligation; 2. Right; 3. Exemption; 4. Power; 5. Privilege; 6. Prerogative; 7. Possession, physical; 8. Possession, legal; 9. Property.

II. CAUSES. 1. Command; 2. Prohibition, Inhibition, etc.; 3. Punishment; 4. Pardon; 5. License; 6. Warrant; 7. Judgement; 8. Division.

All these have for their efficient causes pleasure and pain—but principally pain—in whatsoever shape and from whichsoever of the five sanctions or sources of pleasure or pain derived or expected, *viz.* 1. The physical sanction; 2. The sympathetic sanction, or sanction of sympathy; 3. The popular or moral sanction; 4. The political, including the legal sanction; 5. The religious sanction.

Obligation is the root out of which all these other fictitious entities spring.

Of all the sanctions or sources of pleasure and pain above brought to view, the political sanction being susceptible of being the strongest and surest in its operation, and, accordingly, the obligation derived from it the strongest and most effective, powerful and efficient, this is the sanction which it seems advisable to take for consideration in the first instance; the correspondent obligations of the same name which may be considered as emaning from these other fictitious entities being, in the instance of some of these sanctions, of too weak a nature to act with *any sufficient* force capable of giving to any of those other productions any practical value.

An obligation—understand here that sort of obligation which, through the medium of the will, operates on the active faculty— takes its nature from some act to which it applies itself; it is an obligation to perform or to abstain from performing a certain *act*.

A legal obligation to perform the act in question is said to attach upon a man, to be incumbent upon him, in so far as in the event of his performing the act (understand both at the time and place in question) he will not suffer any pain, but in the event of his not so performing it he will suffer a certain pain, *viz.* the pain that corresponds to it, and by the virtue of which, applying itself eventually as above, the obligation is created.

CHAPTER 2

Exposition[2]

[Bentham uses the term exposition to refer to what we would call analysis. Having examined the nature of fictitious entities in the previous chapter he now goes on to develop a technique of analysing them by relating them to some real entities. Exposition, in his view, can involve a number of thinks like synonymation (tracing synonyms) etymologisation (tracing the origin of a word), phraseoplerosis and archetypation. Only the last two are essential to every mode of logical analysis, and are discussed in some detail in this chapter. It would have been noticed that for Bentham, logic—especially logical analysis—presupposes ontology.]

CLEARNESS IN DISCOURSE, HOW TO PRODUCE IT AND HENCE OF EXPOSITION

Seats of Unclearness. The Words or their Connexion.
Exposition what?

A sentence, in the grammatical sense of the word sentence, consists either of a single proposition, in the logical sense of the word proposition, or of a number of such propositions; if of one only, it may be termed a simple sentence—if of more than one, a compound sentence.

A proposition is clear, in proportion as it is clear—that is, free—at the same time from ambiguity and obscurity.

Where unclearness (why not 'unclearness' as well as 'uncleanness') has place in a discourse, the seat of it will be either in the *words* or in the *syntax*: in some one word, or number of words, each taken singly, *i.e.* without regard to the mode of their connexion, or in that mode itself or in the manner in which they are connected with each other, or in the state of their mutual relations with reference to the import of each other, to each other's import.

In so far as the seat of the unclearness is in the words taken singly, *clearness* has for its *instrument, exposition*; *i.e.* exposition is a name which may, with propriety, be applied to the designation of every operation which has for its object, or end in view, the exclusion or expulsion of unclearness in any shape; to the *operation*, and thereby, for such on the present occasion is the poverty and thence the ambiguity of language, to the portion of discourse by which the end is endeavoured to be accomplished, and by which the operation of accomplishing it is considered as performed.

Of Exposition by Paraphrasis, with its Subsidiary Operations, viz. Phraseopleurosis and Archetypation

EXPLANATION OF THESE MODES OF EXPOSITION, AND OF THE CASE IN WHICH THEY ARE NECESSARY

Paraphrasis is that mode of exposition which is the only instructive mode where the (thing) *expressed*, being the name of a fictitious entity, has not any superior in the scale of logical subalternation.

Connected, and thus necessarily, with paraphrasis, is an operation for the designation of which the word *Phraseoplerosis* (*i.e.* the filling up of the phrase) may be employed.

By the word *paraphrasis* may be designated that sort of exposition which may be afforded by transmuting into a proposition having for its subject some real entity, a proposition which has not for its subject any other than a fictitious entity.

Nothing has no properties. A fictitious entity, being, as this its name imports—being, by the very supposition—a mere nothing, cannot of itself have any properties: no proposition by which any property is ascribed to it can, therefore, be, in itself and of itself, a true one; nor, therefore, an instructive one. Whatsoever of truth is capable of belonging to it cannot belong to it in any other character than that of the representative of—the intended and supposed equivalent and adequate succedaneum of—some proposition having for its subject some real entity.

Of any such fictitious entity or fictitious entities, the real entity with which the import of their respective appellatives is connected, and on the import of which their import depends, may be termed the real *source*, *efficient cause*, or *connecting principle*.

In every *proposition* by which a property or affection of any kind is ascribed to an entity of any kind, real or fictitious, three parts or members are necessarily either expressly or virtually included, *viz.* 1. a *subject*, being the name of the *fictitious entity* in question; 2. a *predicate* by which is designated the property or affection attributed or ascribed to that subject; and 3. the *copula* or sign of the act of the mind by which the attribution or ascription is performed.

By the sort of proposition here in question, *viz.* a proposition which has for its subject some fictitious entity, and for its predicate the name of an attribute attributed to that fictitious entity, some sort of image—the image of some real action or state of things—in every instance is presented to the mind. This image may be termed the *archetype*, (the *emblem*) or *archetypal* (or *emblematic*) *image* appertaining to the fictitious proposition, of which the name of the characteristic fictitious entity constitutes a part.

In so far as of this emblematic image indication is given, the act or operation by which such indication is given may be termed *archetypation*.

Of the subject of the fictitious proposition which is employed as the representative of some real one which, for the exposition of it, requires a paraphrasis, having for its subject a real entity (which paraphrasis, when exhibited, performs, in relation to the name of the fictitious subject, the same sort of office which, for the name of a real entity, is performed by a definition of the ordinary stamp, *viz.* a definition *per genus et differentiam*) the name forms but a part of the fictitious proposition for the exposition or explanation of which the sort of proposition having for its subject a real entity is, in the character of a paraphrastically-expository proposition, required. To compose and constitute such a proposition as shall be ripe and qualified for the receiving for itself, and thereby for its subject, an exposition by *paraphrasis*, the addition of another matter is required, *viz.* besides the name of the subject, the name of the predicate, together with some sign performing the office of the copula is requisite; the operation by which this completion of the phrase is performed, may be termed *phraseoplerosis*.

Phraseoplerosis is thus another of the operations connected with, and subservient to, the main or principal operation, paraphrasis.

To[2] a considerable extent archetypation—i.e. origin of the psychological in some physical idea—is, in a manner, lost; its physical marks being more or less obliterated by the frequency of its use on psychological ground, while it is little and if at all, on the original physical ground.

Such psychological expressions, of which, as above, the physical origin is lost, are the most commodious for psychological use. Why? Because in proportion as it is put out of sight, two psychological expressions, derived from two disparate and incongruous physical sources, are capable of being conjoined without bringing the incongruity to view.

When the expression applied to a psychological purpose is one of which the physical origin remains still prominent and conspicuous, it presents itself to view in the character of a figurative expression; for instance, a metaphor. Carried for any considerable length through its connexions and dependencies, the metaphor becomes an allegory—a figure of speech, the unsuitableness of which to serious and instructive discourse, is generally recognised. But the great inconvenience is that it is seldom that for any considerable length, if any, the physical idea can be moulded and adapted to the psychological purpose.

EXEMPLIFICATION IN THE CASE OF THE FICTITIOUS ENTITY, OBLIGATION

For exposition and explanation of paraphrasis, and of the other modes connected with it and subsidiary to it, that which presents itself as the most instructive of all examples which the nature of the case affords is that which is afforded by the group of ethical fictitious entities, *viz.* obligations, rights, and the other *advantages* dependent on obligation.

The fictitious entities which compose this group have all of them, for their real *source*, one and the same sort of real entity, *viz.* *sensation*; the word being taken in that sense in which it is significant not merely of perception but of perception considered as productive of pain (alone), of pleasure (alone), or of both.

Pain (it is here to be observed) may have for its equivalent, loss of pleasure; pleasure, again, may have for its equivalent, exemption from pain.

An obligation (*viz.* the obligation of conducting himself in a certain manner) is incumbent on a man (*i.e.* is spoken of as incumbent on a man) in so far as, in the event of his failing to conduct himself in that manner, pain, or loss of pleasure, is considered as about to be experienced by him: it being at the same time understood that only in so far as a man is aware of the probability that in the event in question the unpleasant consequence in question will befall him, that the obligation can possess any probability of proving an effective one.

In this example—

1. The exponend, or say the word to be expounded is an *obligation*.

2. It being the name not of a real, but only of a fictitious entity, and that fictitious entity not having any superior genus, it is considered as not susceptible of a definition in the ordinary shape, *per genus et differentiam*, but only of an exposition in the way of paraphrasis.

3. To fit it for receiving exposition in this shape, it is in the character of the subject of a proposition, by the help of the requisite complements, made up into a fictitious proposition. These complements, are (1) the predicate, *incumbent on a man*; (2) the copula *is*: and of these, when thus added to the name of the subject, *viz.* *obligation*, the fictitious proposition which requires to be expounded by paraphrasis, *viz.* the proposition, *An obligation is incumbent on a man*, is composed.

4. Taking the name of the subject for the *basis*, by the addition of this predicate, *incumbent on a man*, and the copula *is*, the phrase is completed—the operation called *phraseoplerosis*, *i.e.* completion of the phrase, [is] performed.

5. The source of the explanation thus given by paraphrasis is the idea of eventual sensation, as expressed by the names of the different and opposite modes of sensation—*viz.* pain and pleasure, with their respective equivalents—and the designation of the event on the happening of which such sensation is considered as being about to take place.

6. For the formation of the variety of fictitious propositions of which the fictitious entity in question, *viz.* obligation, or an

obligation, is in use to constitute the subject, the emblematical, or archetypal image, is that of a man lying down, with a heavy body pressing upon him; to wit, in such sort as either to prevent him from acting at all, or so ordering matters that if so it be that he does act, it cannot be in any other direction or manner than the direction or manner in question—the direction or manner requisite.

The several distinguishable sources from any or all of which the pain and pleasure constitutive of the obligation in question may be expected to be received—*viz.* the several sanctions, distinguished by the names of the physical sanction, the popular, or moral, sanction, the political (including the legal) sanction, and the religious sanction—these particulars belong to another part of the field, and have received explanation in another place.

To that other place it also belongs to bring to view the causes by which the attention and perception of mankind have to so great an extent been kept averted from the only true and intelligible source of obligation—from the only true and intelligible explanation of its nature, as thus indicated.

On the exposition thus given of the term obligation may be built those other expositions of which it will form the basis, *viz.* of rights, quasi-rights or advantages analogous to rights, and their respective modifications, as well as of the several modifications of which the fictitious entity, *obligation*, is itself susceptible.

CHAPTER 3

Phenomena of the Human Mind[1]

Phenomena of the human mind: 1. Experiences, and 2. Operations. Correspondent faculties: perceptive and appetitive.

A. *Experiences*[2]

The whole structure of the mind may be considered as included in two faculties, *viz.* the perceptive and the appetitive.

To the perceptive belong all mental experiences—simple experiences; to the appetitive all mental operations and their results.

In the perceptive faculty the judicial may, in a certain point of view, be considered as included.

To the head of experiences may be referred the following phenomena:

1. Apathematic perceptions: perceptions as they have place in the case in which they do not consist of, nor are attended with, any distinguishable pain or pleasure.

2. Pathematic perceptions: perceptions as they have place in the case where they consist of, or are attended with either pain or pleasure, *i.e.* are attended with pains or painful perceptions, or pleasures or pleasurable perceptions.

Pathematic or apathematic perceptions, may be distinguished into judgement-not-involving, and judgement-involving.

A judgement-involving perception is the perception of a relation, *i.e.* of the existence of a relation between some two objects.

One of the relations most frequently exemplified in this way is the relation of cause and effect.

Between a judgement-involving, and a judgement-not-involving, perception, the differential character is this. In so far as an experience or act of the judicial faculty is not involved in the perception in question, it is not susceptible of error; in so far as any such experience or act is involved, it is susceptible of error.

The case of a judgment-involving perception is exemplified in, and by, every one of the five senses:

1. I open my eyes, I see something before me, it seems to me that it is a distant hill; but in fact it is a cloud. Here is a misjudgment Here is error. But that I see something, *i.e.* that on the retina of my eyes an image is depicted, in this there is no error.

2. I hear a sound—to me it seems the voice of a man at a distance, but in fact it is the cry of an owl.

3. I am sitting in the dark—a piece of drapery is presented to me; I am asked what it is, I pronounce it silk-velvet; but in fact it is cotton-velvet.

4. Left in the dark, a plate of boiled vegetables is placed before me—I am asked what it is; it seems to be spinach, but in fact it is beet leaves.

5. Still in the dark, a flower is presented to me—I am asked what it is; it smells to me to be a pink, but in fact it is a carnation.

In the production of that state of mind in which a perception whether judgment-involving, or judgment-not-involving, has place, objects exterior to the body have, or have not, borne a part. In the first case, the perception may be termed a perception *ab extra*, or say derivative; in the other case, a perception purely *ab intra*, or say indigenous.

Of derivative perceptions, the above five are each of them so many exemplifications.

Of indigenous perceptions examples are: a sense of dilatation in the stomach, a sense of increased or diminished heat: in either of which cases, the perception may be apathematic or pathematic—and, if pathematic, accompanied either with pain or pleasure.

B. *Operations*—Results of the Exercise of the Appetitive Faculty.

Every operation of the mind, and thence every operation of the body, is the result of an exercise of the will, or volitional faculty. The volitional faculty is a branch of the appetitive faculty, *i.e.* that faculty in which desire, in all its several modifications, has place.

Desire has for its object either pleasure or pain, or, what is commonly the case, a mixture of both, in ever varying and un-ascertainable proportions.

The desire which has pleasure for its object, is the desire of the presence of such pleasure. Desire which has pain for its object, is the desire of the absence of such pain.

I see an apple, I conceive a desire to eat, and thence to possess that apple. If not being either hungry or thirsty, my desire is, notwithstanding, excited by the supposed agreeable flavour of the apple, pleasure, and pleasure alone, *viz.* the presence of that pleasure, such as it is, is the object of my desire. If being either hungry or thirsty, or both, and that to a degree of uneasiness, pain, *viz.* the absence of that same uneasiness is moreover the object of my desire.

A desire than has, in every case, an internal object, *viz.* the corresponding pleasure, and in so far as that object has for its expected source an object exterior to the body, an external object.

A desire having pleasure alone, *i.e.* presence of pleasure for its internal object, has place, in so far as, from the presence or productiveness of the supposed source, pleasure is regarded as about to be eventually experienced.

A desire having pain alone, *i.e.* absence of pain for its internal object, has place in so far as, from the presence or productiveness of the supposed source, pain is regarded as being eventually about to be experienced.

A desire having pleasure and pain together for its internal object, has place, in so far as, while from the presence or productiveness of the supposed source, pleasure is regarded as being eventually about to be experienced, pain is, at the same time, experienced from the reflection of the actual absence of that same source; or in so far as, while from the presence of the supposed source, pain is regarded as being eventually about to be experienced, pleasure is at the same time experienced from the reflection of the actual absence of that same source.

If the desire, being a desire having pleasure for its object, is to a certain degree intense, in this case, so long as it remains unsatisfied, it has a certain degree of pain for its inseparable accompaniment, *viz.* the pain of non-possession, or say privation, produced by the absence of the source, and the consequent non-satisfaction of the desire.

If the desire be a desire having pain for its object, *i.e.* the absence of pain from this or that particular source, in this case, if the desire be to a certain degree intense, it has for its inseparable accompaniment, a persuasion more or less intense of the probability of a state of things, in which that pain will be experienced.

Considered as having produced, or as being with more or less probability of success operating towards the production of the result (*viz.* presence of pleasure, or absence of pain), which is the object of it, a desire is termed a motive.

In so far as the production of the state of things which is the immediate object of the desire, is considered as following immediately and certainly upon the existence of the desire, an act of the will is said to take place; the faculty by which this effect is considered as produced, being termed the volitional, or volitive faculty, or, in one word, the will.

The volitional faculty is, therefore, a branch of the appetitive.

But no act of the will can take place but in consequence of a correspondent desire; in consequence of the action of a desire in the character of a motive.

Also, no desire can have place, unless when the idea of pleasure or pain, in some shape or degree, has place. Minute, it is true, minute in the extreme is the quantity of pleasure or pain requisite and sufficient to form the desire of it; but still it is not the less true—take away all pleasure and all pain, and you have no desire.[a]

Pleasure and pain, considered in themselves, belong to the perceptive faculty, *i.e.* to the pathematic branch of it.

But pleasure and pain considered as operating, as above, in the production of desires, operating, as above, in the character of motives, and thus producing volition, and through volition action, internal or external, corporeal, or purely mental, belong to the appetitive faculty.

---

[a] In the production of volition, a desire operating in the character of a motive is either not (certainly) effective or (certainly) effective; if (certainly) effective, an act of the will is the consequence. The cause of my own act is always my own desire; and in this sense my will is free. But the cause of that desire, what is it? In some cases I know what it is; in others not. When I know not what it is, how is my will free? The action of it is in so far dependent upon an unknown cause external to myself.

When I make my choice amongst a multitude of antagonising desires, what is the cause of that choice?

Pleasure and pain compose, therefore, as it were, the bond of union and channel of communication between the two faculties.

Attention is the result of an act of the will; of an exercise of the volitional branch of the appetitive faculty.

In so far as attention has place in so far as attention is applied, either to the direction, or to the observation of an experience, the experience is converted into an operation; or, at any rate, in the field of thought, in the mental field, that place which would otherwise have been the field of an experience and nothing more, becomes now the field of an experience, and of a correspondent operation at the same time—an operation having for its subject the object which was the source or seat of the experience.

In some instances, language affords not as yet any word, or words, by which the difference between the presence or absence of attention, in relation to the effect in question, is denoted.

Here the word judgment—act of the judgment—is the locution employed, as well in the case of those instantaneous and involuntary judgments, which, as above, are commonly confounded with simple perception, and those attentive and elaborate judgments which are pronounced in the senate, on the bench, or in the laboratory of the chemist, or on the library-table of the logician.

Without attention, the memory is but the seat of a mere passive experience, which is termed remembrance. In consequence of an exertion or exercise of the will, importing attention applied to the purpose of searching out and bringing from the storehouse of the mind the impression in question, it becomes the seat and subject of an operation termed recollection.

CHAPTER 4

Springs of Action[1]

I. Pleasures and Pains the basis of all the other entities: these the only real ones; those, fictitious.

Among all the several species of psychological entities, the two which are as it were the roots; the main pillars or foundations of all the rest, the matter of which all the rest are composed—or the receptacles of that matter—whichsoever may be the physical image, employed to give aid, if not existence to conception—will be, it is believed, if they have not been already, seen to be, *Pleasures* and *Pain*. Of these, the existence is matter of universal and constant experience. Without any of the rest, these are susceptible of—and as often as they come unlooked for, do actually come into—existence: without these, no one of all those others ever had, or ever could have had, existence.

True it is, that, when the question is, what in the case in question, are the springs of action, by which, on the occasion in question, the mind in question has been operated upon, or to the operation of which it has been exposed, the species of psychological entity, to be looked out for in the first place—is the motive. But, of the sort of motive, which has thus been in operation, no clear idea can be entertained, otherwise than by reference to the sort of pleasure or pain, which such motive has for its basis: *viz.* the pleasure or pain, the idea, and eventual expectation, of which, is considered as having been operating in the character of a motive.

This being understood, the corresponding interest is at the same time understood: and, if it be to the pleasurable class that the operating cause in question belongs, then so it is that, in its way to become a motive, the interest has become productive of a desire: if to the painful class, of a correspondent aversion: and thus it is, that, on the occasion in question, the operation of a motive of the kind in question, whatever it be (meaning a motive to the will), having had existence, it can not but be, that a corresponding desire or aversion—and the idea, and eventual expectation at least, of a corresponding pleasure or pain and the idea and belief of the existence of a corresponding interest—must also have had existence.

On this basis must also be erected, and to this standard must be referred, whatsoever clear explanations are capable of being suggested, by the other more anomalous apellatives above spoken of; such as emotion, affection, passion, disposition, inclination, propensity, quality (*viz.* moral quality), vice, virtue, moral good, moral evil.

Destitute of reference to the ideas of pain and pleasure, whatever ideas are annexed to the words virtue and vice amount to nothing more than that of groundless approbation or disapprobation. All language in which these appellatives are employed is no better than empty declamation. A virtuous disposition is the disposition to give birth to good—understand always pathological good; or to prevent, or abstain from giving birth to, evil; understand always pathological evil—in so far as the production of the effect requires exertion in the way of self-denial: *i.e.* sacrifice of supposed lesser good to supposed greater good. In so far as the greater good, to which the less is sacrificed, is considered as being the good of others, the virtue belongs to the head of probity or beneficence: in so far as it is considered as being the good of self, to that of self-regarding prudence. Means selecting is the name by which the other branch of prudence may be designated: *viz.* that which, being subservient in its nature, and being so with reference to some interest, is equally capable of being understood to be so, whether that interest be of the self-regarding class, or of the extra-regarding; *viz.* of the social or of the dissocial class.

II. No Act Properly Speaking Disinterested.

If so it be, that, of the view here given of the causes of human action, the general tenor is conformable to the truth of things, than so it is, that, by means of it, divers psychological phaenomena—divers phaenomena of the human mind—which till now have been either not at all or but indistinctly perceived—phaenomena of the most unquestionable importance with reference to practice—will, now for the first time, have become distinctly visible.

1. In regard to interest, in the most extended—which is the original and only strictly proper sense—of the word disinterested, no human act ever has been or ever can be disinterested. For there exists not ever any voluntary action, which is not the result of the operation of some motive or motives: nor any motive, which has not for its accompaniment a corresponding interest, real or imagined.

2. In the only sense in which disinterestedness can with truth be predicated of human action, it is employed in a sense more confined than the only one which the etymology of the word suggests, and can with propriety admit of: what, in this sense, it must be understood to denote, being—not the absence of all interest, a state of things which, consistently with voluntary action, is not possible—but only the absence of all interest of the self-regarding class. Not but that it is very frequently predicated of human action in cases in which divers interests, to no one of which the appellation of self-regarding can with proprietary be denied, have been exercising their influence: and in particular (No. 9) fear of God or hope from God, and (No. 8) fear of ill-repute or hope of good repute.

3. If what is above be correct, the most disinterested of men is not less under the domination of interest than the most interested. The only cause of his being styled disinterested is—its not having been observed that the sort of motive (suppose its sympathy for an individual or a class of individuals) has as truly a corresponding interest belonging to it, as any other species of motive has. Of this contradiction, between the truth of the case, and the language employed in speaking of it, the cause is that, in the one case, men have not been in the habit of making—as in point of consistency they ought to have made—of the word interest that use which, in the other case, they have been in the habit of making of it.

4. At the same time, by its having been as properly, and completely, and indisputably, the product of interest, as any other action ever is or can be, whatsoever merit may happen to belong to any action, to which, in the loose and ordinary way of speaking, the epithet disinterested would be applied, is not in any the slightest degree lessened.

Not that, in the case where sympathy is the motive, there is less need of—nor even less actual demand for—such a word as interest, than in the case, where the motive and interest are of the self-regarding class. Not but that, even in the case of sympathy, conjugates of the word interest are employed, and even the word itself. Witness these expressions among so many: There stands a man, in whose behalf I feel myself strongly interested; a man, in whose fate—in whose sorrows—I take a lively interest, etc. etc.

CHAPTER 5[1]

A. Of the Principle of Utility

1. Nature has placed mankind under the governance of two sovereign masters, *pain* and *pleasure*. It is for them alone to point out what we ought to do, as well as to determine what we shall do. On the one hand the standard of right and wrong, on the other the chain of causes and effects, are fastened to their throne. They govern us in all we do, in all we say, in all we think: every effort we can make to throw off our subjection, will serve but to demonstrate and confirm it. In words a man may pretend to abjure their empire: but in reality he will remain subject to it all the while. The *principle of utility*[a] recognises this subjection, and assumes it for the foundation of that system, the object of which is to rear the fabric of felicity by the hands of reason and of law. Systems which

---

[a] Note by the author, July 1822.

To this denomination has of late been added, or substituted, the *greatest happiness* or *greatest felicity* principle: this for shortness, instead of saying at length *that principle* which states the greatest happiness of all those whose interest is in question, as being the right and proper, and only right and proper and universally desirable, end of human action in every situation, and in particular in that of a functionary or set of functionaries exercising the powers of Government. The word *utility* does not so clearly point to the ideas of *pleasure* and *pain* as the words *happiness* and *felicity* do: nor does it lead us to the consideration of the *number*, of the interests affected; to the *number*, as being the circumstance, which contributes, in the largest proportion, to the formation of the standard here in question; the *standard of right and wrong*, by which alone the propriety of human conduct, in every situation, can with propriety be tried. This want of a sufficiently manifest connexion between the ideas of *happiness* and *pleasure* on the one hand, and the idea of *utility* on the other, I have every now and than found operating, and with but too much efficiency, as a bar to the acceptance, that might otherwise have been given, to this principle.

attempt to question it, deal in sounds instead of sense, in caprice instead of reason, in darkness instead of light.

But enough of metaphor and declamation: it is not by such means that moral science is to be improved.

2. The principle of utility is the foundation of the present work: it will be proper therefore at the outset to give an explicit and determinate account of what is meant by it. By the principle[b] of utility is meant that principle which approves or disapproves of every action whatsoever, according to the tendency which it appears to have to augment or diminish the happiness of the party whose interest is in question: or, what is the same thing in other words, to promote or to oppose that happiness. I say of every action whatsoever; and therefore not only of every action of a private individual, but of every measure of government.

3. By utility is meant that property in any object, whereby it tends to produce benefit, advantage, pleasure, good, or happiness, (all this in the present case comes to the same thing) or (what comes again to the same thing) to prevent the happening of mischief, pain, evil, or unhappiness to the party whose interest is considered: if that party be the community in general, then the happiness of the community: if a particular individual, then the happiness of that individual.

4. The interest of the community is one of the most general expressions that can occur in the phraseology of morals: no wonder that the meaning of it is often lost. When it has a meaning, it is

---

[b] (Principle) The word principle is derived from the Latin *principium*: which seems to be compounded of the two words *primus*, first, or chief, and *cipium*, a termination which seems to be derived from *capio*, to take, as in *mancipium, municipium*; to which are analogous *auceps, forceps*, and others. It is a term of very vague and very extensive signification: it is applied to any thing which is conceived to serve as a foundation or beginning to any series of operations: in some cases, of physical operations; but of mental operations in the present case.

The principle here in question may be taken for an act of the mind; a sentiment; a sentiment of approbation; a sentiment which, when applied to an action, approves of its utility, as that quality of it by which the measure of approbation or disapprobation bestowed upon it ought to be governed.

this. The community is a fictitious *body*, composed of the individual persons who are considered as constituting as it were its *members*. The interest of the community then is, what?—the sum of the interests of the several members who compose it.

5. It is in vain to talk of the interest of the community, without understanding what is the interest of the individual.[c] A thing is said to promote the interest, or to be *for* the interest, of an individual, when it tends to add to the sum total of his pleasures: or, what comes to the same thing, to diminish the sum total of his pains.

6. An action then may be said to be conformable to the principle of utility, or, for shortness sake, to utility (meaning with respect to the community at large), when the tendency it has to augment the happiness of the community is greater than any it has to diminish it.

7. A measure of government (which is but a particular kind of action, performed by a particular person or persons) may be said to be conformable to or dictated by the principle of utility, when in like manner the tendency which it has to augment the happiness of the community is greater than any which it has to diminish it.

8. When an action, or in particular a measure of government, is supposed by a man to be conformable to the principle of utility, it may be convenient, for the purposes of discourse, to imagine a kind of law or dictate, called a law or dictate of utility: and to speak of the action in question, as being conformable to such law or dictate.

9. A man may be said to be a partisan of the principle of utility, when the approbation or disapprobation he annexes to any action, or to any measure, is determined by, and proportioned to the tendency which he conceives it to have to augment or to diminish the happiness of the community: or in other words, to its conformity or unconformity to the laws or dictates of utility.

10. Of an action that is conformable to the principle of utility, one may always say either that it is one that ought to be done, or at least that it is not one that ought not to be done. One may say also, that it is right it should be done; at least that it is not wrong it should be done: that it is a right action; at least that it is not a wrong action. When thus interpreted, the words *ought*, and *right*

---

[c] (Interest.) Interest is one of those words, which not having any superior *genus*, cannot in the ordinary way be defined.

and *wrong*, and others of that stamp, have a meaning: when otherwise, they have none.

11. Has the rectitude of this principle been ever formally contested? It should seem that it had, by those who have not known what they have been meaning. Is it susceptible of any direct proof? it should seem not: for that which is used to prove every thing else, cannot itself be proved: a chain of proofs must have their commencement somewhere. To give such proof is as impossible as it is needless.

12. Not that there is or ever has been that human creature breathing, however stupid or perverse, who has not on many, perhaps on most occasions of his life, deferred to it. By the natural constitution of the human frame, on most occasions of their lives men in general embrace this principle, without thinking of it: if not for the ordering of their own actions, yet for the trying of their own actions, as well as of those of other men. There have been, at the same time, not many, perhaps, even of the most intelligent, who have been disposed to embrace it purely and without reserve There are even few who have not taken some occasion or other to quarrel with it, either on account of their not understanding always how to apply it, or on account of some prejudice or other which they were afraid to examine into, or could not bear to part with. For such is the stuff that man is made of: in principle and in practice, in a right track and in a wrong one, the rarest of all human qualities is consistency.

13. When a man attempts to combat the principle of utility, it is with reasons drawn, without his being aware of it, from that very principle itself.[d] His arguments, if they prove any thing, prove not that the principle is *wrong*, but that, according to the applications he supposes to be made of it, it is *misapplied*. Is it possible for a man to move the earth? Yes; but he must first find out another earth to stand upon.

---

[d] 'The principle of utility (I have heard it said) is a dangerous principle: it is dangerous on certain occasions to consult it.' This is as much as to say, what? that it is not consonant to utility, to consult utility: in short, that it is *not* consulting it, to consult it. [A long footnote Bentham added in 1822 and included in the 1823 edition has been omitted.]

14. To disprove the propriety of it by arguments is impossible; but, from the causes that have been mentioned, or from some confused or partial view of it, a man may happen to be disposed not to relish it. Where this is the case, if he thinks the settling of his opinions on such a subject worth the trouble, let him take the following steps, and at length, perhaps, he may come to reconcile himself to it.

(1) Let him settle with himself, whether he would wish to discard this principle altogether; if so, let him consider what it is that all his reasonings (in matters of politics especially) can amount to?

(2) If he would, let him settle with himself, whether he would judge and act without any principle, or whether there is any other he would judge and act by?

(3) If there be, let him examine and satisfy himself whether the principle he thinks he has found is really any separate intelligible principle; or whether it be not a mere principle in words, a kind of phrase, which at bottom expresses neither more nor less than the mere averment of his own unfounded sentiments; that is, what in another person he might be apt to call *caprice*?

(4) If he is inclined to think that his own approbation or disapprobation, annexed to the idea of an act, without any regard to its consequences, is a sufficient foundation for him to judge and act upon, let him ask himself whether his sentiment is to be a standard of right and wrong, with respect to every other man, or whether every man's sentiment has the same privilege of being a standard to itself?

(5) In the first case, let him ask himself whether his principle is not despotical, and hostile to all the rest of human race?

(6) In the second case, whether it is not anarchial, and whether at this rate there are not as many different standards of right and wrong as there are men? and whether even to the same man, the same thing, which is right today, may not (without the least change in its nature) be wrong tomorrow? and whether the same thing is not right and wrong in the same place at the same time? and in either case, whether all argument is not at an end? and whether, when two men have said, 'I like this', and 'I don't like it', they can (upon such a principle) have anything more to say?

(7) If he should have said to himself, No: for that the sentiment

which he proposes as a standard must be grounded on reflection, let him say on what particulars the reflection is to turn? if on particulars having relation to the utility of the act, then let him say whether this is not deserting his own principle, and borrowing assistance from that very one in opposition to which he sets it up: or if not on those particulars, on what other particulars?

(8) If he should be for compounding the matter, and adopting his own principle in part, and the principle of utility in part, let him say how far he will adopt it?

(9) When he has settled with himself where he will stop, then let him ask himself how he justifies to himself the adopting it so far? and why he will not adopt it any farther?

(10) Admitting any other principle than the principle of utility to be a right principle, a principle that it is right for a man to pursue; admitting (what is not true) that the word *right* can have a meaning without reference to utility, let him say whether there is any such thing as a *motive* that a man can have to pursue the dictates of it: if there is, let him say what that motive is, and how it is to be distinguished from those which enforce the dictates of utility: if not, then lastly let him say what it is this other principle can be good for?

B. Of Principles Adverse to that of Utility

1. If the principle of utility be a right principle to be governed by, and that, in all cases, it follows from what has been just observed, that whatever principle differs from it in any case must necessarily be a wrong one. To prove any other principle, therefore, to be a wrong one, there needs no more than just to show it to be what it is, a principle of which the dictates are in some point or other different from those of the principle of utility: to state it is to confute it.

2. A principle may be different from that of utility in two ways: 1. By being constantly opposed to it: this is the case with a principle which may be termed the principle of *asceticism*.[e] 2. By being sometimes opposed to it, and sometimes not, as it may happen:

---

e (Asceticism) ascetic is a term that has been sometimes applied to monks. It comes from a Greek word which signifies *exercise*. The practices by which monks sought to distinguish themselves from other men were called their exercises. These exercises consisted in so many contrivances they had for tormenting themselves. By this they thought to ingratiate themselves with the Deity. For the Deity, said they, is a Being of infinite benevolence: now a Being of the most ordinary benevolence is pleased to see others make themselves as happy as they can: therefore to make ourselves as unhappy as we can is the way to please the Deity. If any body asked them, what motive they could find for doing all this? Oh! said they, you are not to imagine that we are punishing ourselves for nothing: we know very well what we are about. You are to know, that for every grain of pain it costs us now, we are to have a hundred grains of pleasure by and by. The case is, that God loves to see us torment ourselves at present: indeed he has as good as told us so. But this is done only to try us, in order just to see how we should behave: which it is plain he could not know, without making the experiment. Now then, from the satisfaction it gives him to see us make ourselves as unhappy as we can make ourselves in this present life, we have a sure proof of the satisfaction it will give him to see us as happy as he can make us in a life to come.

this is the case with another, which may be termed the principle of *sympathy* and *antipathy*.

3. By the principle of asceticism I mean that principle, which, like the principle of utility, approves or disapproves of any action, according to the tendency which it appears to have to augment or diminish the happiness of the party whose interest is in question; but in an inverse manner: approving of actions in as far as they tend to diminish his happiness; disapproving of them in as far as they tend to augment it.

4. It is evident that any one who reprobates any the least particle of pleasure, as such, from whatever source derived, is *pro tanto* a partisan of the principle of asceticism. It is only upon that principle, and not from the principle of utility, that the most abominable pleasure which the vilest of malefactors ever reaped from his crime would be to be reprobated, if it stood alone. The case is, that it never does stand alone; but is necessarily followed by such a quantity of pain (or, what comes to the same thing, such a chance for a certain quantity of pain) that the pleasure in comparison of it, is as nothing: and this is the true and sole, but perfectly sufficient, reason for making it a ground for punishment.

5. There are two classes of men of very different complexions, by whom the principle of asceticism appears to have been embraced; the one a set of moralists, the other a set of religionists. Different accordingly have been the motives which appear to have recommended it to the notice of these different parties. Hope, that is the prospect of pleasure, seems to have animated the former: hope, the ailment of philosophic pride: the hope of honour and reputation at the hands of men. Fear, that is the prospect of pain, the latter: fear, the offspring of superstitious fancy: the fear of future punishment at the hands of a splenetic and revengeful Deity. I say in this case fear: for of the invisible future, fear is more powerful than hope. These circumstances characterize the two different parties among the partisans of the principle of asceticism; the parties and their motives different, the principle the same.

6. The religious party, however, appear to have carried it farther than the philosophical: they have acted more consistently and less wisely. The philosophical party have scarcely gone farther than to reprobate pleasure: the religious party have frequently gone so

far as to make it a matter of merit and of duty to court pain. The philosophical party have hardly gone farther than the making pain a matter of indifference. It is no evil, they have said: they have not said, it is a good. They have not so much as reprobated all pleasure in the lump. They have discarded only what they have called the gross; that is, such as are organical, or of which the origin is easily traced up to such as are organical: they have even cherished and magnified the refined. Yet this, however, not under the name of pleasure: to cleanse itself from the sordes of its impure original, it was necessary it should change its name: the honourable, the glorious, the reputable, the becoming, the *honestum*, the *decorum*, it was to be called: in short, any thing but pleasure.

7. From these two sources have flowed the doctrines from which the sentiments of the bulk of mankind have all along received a tincture of this principle; some from the philosophical, some from the religious, some from both. Men of education more frequently from the philosophical, as more suited to the elevation of their sentiments: the vulgar more frequently from the superstitious, as more suited to the narrowness of their intellect, undilated by knowledge: and to the abjectness of their condition, continually open to the attacks of fear. The tinctures, however, derived from the two sources, would naturally intermingle, insomuch that a man would not always know by which of them he was most influenced: and they would often serve to corroborate and enliven one another. It was this conformity that made a kind of alliance between parties of a complexion otherwise so dissimilar: and disposed them to unite upon various occasions against the common enemy, the partisan of the principle of utility, whom they joined in branding with the odious name of Epicurean.

8. The principle of asceticism, however, with whatever warmth it may have been embraced by its partisans as a rule of private conduct, seems not to have been carried to any considerable length, when applied to the business of government. In a few instances it has been carried a little way by the philosophical party: witness the Spartan regimen. Though then, perhaps, it may be considered as having been a measure of security: and an application, though a precipitate and perverse application, of the principle of utility. Scarcely in any instances, to any considerable length, by the

religious: for the various monastic orders, and the societies of the Quakers, Dumplers, Moravians, and other religionists, have been free societies, whose regimen no man has been astricted to without the intervention of his own consent. Whatever merit a man may have thought there would be in making himself miserable, no such notion seems ever to have occurred to any of them, that it may be a merit, much less a duty, to make others miserable: although it should seem, that if a certain quantity of misery were a thing so desirable, it would not matter much whether it were brought by each man upon himself, or by one man upon another. It is true, that from the same source from whence, among the religionists, the attachment to the principle of asceticism took its rise, flowed other doctrines and practices, from which misery in abundance was produced in one man by the instrumentality of another: witness the holy wars, and the persecutions for religion. But the passion for producing misery in these cases proceeded upon some special ground: the exercise of it was confined to persons of particular descriptions: they were tormented, not as men, but as heretics and infidels. To have inflicted the same miseries on their fellow-believers and fellow-sectaries, would have been as blameable in the eyes even of these religionists, as in those of a partisan of the principle of utility. For a man to give himself a certain number of stripes was indeed meritorious: but to give the same number of stripes to another man, not consenting, would have been a sin. We read of saints, who for the good of their souls, and the mortification of their bodies, have voluntarily yielded themselves a prey to vermin: but though many persons of this class have wielded the reins of empire, we read of none who have set themselves to work, and made laws on purpose, with a view of stocking the body politic with the breed of highwaymen, housebreakers, or incendiaries. If at any time they have suffered the nation to be preyed upon by swarms of idle pensioners, or useless placemen, it has rather been from negligence and imbecility, than from any settled plan for oppressing and plundering of the people.[f] If at any time they have sapped the

---

[f] So thought A⁰ 1780 and 1789; not so A⁰ 1814. [This note that Bentham inserted in his copy of the 1789 edition was overlooked in the 1823 edition. Bowring, however, inserted it in Vol. I of his collected works.]

sources of national wealth, by cramping commerce, and driving the inhabitants into emigration, it has been with other views, and in pursuit of other ends. If they have declaimed against the pursuit of pleasure, and the use of wealth, they have commonly stopped at declamation: they have not, like Lycurgus, made express ordinances for the purpose of banishing the precious metals. If they have established idleness by a law, it has been not because idleness, the mother of vice and misery, is itself a virtue, but because idleness (say they) is the road to holiness. If under the notion of fasting, they have joined in the plan of confining their subjects to a diet, thought by some to be of the most nourishing and prolific nature, it has been not for the sake of making them tributaries to the nations by whom that diet was to be supplied, but for the sake of manifesting their own power, and exercising the obedience of the people. If they have established, or suffered to be established, punishments for the breach of celibacy, they have done no more than comply with the petitions of those deluded rigorists, who, dupes to the ambitions and deep-laid policy of their rulers, first laid themselves under that idle obligation by a vow.

9. The principle of asceticism seems originally to have been the reverie of certain hasty speculators, who having perceived, or fancied, that certain pleasures, when reaped in certain circumstances, have, at the long run, been attended with pains more than equivalent to them, took occasion to quarrel with every thing that offered itself under the name of pleasure. Having then got thus far, and having forgot the point which they set out from, they pushed on, and went so much further as to think it meritorious to fall in love with pain. Even this, we see, is at bottom but the principle of utility misapplied.

10. The principle of utility is capable of being consistently pursued; and it is but tautology to say, that the more consistently it is pursued, the better it must ever be for human-kind. The principle of asceticism never was, nor ever can be, consistently pursued by any living creature. Let but one tenth part of the inhabitants of this earth pursue it consistently, and in a day's time they will have turned it into a hell.

11. Among principles adverse to that of utility, that which at this day seems to have most influence in matters of government, is

what may be called the principle of sympathy and antipathy.[g] By

---

[g] The following Note was first printed in January 1789.[2]

It ought rather to have been styled, more extensively, the principle of *caprice*. Where it applies to the choice of actions to be marked out for injunction or prohibition, for reward or punishment (to stand, in a word, as subjects for *obligations* to be imposed), it may indeed with propriety be termed, as in the text, the principle of *sympathy* and *antipathy*. But this appellative does not so well apply to it, when occupied in the choice of the *events* which are to serve as sources of *title* with respect to *rights*: where the actions prohibited and allowed the obligations and rights, being already fixed, the only question is, under what circumstances a man is to be invested with the one or subjected to the other? From what incidents occasion is to be taken to invest a man, or to refuse to invest him, with the one, or to subject him to the other? In this latter case it may more appositely be characterized by the name of the *phantastic principle*. Sympathy and antipathy are affections of the *sensible* faculty. But the choice of *titles* with respect to *rights*, especially with respect to proprietary rights, upon grounds unconnected with utility, has been in many instances the work, not of the affections but of the imagination.

When, in justification of an article of English Common Law, calling uncles to succeed in certain cases in preference to fathers, Lord Coke produced a sort of ponderosity he had discovered in rights, disqualifying them from ascending in a straight line, it was not that he *loved* uncles particularly, or *hated* fathers, but because the analogy, such as it was, was what his imagination presented him with, instead of a reason, and because, to a judgment unobservant of the standard of utility, or unacquainted with the art of consulting it, where affection is out of the way, imagination is the only guide.

When I know not what ingenious grammarian invented the proposition *Delegatus non potest delegare*, to serve as a rule of law, it was not surely that he had any antipathy to delegates of the second order, or that it was any pleasure to him to think of the ruin which, for want of a manager at home, may befall the affairs of a traveller, whom an unforeseen accident has deprived of the object of his choice: it was, that the incongruity, of giving the same law to objects so contrasted as *active* and *passive* are, was not to be surmounted, and that *-atus* chimes, as well as it contrasts, with *-are*.

When that inexorable maxim (of which the dominion is no more to be defined, than the date of its birth, or the name of its father, is to the principle of sympathy and antipathy, I mean that principle which approves or disapproves of certain actions, not on account of their tending to augment the happiness, nor yet on account of their tending to diminish the happiness of the party whose interest is in question, but merely because a man finds himself disposed to approve or disapprove of them: holding up that approbation or disapprobation as a sufficient reason for itself, and disclaiming the necessity of looking out for any extrinsic ground. Thus far in the general department of morals: and in the particular department of politics, measuring out the quantum (as well as determining the ground) of punishment, by the degree of the disapprobation.

12. It is manifest, that this is rather a principle in name than in reality: it is not a positive principle of itself, so much as a term employed to signify the negation of all principle. What one expects to find in a principle is something that points out some external consideration, as a means of warranting and guiding the internal sentiments of approbation and disapprobation: this expectation is but ill fulfilled by a proposition, which does neither more nor less than hold up each of those sentiments as a ground and standard for itself.

13. In looking over the catalogue of human actions (says a partisan of this principle) in order to determine which of them are to be marked with the seal of disapprobation, you need but to take counsel of your own feelings: whatever you find in yourself a propensity to condemn, is wrong for that very reason. For the same reason it is also meet for punishment: in what proportion it is adverse to utility, or whether it be adverse to utility at all, is a matter that makes no difference. In that same *proportion* also is it meet for punishment: if you hate much, punish much: if you hate

---

be found) was imported from England for the government of Bengal, and the whole fabric of judicature was crushed by the thunders of *ex post facto* justice, it was not surely that the prospect of a blameless magistracy perishing in prison afforded any enjoyment to the unoffended authors of their misery; but that the music of the maxim, absorbing the whole imagination, had drowned the cries of humanity along with the dictates of common sense.[3] *Fiat Justitia, ruat caelum*, says another maxim, as full of extravagance as it is of harmony: Go heaven to wreck—so justice be but done:—and what is the ruin of kingdoms, in comparison of the wreck of heaven?[4]

little, punish little: punish as you hate. If you hate not at all, punish not at all: the fine feelings of the soul are not to be overborne and tyrannized by the harsh and rugged dictates of political utility.

14. The various systems that have been formed concerning the standard of right and wrong, may all be reduced to the principle of sympathy and antipathy. One account may serve for all of them. They consist all of them in so many contrivances for avoiding the obligation of appealing to any external standard, and for prevailing upon the reader to accept of the author's sentiment or opinion as a reason and that a sufficient one[5] for itself. The phrases different, but the principle the same.[h]

---

[h] It is curious to observe the variety of inventions men have hit upon, and the variety of phrases they have brought forward, in order to conceal from the world, and, if possible, from themselves, this very general and therefore very pardonable self-sufficiency:

1. One man (Lord Shaftesbury, Hutchinson, Hume, etc.)[6] says, he has a thing made on purpose to tell him what is right and what is wrong: and that it is called a *moral sense*: and then he goes to work at his ease, and says, such a thing is right, and such a thing is wrong —why? 'because my moral sense tells me it is'.

2. Another man (Dr Beattie) comes and alters the phrase: leaving out *moral*, and putting in *common*, in the room of it. He then tells you, that his common sense teaches him what is right and wrong, as surely as the other's moral sense did: meaning by common sense, a sense of some kind or other, which, he says, is possessed by all mankind: the sense of those, whose sense is not the same as the author's, being struck out of the account as not worth taking. This contrivance does better than the other; for a moral sense, being a new thing, a man may feel about him a good while without being able to find it out: but common sense is as old as the creation; and there is no man but would be ashamed to be thought not to have as much of it as his neighbours. It has another great advantage: by appearing to share power, it lessens envy: for when a man gets up upon this ground, in order to anathematize those who differ from him, it is not a *sic volo sic jubeo*, but by a *velitis jubeatis*.

3. Another man (Dr Price) comes, and says, that as to a moral sense indeed, he cannot find that he has any such thing: that however he has an *understanding*, which will do quite as well. This understanding, he says, is the standard of right and wrong: it tells him so and so. All good and wise men understand as he does:

footnote continued—

if other men's understandings differ in any point from his, so much the worse for them: it is a sure sign they are either defective or corrupt.

4. Another man says that there is an eternal and immutable Rule of Right: that that rule of right dictates so and so: and then he begins giving you his sentiments upon anything that comes uppermost: and these sentiments (you are to take for granted) are so many branches of the eternal rule of right.

5. Another man (Dr Clark), or perhaps the same man (it's no matter) says, that there are certain practices conformable, and others repugnant, to the Fitness of Things; and then he tells you, at his leisure, what practices are conformable and what repugnant: just as he happens to like a practice or dislike it.

6. A great multitude of people are continually talking of the Law of Nature; and then they go on giving you their sentiments about what is right and what is wrong: and these sentiments, you are to understand, are so many chapters and sections of the Law of Nature.

7. Instead of the phrase, Law of Nature, you have sometimes, Law of Reason, Right Reason, Natural Justice, Natural Equity, Good Order. Any of them will do equally well. This latter is most used in politics. The three last are much more tolerable than the others, because they do not very explicitly claim to be any thing more than phrases: they insist but feebly upon the being looked upon as so many positive standards of themselves, and seem content to be taken, upon occasion, for phrases expressive of the conformity of the thing in question to the proper standard, whatever that may be. On most occasions, however, it will be better to say *utility*: *utility* is clearer, as referring more explicitly to pain and pleasure.

8. We have one philosopher (Woolaston), who says, there is no harm in any thing in the world but in telling a lie: and that if, for example, you were to murder your own father, this would only be a particular way of saying, he was not your father. Of course, when this philosopher sees any thing that he does not like, he says, it is a particular way of telling a lie. It is saying, that the act ought to be done, or may be done, when, *in truth*, it ought not to be done.

9. The fairest and openest of them all is that sort of man who speaks out, and says, I am of the number of the Elect: now God himself takes care to inform the Elect what is right: and that with so good effect, that let them strive ever so, they cannot help not only knowing it but practising it. If therefore a man wants to know what is right and what is wrong, he has nothing to do but to come to me.

footnote continued—

It is upon the principle of antipathy that such and such acts are often reprobated on the score of their being *unnatural*: the practice of exposing children, established among the Greeks and Romans, was an unnatural practice. Unnatural, when it means any thing, means unfrequent: and there it means something; although nothing to the present purpose. But here it means no such thing: for the frequency of such acts is perhaps the great complaint. It therefore means nothing; nothing, I mean, which there is in the act itself. All it can serve to express is, the disposition of the person who is talking of it: the disposition he is in to be angry at the thoughts of it. Does it merit his anger? Very likely it may: but whether it does or no is a question, which, to be answered rightly, can only be answered upon the principle of utility.

Unnatural, is as good a word as moral sense, or common sense; and would be as good a foundation for a system. Such an act is unnatural; that is, repugnant to nature: for I do not like to practise it; and, consequently, do not practise it. It is therefore repugnant to what ought to be the nature of every body else.

The mischief common to all these ways of thinking and arguing (which, in truth, as we have seen, are but one and the same method, couched in different forms of words) is their serving as a cloak, and pretence, and ailment, to despotism: if not a despotism in practice, a despotism however in disposition: which is but too apt, when pretence and power offer, to show itself in practice. The consequence is, that with intentions very commonly of the purest kind, a man becomes a torment either to himself or his fellow-creatures. If he be of the melancholy cast (Dr Price), he sits in silent grief, bewailing their blindness and depravity: if of the irascible (Dr Beattie), he declaims with fury and virulence against all who differ from him; blowing up the coals of fanaticism, and branding with the charge of corruption and insincerity, every man who does not think, or profess to think, as he does.

If such a man happens to possess the advantages of style, his book may do a considerable deal of mischief before the nothingness of it is understood.

These principles, if such they can be called, it is more frequent to see applied to morals than to politics: but their influence extends itself to both. In politics, as well as morals, a man will be at least equally glad of a pretence for deciding any question in the manner that best pleases him, without the trouble of inquiry. If a man is an infallible judge of what is right and wrong in the actions of private individuals, why not in the measures to be observed by public men

footnote continued—

in the direction of such actions?[7] accordingly (not to mention other chimeras) I have more than once known the pretended law of nature set up in legislative debates, in opposition to arguments derived from the principle of utility.

'But is it never, then, from any other considerations than those of utility, that we derive our notions of right and wrong?' I do not know: I do not care. Whether a moral sentiment can be originally conceived from any other source than a view of utility, is one question: whether upon examination and reflection it can, in point of fact, be actually persisted in and justified on any other ground, by a person reflecting within himself, is another: whether in point of right it can properly be justified on any other ground, by a person addressing himself to the community, is a third. The two first are questions of speculation: it matters not, comparatively speaking, how they are decided. The last is a question of practice: the decision of it is of as much importance as that of any can be.

'I feel in myself', (say you) 'a disposition to approve of such or such an action in a moral view: but this is not owing to any notions I have of its being a useful one to the community. I do not pretend to know whether it be a useful one or not: it may be, for aught I know, a mischievous one.' 'But it is then', (say I) 'a mischievous one? examine; and if you can make yourself sensible that it is so, then, if duty means anything, that is, moral duty, it is your *duty* at least to abstain from it: and more than that, if it is what lies in your power, and can be done without too great a sacrifice, to endeavour to prevent it. It is not your cherishing the notion of it in your bosom, and giving it the name of virtue, what will excuse you.'

'I feel in myself', (say you again) 'a disposition to detest such or such an action in a moral view; but this is not owing to any notions I have of its being a mischievous one to the community. I do not pretend to know whether it be a mischievous one or not: it may be not a mischievous one: it may be, for aught I know, an useful one.'— 'May it indeed?' (say I) 'an useful one? but let me tell you then, that unless duty, and right and wrong, be just what you please to make them, if it really be not a mischievous one, and any body has a mind to do it, it is no duty of yours, but, on the contrary, it would be very wrong in you, to take upon you to prevent him: detest it within yourself as much as you please; that may be a very good reason (unless it be also a useful one) for your not doing it yourself: but if you go about, by word or deed, to do any thing to hinder him, or make him suffer for it, it is you, and not he, that have done wrong: it is not your setting yourself to blame his conduct, or

15. It is manifest that the dictates of this principle will frequently coincide with those of utility, though perhaps without intending any such thing. Probably more frequently than not: and hence it is that the business of penal justice is carried on upon that tolerable sort of footing upon which we see it carried on in common at this day. For what more natural or more general ground of hatred to a practice can there be, than the mischievousness of such practice? What all men are exposed to suffer by, all men will be disposed to hate. It is far yet, however, from being a constant ground: for when a man suffers, it is not always that he knows what it is he suffers by. A man may suffer grievously, for instance, by a new tax, without being able to trace up the cause of his sufferings to the injustice of some neighbour, who has eluded the payment of an old one.

16. The principle of sympathy and antipathy is most apt to err on the side of severity. It is for applying punishment in many cases which deserve none: in many cases which deserve some, it is for applying more than they deserve. There is no incident imaginable, be it ever so trivial, and so remote from mischief, from which this principle may not extract a ground of punishment. Any difference in taste: any difference in opinion: upon one subject as well as upon another. No disagreement so trifling which perseverance and altercation will not render serious. Each becomes in the other's eyes an enemy, and, if laws permit, a criminal.[1] This is one of the

branding it with the name of vice, that will make him culpable, or you blameless. Therefore, if you can make yourself content that he shall be of one mind, and you of another, about that matter, and so continue, it is well: but if nothing will serve you, but that you and he must needs be of the same mind, I'll tell you what you have to do: it is for you to get the better of your antipathy, not for him to truckle to it.'

[1] King James the First of England had conceived a violent antipathy against Arians: two of whom he burnt.* This gratification he procured himself without much difficulty: the notions of the times were favourable to it. He wrote a furious book against Vorstius, for being what was called an Arminian: for Vorstius was at a distance. He also wrote a furious book, called *A Counterblast to Tobacco*, against the use of that drug, which Sir Walter Raleigh had then lately introduced. Had the notions of the times co-operated

* Hume's History Vol 6.

circumstances by which the human race is distinguished (not much indeed to its advantage) from the brute creation.

17. It is not, however, by any means unexampled for this principle to err on the side of lenity. A near and perceptible mischief moves antipathy. A remote and imperceptible mischief, though not less real, has no effect. Instances in proof of this will occur in numbers in the course of the work.[j] It would be breaking in upon the order of it to give them here.

18. It may be wondered, perhaps, that in all this while no mention has been made of the *theological* principle; meaning that principle which professes to recur for the standard of right and wrong to the will of God. But the case is, this is not in fact a distinct principle. It is never any thing more or less than one or other of the three before-mentioned principles presenting itself under another shape. The *will* of God here meant cannot be his revealed will, as contained in the sacred writings: for that is a system which nobody

---

with him he would have burnt the Anabaptist and the smoker of tobacco in the same fire. However he had the satisfaction of putting Raleigh to death afterwards, though for another crime.

Disputes concerning the comparative excellence of French and Italian music have occasioned very serious bickerings at Paris. One of the parties would not have been sorry (says Mr D'Alembert*) to have brought government into the quarrel. Pretences were sought after and urged. Long before that, a dispute of like nature, and of at least equal warmth, had been kindled at London upon the comparative merits of two composers at London; where riots between the approvers and disapprovers of a new play are, at this day, not unfrequent. The ground of quarrel between the Big-endians and the Little-endians in the fable, was not more frivolous than many an one which has laid empires desolate. In Russia, it is said, there was a time when some thousands of persons lost their lives in a quarrel, in which the government had taken part, about the number of fingers to be used in making the sign of the cross. This was in days of yore: the ministers of Catherine II† are better *instructed* than to take any other part in such disputes, than that of preventing the parties concerned from doing one another a mischief.

---

[j] See Ch. XVI (Division) par. 42, 44.

* Melanges *Essai sur la Liberte de la Musique.*
† Instruct. art. 474, 475, 476.

ever thinks of recurring to at this time of day, for the details of political administration: and even before it can be applied to the details of private conduct, it is universally allowed, by the most eminent divines of all persuasions, to stand in need of pretty ample interpretations; else to what use are the works of those divines? And for the guidance of these interpretations, it is also allowed, that some other standard must be assumed. The will then which is meant on this occasion, is that which may be called the *presumptive* will: that is to say, that which is presumed to be his will on account of the conformity of its dictates to those of some other principle. What then may be this other principle? it must be one or other of the three mentioned above: for there cannot, as we have seen, be any more. It is plain, therefore, that, setting revelation out of the question, no light can ever be thrown upon the standard of right and wrong, by anything that can be said upon the question, what is God's will. We may be perfectly sure, indeed, that whatever is right is conformable to the will of God: but so far is that from answering the purpose of showing us what is right, that it is necessary to know first whether a thing is right, in order to know from thence whether it be conformable to the will of God.[k]

---

[k] The principle of theology refers everything to God's pleasure. But what is God's pleasure? God does not, he confessedly does not now, either speak or write to us. How then are we to know what is his pleasure? By observing what is our own pleasure, and pronouncing it to be his. Accordingly, what is called the pleasure of God, is and must necessarily be (revelation apart) neither more nor less than the good pleasure of the person, whoever he be, who is pronouncing what he believes, or pretends, to be God's pleasure. How know you it to be God's pleasure that such an act should be abstained from? whence come you even to suppose as much? 'Because the engaging in it would, I imagine, be prejudicial upon the whole to the happiness of mankind'; says the partisan of the principle of utility, 'Because the commission of it is attended with a gross and sensual, or at least with a trifling and transient satisfaction'; says the partisan of the principle of asceticism: 'Because I detest the thoughts of it; and I cannot, neither ought I to be called upon to tell why'; says he who proceeds upon the principle of antipathy. In the words of one or other of these must that person necessarily answer (revelation apart) who professes to take for his standard the will of God.

19. There are two things which are very apt to be confounded, but which it imports us carefully to distinguish: the motive or cause, which, by operating on the mind of an individual, is productive of any act: and the ground or reason which warrants a legislator, or other by-stander, in regarding that act with an eye of approbation. When the act happens, in the particular instance in question, to be productive of effects which we approve of, much more if we happen to observe that the same motive may frequently be productive, in other instances, of the like effects, we are apt to transfer our approbation to the motive itself, and to assume, as the just ground for the approbation we bestow on the act, the circumstance of its originating from that motive. It is in this way that the sentiment of antipathy has often been considered as a just ground of action. Antipathy, for instance, in such or such a case, is the cause of an action which is attended with good effects: but this does not make it a right ground of action in that case, any more than in any other. Still farther. Not only the effects are good, but the agent sees beforehand that they will be so. This may make the action indeed a perfectly right action: but it does not make antipathy a right ground of action. For the same sentiment of antipathy, if implicitly deferred to, may be, and very frequently is, productive of the very worst effects. Antipathy, therefore, can never be a right ground of action. No more, therefore, can resentment, which, as will be seen more particularly hereafter, is but a modification of antipathy. The only right ground of action, that can possibly subsist, is, after all, the consideration of utility, which, if it is a right principle of action, and of approbation, in any one case, is so in every other. Other principles in abundance, that is, other motives, may be the reasons why such and such an act *has* been done: that is, the reasons or causes of its being done: but it is this alone that can be the reason why it might or ought to have been done. Antipathy or resentment requires always to be regulated, to prevent its doing mischief: to be regulated by what? always by the principle of utility. The principle of utility neither requires nor admits of any other regulator than itself.

CHAPTER 6

Virtue

A. [NATURE OF VIRTUE][1]

Virtue is an appellative by which a fictitious entity is wont to be designated. The entity signified by it having no superior genus, the term is not susceptible of what is commonly meant by a definition: *viz.* indication given of a generic appellative, within the import of which that of the term defined is comprehended, together with an indication of some property by which the thing so indicated is distinguished from all other things designated by the same generic appellative.

Thus it is that, in a direct way, it is by itself incapable of being defined or so much as in any other way expounded.

But in a direct way through the medium of this or that conjugate belonging to the same cast, it is capable of being expounded.

A virtuous act, a virtuous habit, a virtuous disposition—in these several ways—by means of these several locutions its conjugate virtuous is susceptible of being expounded and by means of it a tolerably determinate and correct conception of it may be indicated by it.

Virtue in the common acceptation of the word is not only the name of a fictitious entity, but that fictitious entity is a fictitious personage. It is a member of a sort of fictitious family. For those who speak of virtue in the singular speak also of the virtues in the plural: of an indefinitely extensive family, of which the several virtues are the members. In a word, the scene presented to the imagination is that of a parent with a family of children. The Latin language being the parent soil of this appellative, and the gender of the appellative, the feminine, the image presented is that of a mother, surrounded by a family of daughters. Virtue in the abstract sense and singular number, the mother: the virtues in the plural number, her daughters. Many a person, by whom the unavoidable and almost incurable imperfections of the instrument called language has not been sufficiently considered, will here be apt to be shocked by the proposition that virtue is a fictitious entity. What (will he say), deny the existence of virtue? Virtue an empty name? No such thing as virtue? Oh horrible! What an opinion must this man have of human nature. What good, what useful information can be expected from him? What of any other sort, but the most pernicious conceivable? But if virtue is a mere imaginary thing, so will be its correspondent and opposite, vice. Thus will virtue and vice be on a level. Both alike creatures of the imaginations, alike objects of indifference: peace, good sir, no such horrible consequences will follow.

When speaking of an act, a habit, a disposition or a propensity, a man speaks of it at the same time as being virtuous, what he means by it, if it is his own opinions alone that it is his intention to express, and not the opinion of any other person, is that in his mind a sentiment of approbation is associated with the idea of it. And at the same time that, to the act, habit, disposition or propensity in question, a degree of importance not altogether inconsiderable belongs; so far, so good: but thereupon comes the question of the sentiment of approbation thus connected with the idea of the object in question, what is the efficient cause, or in one word, what is the ground?

My answer is in different states of society, in different individuals belonging to the same society; the ground has everywhere as yet been very considerably different. Therefore, to this question no single answer can be given, and be at the same time a true one. To be all true, or even in any considerable number true, different answers will require to be given: and for the collections of them, intricate and all comprehensive, would require to be the researches made into the several fields of geography and history.

Therefore it is that when to the question above mentioned an answer is required, all the satisfaction that a man who is duly solicitous for the correctness of the propositions which on so important a subject he delivers, will be—to give what, according to his own opinion is that same desired efficient cause or ground. In the present instance, this exclusively true answer will be given without difficulty. The efficient cause or, say, ground for whatever sentiment of approbation is in any mind associated with the idea of

any act, habit, disposition or propensity, is its tendency to give a
net increase to the aggregate quantity of happiness in all its shapes
taken together, about to have place in the community, whatsoever it
be that is in question: thence, if it be of the human species, of the
whole human species: and this effect is produced, if any particle,
howsoever small, of happiness is produced on the part of any one
individual, without the production of an equal quantity of unhappiness in any other. Thus much accords with truth as far as it
goes. But when this exposition is applied to the explanation of the
import of the word virtue and its conjugate virtues, as above, an
indication of one circumstance must be super-added. When an
act, a habit, a disposition, a propensity, is spoken of as virtuous, the
idea of something of difficulty in the task implied, and of consequent
exertion and effort employed in the surmounting of that difficulty,
seems to be in every case implied.

For example, that by those acts, habits, dispositions and propensities, which have for their effect the preservation of the existence of the individual, by the introsusception of nourishment, very
considerable addition to the quantity of happiness is produced, and
this on the part of every individual without exception during at the
worst the greatest part of his life, is what no one assuredly can
entertain a doubt of. Yet to no such acts or at any rate to no such
habits, or dispositions or propensities, will he attach the name of
virtuous. These things being promised, and to the word virtue a
tolerably clear as well as correct and comprehensive idea endeavoured to be attached, we will next proceed to the consideration
of the different virtues, or, changing a little the phrase and the image,
we will consider virtue as an aggregate of all the virtues, and the
individual objects contained in it as divisible into different groups.

[*Virtue and effort*][2]

Actions, virtuous and vicious—virtues and vices—vice—the ideas
whence and how deduced: every virtuous action is in effect or in
tendency beneficial to the community: every vicious action
pernicious.

To be virtuous every action must then be either in effect or in
tendency beneficial as above. But of actions that are beneficial to the
community, it is not every one that is virtuous. For a beneficial

action to be virtuous, some effort must accompany the performance of it. The actions that are most beneficial to the community are those by which the individual is preserved and those by which the species is preserved. To neither of these two species of acts as such is any such epithet as that of virtuous ever attributed. For a species of action to be regarded as having a claim to the appellation of virtuous, it seems necessary that some effort should in some degree have accompanied it. Of this effort, the nature would be different according to the mode in which the action is virtuous, of which presently. To be beneficial, an action must be so either to the agent himself or to another person or other persons or to both. In so far as being thus beneficial to the agent himself it is virtuous, a virtue is considered as being exercised by the performance of it; and this virtue is termed prudence, in particular, self-regarding prudence. In so far as being beneficial to others it is also virtuous, virtue in another shape is considered as exercised by the performance of it. This virtue is termed beneficence.

In so far as the intention or disposition, in so far as the effect which it is the intention or disposition to produce, is regarded as being in the opinion *of the agent* beneficial to others, the action is termed benevolent and the virtue benevolence: and this whether any benefit to any other person be or be not among the effects of it.

In regard to efforts, however, thus much is to be understood. Though effort is necessary, what is *not* necessary is that the time of the effort should be the very time when the exercise in question is given to the virtue. All that is necessary is that the act in question should be of the sort of some of those to the exercise of which an effort in most men is necessary. By habit that which in the first instance required effort, comes by degrees to be done without effort. Take for instance the confining of anger within the limits prescribed by prudence and benevolence. If in this instance there could be no virtue without effort exerted by the individual in question at the very time in question, on that supposition virtue in its most consummate state would cease to be virtue.

[*Virtue and Self-denial*][3]

Virtue is under every system of morals a common epithet attributed to human action considered in the light of this being apt to be repugnant to the inclination of the agent; *i.e.*, to a certain degree and in a certain respect painful to him. Under the system of utility, virtuous is a common epithet attributed to such [actions] only as are meant[4] to be of a tendency beneficial to the community upon the whole, considered in the light of their being apt to be repugnant to the inclination of the agent. Utility alone, though ever so great, cannot be understood even under the system of utility to bring an action under the denomination of virtuous. No act so useful as the act of eating. It is more than useful; it is absolutely necessary. Without it the species would soon perish. Yet neither under the system of utility nor under any other system was the act of eating what one liked to eat ever considered as an act of virtue, ever set down in the catalogue of virtuous acts. It may be reckoned an act of virtue in a man to *abstain* from eating what he likes: for instance in order that a friend or other fellow creature who is in want may eat the more, or in order to save himself from an indisposition which he may apprehend would be the consequence of such an indulgence. In the one case the abstinence is an exercise of the social virtue of benevolence; in the other, of the self-regarding virtue of temperance. It may be reckoned an act of virtue in a man to eat what he does *not* like: for instance, to take a bolus recommended to him in the way of medicine. This virtue, as far as it goes, is of the self-regarding class and may be referred to the general head of prudence.

Self-denial, then, under the system of utility not less than under the system of asceticism itself, is essentially included in the idea of virtue. Not that it is necessary to an act's coming under the denomination of a virtuous act that the individual act in question should be attended with pain, should be an act of self-denial: all that is necessary [is] that it should be of a species of act which in the individual instances of its exercise is *apt* to be so attended: on the contrary, provided it be of such a species, the more pure from al pain, the more highly fraught with pleasure the exercise of it is in the individual instance, the more exalted the virtue. Take for instance, *generosity*. Generosity cannot, in the general exercise of it *but* be attended with a certain degree of uneasiness and self-denial: since it is of the essence of it to be attended with the sacrifice of a portion of that which is the universal object of desire. Yet the purer the pleasure it is understood to be attended with, the freer from everything of uneasiness and regret, the stronger is the proof it is understood to afford of a virtuous mind, of a mind habitually inured to the exercise of virtue. Why? because the purer pleasure with which an act (of a species to which uneasiness is so natural and in the first instance universal a concomitant) is accompanied in any individual instance, the stronger the proof it affords of an habitual exercise of virtue, since it is habit and habit alone that can get the better of original repugnance and convert acts which on first trial are unpleasurable into pleasurable ones.

B. THE VIRTUES OR SPECIES OF VIRTUE CLASSED[5]

Intrinsically useful virtues; subservient or ancillary virtues. Under one or other of these heads will every thing which is entitled to the appellation of virtue, and with few if any exceptions every thing that has ever worn the name of *virtue*, be comprised: every act which being possessed of that other property which has been above spoken of as essential to virtue, as essential ingredient in the composition of an act of virtue can, upon the principle of utility, be regarded as capable of being with propriety designated by that appellation: every thing which, taking for the standard and act of virtue conduciveness to well-being, can with propriety and consistency be regarded as entitled to the name of virtue.

Prudence, in respect of the greater part of its application, probity and beneficence—to one or other of these appellations will virtues that are intrinsically valuable be found it is believed comparable. To prudence, in so far as the person to whose well-being the virtue, and accordingly the act which is regarded as being virtuous, is regarded as conducive is that person himself; in which respect the virtue may be said to be of the self-regarding kind: *probity* and *benefice*, in so far as the party or parties, to whose well-being it is regarded as conducive are any party or parties other than the person himself whose act is in question, probity in so far as the act in question, the act regarded as an act of probity, is of the number of those acts which are considered as obligatory, *i.e.* as being rendered so by the force of one or more of the above mentioned four sanctions: free beneficence, say for shortness beneficence, in so far as it is considered as not comprised within the field of any of those obligations.

Subservient and in certain respects reducible to one or more of the above three, with few or no exceptions, will, it is believed, be found every other moral quality the name of which has ever been considered as the name of species included under the genus designated by the terms virtuous and virtue.

Primary virtues, principal virtues, virtues of the first rank, virtues of the first order; by all these several denominations may the virtues here designated by the name of *intrinsically useful* virtues be occasionally designated. Secondary virtues or virtues of the second order or ancillary virtues—by these several designations may the whole tribe of virtues, the value of which depends upon their subserviency to these primarily and intrinsically useful, be designated.

Of this class of secondary virtues the following properties (deduced from the relation they bear to those of the primary class) may be stated as the characteristics.[6]

1. If those of primary class were not useful, neither would those of the secondary class be so.

2. Their utility consists in their subserviency to those ends which are the same ends as those of the primary class.

3. With reference to some person or other, whether useful or not to human society upon the whole, the virtues of the primary class are always in all cases of a useful tendency.

4. Of those of the secondary class in so far as the tendency is useful, it is so no otherwise than in so far as it is their tendency to be productive of some one or more of the effects which it is the tendency of those of the first class to be productive.

5. Their utility has for its measure the degree in which they contribute or tend to contribute to the advancement of one or more of those ends which are the ends of the primary virtues.

[*Primary virtues*]

Prudence and benevolence (or beneficence) the virtues to which all others are reducible—of which all others are but modifications. Prudence and Benevolence, the two all-comprehensive Virtues.

If their conduciveness to happiness is the test of virtue, if all happiness is either the happiness of the agent himself or the happiness of others, if conduciveness to a man's own happiness is prudence, to the happiness of others benevolence, and in so far as productive of effect, beneficence, all other virtues howsoever denominated are but so many modifications of prudence or benevolence or both together. Here then is the lot of virtues divided, the whole of it into two branches: forming together a test by which everything else that has ever borne the name of virtue may be traced: those which have no value condemned and discarded, and of those which have value, the value proved and the quantum of it measured.

Four virtues have been known under the name of cardinal virtues: *cardo* being taken for a hinge, virtues on which, as doors on hinges, all other virtues were said to turn. On the two above mentioned ones, to wit prudence and benevolence, yes; on the four in question, no. This will in its order be shown at large. Note mean time that in Aristotle's list, no such virtue as benevolence or beneficence is to be found: nothing nearer to it than justice, which is but a portion of benevolence in disguise.

In this way and this way alone—namely by indication of the relation borne to happiness, that is, to pleasures and pains, can any clear conception be attached to the words virtue and virtues, vice and vices. But for this principle of order, not one of these names, familiar as they are, the meaning of which is not unsettled and indeterminate.

[*Prudence*][8]

Prudence purely self-regarding regards either actions or thoughts: actions, to wit, bodily or external actions, for mental or internal actions are thought.[9]

In so far as actions are in question, that which prudence can do and all that it can do (that prudence which consists in the choice of means being out of the question) consists in the sacrifice of the present to the future: in this sacrifice, *i.e.* in so far as and no further than the aggregate of happiness is thus increased, to wit, by the sacrifice of the lesser present (sacrifice) to the greater future. Of two portions of happiness equal in magnitude, one present the other not present, that which is present will always be greater in value than that which is but future: of that which is but future, the value being lessened by, and in proportion to, in the first place remoteness and in case of uncertainty by the uncertainty. In so far as no portion of time is considered but the present, or if as between pleasure and pleasure, pain and pain, or pleasure and pain, the future is regarded as continuing on the same footing in respect of magnitude and certainty as the present and in the same degree of propinquity and certainty in all the several cases, virtue is out of the question: the case comes under the dominion not of virtue but of taste.

Under this general head, to wit, the head of purely self-regarding prudence come several of the particular virtues put by Aristotle and thence by other moralists to this day on a line with prudence.

These are 1. Temperance 2. Continence 3. Fortitude 4. Magnanimity 5. Veracity: to wit in so far as by the effects of actions considered as regulated by those virtues the happiness of no being other than the agent in question is considered as being affected.

In so far as the interest[s] of others are connected with and dependent on that of the person in question, beneficence, to wit, as towards those others comes under the head of prudence, even self-regarding prudence. But in this case the sort of prudence in question is not purely self-regarding but extra-regarding prudence. In so far as neither the greatest[10] future happiness of the agent in question is considered as being promoted or endeavoured to be promoted, nor the happiness of others a sacrifice of happiness whether present or future, is asceticism—the very opposite to prudence: the offspring of delusion: the very opposite of prudence.

To give up any the least particle of pleasure for any other purpose than that of obtaining for a man's self or some other person a greater quantity of pleasure, or of saving oneself or some other person from a more than equivalent quantity of pain, is not virtue but folly.

To cause or endeavour to cause any other person to give up any particle of pleasure for any other purpose than that of obtaining for a man's self or some other person a greater quantity of pleasure, or of saving oneself or some other person from a more than equivalent quantity of pain, is not virtue but vice, is not beneficence or benevolence but maleficence or malevolence.

Of Beneficence and Benevolence: (and the opposite vices maleficence and malevolence)[11]

Positive and *negative*: into these two branches the field of beneficence requires, it will be seen, to be divided.

Positive beneficence is the quality which a man is considered as possessing in proportion to the importance of the positive acts of a serviceable nature exercised by him in relation to the persons towards whom the virtue is considered as expressing itself.

Negative beneficence is the quality which a man is considered as possessing in respect of all or any such acts as, without being repugnant to the virtue of probity, *i.e.* modifications of the *vice* of improbity, would be productive of annoyance, *i.e.* of pain or uneasiness to other men.

By[12] the word *benevolence* seems to be designated the disposition to perform those same acts in the actual exercise of which beneficence consists. Its field coincides therefore exactly with the field of beneficence. Not that either of them has necessarily for its accompaniment the other.[13] That benevolence may have place without beneficence is but too certain and sufficiently obvious. Be the action, if performed, beneficial or pernicious, the endeavour is liable to fail of corresponding to intention, much more the bare desire or wish.

On the other hand, so may beneficence without benevolence. In truth in the whole mass of human affairs the good which has for its spring the benevolent, the sympathetic affection, would upon examination be found to bear a very small proportion to that which has its source in the influence of the self-regarding class of motives. The quantity of the matter of wealth, of subsistence and abundance which is transferred without equivalent, bears but a small proportion to that which is not obtained but for an equivalent, *viz.* in the way of trade (even if the donation made in favour of children by their parents be reckoned into the account).[14] The quantity voluntarily offered up to government to be employed for the benefit of the public at large bears but a small proportion to the quantity paid in in obedience to compulsory requisitions.

In the account of the sentimentalist, as between beneficence and benevolence, as between benevolence and beneficence; benevolence, whether accompanied or not by beneficence, is apt to experience the larger portion of popular favour. Only however in proportion as it is accompanied by beneficence is benevolence of use.

C. ANALYSIS OF MORAL EMOTIONS

[Many critics of Utilitarianism have rightly asked how it would analyse familiar moral concepts and emotions like justice, love of liberty, anger and envy. In this section are included a few manuscripts in which Bentham offers his account of them. Ed.]

On the supposed love of Justice[15]

By Love of Justice is meant regard for human happiness considered as promoted by observance of fixed rules, especially rules laid down by authority of government: but justice having two different imports according as it is by the civil or, say, non-penal branch of law, or by the penal branch of law, that these rules are considered as laid down, hence it is that in correspondence with this distinction, justice, and the love of it require two very different descriptions: nor is there any one description that can with propriety be applied in both cases.

In matters of civil law, justice consists in adherence to or in observance of the non-disappointment principle: by observing on all occasions that line of conduct by which, to expectation of the enjoyment of that article, belonging to the lists of the several objects of general desire which is in question, either no disappointment whatsoever or, if some it cannot but be produced, the minimum of disappointment that can be produced [is produced]. So much for justice according to the import given to the word in the sort of case called a civil case.

Now as to justice in the sense in which the word is employed in the sort of case called a penal case. In a penal case existence and employment is supposed to be purposely given to a portion of the matter of evil: and if the greatest happiness principle be the ruling principle, it is always with the view and for the purpose of putting an exclusion upon a mass of evil in greater quantity and value or what comes to the same thing the giving existence to a preponderant portion of the matter of good. This being the case only in the character of a remedy or as above what is equivalent to a remedy, is evil under the name of punishment ever applied. But punishment is but one of four distinguishable sorts of remedies by which the supposed evil of a species of act regarded as maleficent is capable of being combated: these are 1. the preventive, 2. the suppressive, 3. the satisfactive, 4. the punitive or, say, subsequentially preventive: in order of time 1st. the preventive, then in so far as that has failed of its effects, secondly, the suppressive, thirdly, the

4

satisfactive, and subsequentially preventive, for these two last are capable of being applied at the same moment of time. Of the satisfactive species of remedy there are several modifications, but these belong not to the present purpose.

What, then, in regard to these several sorts of remedies is it that justice in a penal case requires? In regard to all four of these sorts of remedies but more particularly the satisfactive and the punitive—what it requires is: 1. that in every case in which the evil so applied promises to be productive of preponderant good, application be made of it accordingly; 2. that in no case in which it does not afford such promise, application be made of it; 3. that where application is made of it, application be not made of any more of it than what is necessary to the production of that effect.

1. Coincident with the first of these three cases is that in which an individual charged with having committed a certain offence to which, by law, punishment is attached, has really committed it, and in that persuasion has in relation to it been deemed guilty.

2. Coincident with the present case is that in which it does not afford such promise, and in that persuasion has in relation to it been deemed *not* guilty.

3. Coincident with the third case is that where application is made of it, application be not made of any more of it than what is necessary to the production of that effect.

This is the case in which justice is frequently spoken of as being tempered with mercy.

True it is that another case in which mercy is said to be exercised is that in which punishment which would otherwise be applied is, instead of being diminished, withholden altogether. But in this case, a quantity of punishment customarily applied to the species of offence in question, is considered in aggregate mass; and in this case so it is, that while to the individual lot, total exclusion is applied, to the aggregate mass not total exclusion, but only diminution is applied.

A sort of error pervading the whole field of language is, from the observation of a sign, *i.e.* a substantive, constitutive of a name, common or proper, inferring without reflexion, and by the mere force of the association principle, the existence of a correspondent object signified. Thus, in the present case, the word justice used as the name of a thing, being in continnal use, is seen to be in existence:

here we have the antecedent; therefore, so is a thing, so is the thing signified by it: here we have the consequence.

As it is with justice in this respect, so is it with power—liberty, and many others.

1. First as to power. In Locke's *Essay*, by the word *power*, if memory is not deceitful, no small quantity of matter is occupied, and from this cause, no small degree of obscurity produced. Power is the name of a particular sort of fictitious entity, and as it is with other fictitious entities, so with this that to get rid of the fiction and to the language of fiction to substitute that of realities, a proposition in which no name of a fictitious entity has place must be employed.

So in the case of love of liberty. By love of liberty, two very different affections are denoted, according to the person whose liberty is in question. Is it the lover himself? If yes, love of liberty is so far love of power—of power over his own actions and his own feelings. In this case, the affection is a self-regarding one. Is it a person other than that same lover, an assemblage of any such persons, small or large, assignable on unassignable, it is then a modification of sympathy for the happiness of those same persons. In this case, the affection is of the extra-regarding, and therein of the benevolent kind.

To the same erroneous propensity it should seem that language is indebted for the terms *moral* sense—a term which constituted the basis of a system antagonising with that the basis of which is expressed by the words *greatest happiness principle*.

If justice be admitted in the character of an independent subject of love, where shall we stop—what limit can there be to the number of these objects? To justice must we not add in like manner Equity—right reason—legitimacy and so on. The catalogue of these supposed innate and universal objects of love, may not be various in the various languages some or all of them—may it not, in a word, vary with the language?

Love of Liberty[16]

In so far as when the *ruling principle* is the *maximum of utility*, the corresponding affection, the affection from which it receives its support, and by the cultivation and exercise of which it is strengthened, is *philanthropy*. When the *ruling principle* is the *love of liberty*, the corresponding affection, the affection from which it receives its support, and by the cultivation and exercise of which it is strengthened, is but self-regarding interest. Love of liberty is but *impatience of control*. But control is necessary not only to the well-being but to the being of society. Control is necessary to the being of every government: of the best not less so than of the worst. The exercise of control is the essential character of all government.

The spirit of liberty is the spirit of opposition. But the spirit of opposition is not philanthropy. To a first view it is more manifestly adverse to philanthropy than coincident with it or subservient to it. The spirit of opposition—a constantly existing howsoever moderated and regulated spirit of opposition—is indeed necessary to good government and as such, in so far as it is under the guidance of philanthropy, is coincident with and subservient to philanthropy. But in so far as it is not under the guidance of philanthropy, it is adverse to philanthropy; and the fruit of it in so far as it prevails is weak government, bad government—mischief.[17]

Love of liberty is not a primary or independent principle; is not capable of serving in the character of a primary (ruling) principle. It is but a secondary and as it were a negative principle, a principle of reaction, not of original action. In its existence is included and supposed the existence, present, past or probably future, of a bad government, of a government supported by a different principle and that a bad one, *viz.* a government adverse to liberty—in a word tyranny, whether in the hands of one or more than one. The view, therefore, which is taken of the subject by him by whom a public man is considered as guided in his conduct by this principle and nothing else, is necessarily and proportionally a partial one. It is a principle of opposition, a principle under which the motives and schemes of those who are guided by it are determined by foreign accidents and considerations, are determined by the motives expected at the hands of the power against which the opposition is directed. It can go no further, at least without doing mischief instead of good. It is therefore, if taken by itself, taken as the sole or even the predominantly ruling principle, a dangerous principle (a mischievous affection). In[18] that character, it never can be received without mischief: philanthropy, and that alone, is the affection which without mischief or danger can be received as the predominant one.

[*Suicide*[19]]

Quantity of well-being in human life—its preponderance over that of ill-being.

Taking the whole of mankind together on which side of the account does the balance lie? On the well-being or on the ill-being side?

If religion were out of the question, the answer would require scarce a moment's thought: on the side of well-being beyond dispute: of well-being existence is of itself a conclusive proof. So small is the quantity of pain necessarily accompanying the termination of existence.

But under the guidance of religion men have made to themselves an almighty being, whose delight is in human misery; and who, to prevent a man's escaping from whatsoever misery he may be threatened with in the present life, has without[20] having denounced it [declared his sinister] determination in the event of any such escape, to plunge him into infinitely greater misery in a life to come.

Even taking the Christian religion for true, this notion is a most vain and groundless conceit. For the Christian scripture is open to every eye, and in no one part of it is any intimation given of any such doom.

By no precept has Jesus been represented as forbidding suicide. By his own example he is represented as approving of it. Possessed even of superhuman power, Jesus, having power, though it were for ever, to exempt himself from death, Jesus, purposely and spontaneously subjected himself to it. What he then did, it was for all men, *i.e.* to promote the well-being of all men that he did it. Will this be said? What he thought right that by one person it should be done by [for?] all men, how could he think it otherwise than right that by each person it should upon occasion be done for himself.

A manufacturer of human misery is every man who joins in the declamation against suicide. In what proportion? In the exact proportion of the extent of his influence.

The Passions[21]

For the nature of the passions, references will be made to the list of pleasures and pains; for the principles by which they are to be governed, to the list of virtues and vices.

Take for example the passion of anger. When operated upon by that passion, a man is suffering a pain—a pain of mind produced by the consideration of the act of some other person—of an act by which the passion has been excited.

Of the pain thus suffered one consequence is a desire to produce n the breast of the party, by whom the anger has been excited, a pain in some shape or other according to circumstances. Here then are two constant ingredients in the case of anger—pain suffered by one *viz.* the angry men; a desire to produce pain in another, *viz.* the person by whom he has been made angry.

Now as to the virtues and vices which have application to the case, *viz.* the two all-comprehensive virtues and the two vices their respective opposites.

In the first place no anger without pain, but to do anything by which a man draws pain upon himself, that pain not being compensated and over balanced by more than equivalent pleasure, is what cannot be done without imprudence; without violation of the law of self-regarding prudence.

Turn now to the next effect, *viz.* the desire to produce pain in the breast of the person by whose act or supposed act the passion has been excited. Here then is a desire to produce pain on the part of another. But setting aside any pleasure that may be produced or pain that may be excluded in consequence of the pain desired to be produced, here we have a desire which is endeavoured to be gratified and which cannot be gratified without an act of malevolence and maleficence: without a violation of the law of benevolence. Thus in the case of anger we have an exemplification of the relation which has place on the one hand between passion on one part and pain and pleasure on the other, on the other hand between passion on the [one] part and vice and virtue on the other.

Question. Is it then true that no anger can have place without vice in both its modes; without violation of virtue in both its modes; without violation in the first place of the law of self-regarding prudence, in the next place of the law of benevolence.

The answer is, no; in so far as the emotion rises to the height of passion, and here should be added another and though more remote yet commonly much more mischievous violation of the law of self-regarding prudence. The passion can not receive its gratification but pain is produced in the breast of the individual by whose act the passion has been excited; but neither in-his breast can it have been productive of that effect without producing in that same breast, in so far as he is apprised of the cause whereby that pain has been produced, a counter desire to give birth on his part to pain in the breast of him by whom his pain has been produced. To the first pain *viz.* that which has accompanied the birth of the passion of anger there is always a termination and that commonly a speedy one; but to the second and remote pain which may have constituted the third link in this chain of causes and effects there is no certain termination; in the breast of the party of whom vengeance, as the phrase is, has been taken, anger in the more durable form, in which it is called enmity, has been created, and to the duration of this permanent passion or to the quantity of mischief to which it may happen to give birth no determinate limit can be assigned.

Since, then, anger cannot have place without vice in both shapes, what is to be done? Can man exist without anger? Without anger can injuries be averted, can self-defence, can self-preservation be provided for?

Answer. Certainly not without production of pain in the breast of the individual by whom injury has been inflicted, but to the production of this pain anger is not necessary. Anger is not necessary any more than on the part of a surgeon, by whom to save life a limb is amputated, anger excited by view of the suffering of the patient and by contemplation of the still greater evil which without such amputation is about to have place is necessary. That anger never should have place is not possible; is not consistent with the structure of the human mind. This however may be said and without exception that in every case the less there is of it, the better: for whatsoever of pain is necessary to the production of the useful effect, will be much better measured out without the passion than by it.

Circumstances it may be said there are, in which not merely pain, the natural fruit of anger—pain purposely produced—but anger itself the passion, is not merely useful to society but even necessary to its existence: the passion itself, and this, so conditioned as not to be regulated according to the dictates either of self-regarding prudence or benevolence. These circumstances are no other than those which have place in this country throughout the whole field of penal jurisprudence. I have been robbed: the circumstances of the offence are such as, in case of conviction, subject the offender either to capital punishment or at least to transportation in a state of servitude: shall I prosecute the offender? Not if self-regarding prudence, and this alone is to be my counsellor; for what would be the result? To the loss sustained by the robbery I should add the further loss inflicted upon the prosecutor by the prosecution. Not, if benevolence is to be my counsellor; for of benevolence, in any view of it, the response may be that the punishment is too great for the offence. Such accordingly is the response which as every body knows is to a great extent considered by man as actually given in this case, in particular where the punishment is death. But, of benevolence, if the matter were rightly considered, the response, it may be said, would be that prosecution should take place notwithstanding; and that for so important a good to the public at large neither the suffering of the offender in the shape of punishment, nor the suffering of the prosecutor in respect of expense and vexation should be grudged. Good. But in the first place, I can very ill afford it: so ill that the suffering produced by the pecuniary burden upon me may be greater than any good, the uncertain and imponderable nature of it considered, that can be clearly seen should be sufficiently promised by the prosecution and its result.

In the next place the responses of benevolence, be they ever so decisive, have no influence on me, or what comes to the same thing, have no adequate influence: here, then, in neither shape has virtue sufficient force to produce the effect in question: and yet without the frequent production of such an effect, the security of society would suffer a shock more or less grievous according to the failure in respect of frequency, and supposing it never produced at all, security would be entirely destroyed, and the general destrucion of property would be the result. This supposed, virtue in both its forms is insufficient for the preservation of society: anger, the passion, dissocial as it seems to be on first appearance, is indispensably necessary. To these observations it seems not to oppose a refutative reply: But in this country in the present state of the laws, others there are by which it may be made [to] appear that the necessity of the passion does not at any rate arise altogether out of the nature of the case, but is in no small degree produced by the imperfect state of the laws: insomuch that if in the particulars in question the laws were in the state in which they might be, the demand for anger, the passion, would in no inconsiderable degree be reduced.

In the first place comes the factitious part of the expense and vaxation produced to the prosecutor by the prosecution; and so great is this factitious part that in many instances, were it taken away, the response given by self-regarding prudence might be opposite to what it is.

In the next place comes the punishment, and so excessive in many cases is its severity, that if the excess were removed, in cases to no inconsiderable extent, if general opinion is to be trusted to the response of benevolence would be opposite to what it is.

One thing is to be considered, that if you suppose a state in which the passion of anger were, generally speaking, in a state of subjection to the constant influence of the two all-comprehensive virtues, self-regarding prudence and benevolence, you would thereby suppose a state in which offences of the sort in question, and consequently the demand for anger in a state of excess beyond the limits prescribed by self-regarding prudence and benevolence, would be proportionally rare.

Note that in the present state of society this is not the only case in which the dictates of general utility present an appearance of being in opposition to the dictates of the two virtues in question, all-comprehensive as, when taken together, they are. Thus would it stand if the welfare of society depended altogether upon the quantum of these two virtues having place in the breasts of individuals; but here comes the demand for the two virtues, and in particular for the virtue of benevolence, acting upon the national scale; though in the breasts of individuals, individually taken, both virtues might join in inhibiting the gratification of the passion to the extent in question, benevolence acting in the breast of the legislator upon the national scale, recommends the doing what seems conducive and necessary to the keeping it up beyond those limits to the extent required for the public purpose, of keeping delinquency in general bounds.

4*

[*Envy*[22]]

Envy and jealousy seem to require to be spoken of together, both of them bear reference to some good, and to some other person considered in respect of it.

Envy supposes the good to be in possession of that other person: jealousy supposes it not to be in his possession. Suppose I am the jealous person; you the person who is the object of my jealousy: jelaousy as towards you may equally have place in my breast whether I am in possession of the good in question or not.

Be the degree in either case what it may, envy and jealousy agree in this; namely that they have suffering, evil in the shape of suffering, for their inseparable accompaniment. The consequence is to repress the emotion as far as may be, if possible even to suppress or prevent it altogether, is on every occasion among the dictates of prudence.

Supposing the emotion, the affection, the passion, whatever be the name applied to it—suppose it to remain in the breast in which it has been excited, in an unproductive state, without giving rise to acts productive of any effect on the feelings of any other person; on this supposition benevolence has no application to it. Suppose it about to produce or liable to produce acts exercising a maleficent influence on the feelings of any other person or persons, here then the repressing it as far as may be, is among the dictates of benevolence.

[*Vanity and Pride*][23]

Vanity is more nearly allied to benevolence: pride to self-regard and malevolence.

To each the object or end in view—final cause of action—is the pleasure of the popular or moral sanction: esteem and respect at the hands of those with whom they have or expect to have to do.

The vain man regards himself as comparatively ill-assured of the advantages which he is thus looking for at their hands: he is proportionably anxious to do what depends upon him towards the attainment of them: and for that purpose takes every occasion for making display of those attainments of his which in his eyes are the efficient causes of his title to those benefits and on which his hopes of obtaining them are accordingly founded. But to this purpose it is necessary that he should to a certain degree possess their good will:

at any rate that he should not be an object of their ill will: hence it is necessary in effect and at any rate in his eyes that towards the persons in question his deportment should be conformable to the dictates of benevolence: of negative at least if not of positive benevolence: that the sentiments produced by it as towards himself should be as far as possible those of esteem, which in its higher degree is admiration, and by ill will or antipathy by whatsoever causes produced, the esteem and admiration if not entirely excluded are so in a greater or less degree.

As it is in general the object, so in general is it the effect of the display he makes to afford more or less of pleasure to those in the eyes of whom he makes it. For by admiration, surprise is excited and a certain appetite, the appetite of curiosity the love of the marvellous, more or less gratified.

But there are two cases in which this effect is liable to be not only counteracted and diminished but reversed: 1. where the superiority displayed or the manner in which it is displayed is such as to produce humiliation—the sense of inferiority—in the breast of those before whom the display is made: 2. this effect is proportionably increased if in respect of the particular endowment in question any particular competition as between a vain man and the persons in question happens to have place.

In so far as this is the case, benevolence and prudence concur in recommending to him to abstain from his displays: benevolence because thereby on his part a pain of humiliation will be produced; prudence because in that case the passions of envy and jealousy as towards himself will be apt to be excited, and towards himself a sentiment of ill-will whence upon occasion the correspondent ill offices or withholding of good ones will be apt to be produced.

To[24] the proud man as such, and to the vain man as such, esteem is an object of *love* and *relish*; consequently more or less so of *desire*.

But, in the proud man, as such, this desire of esteem is accompanied with a contempt, that is, the absence of esteem (disesteem), for the persons whose esteem is the object of the desire: which, on the part of the vain man as such, is not the case.

Bulk for bulk, the value of the object being so much less in the eyes of the proud man than in those of the vain man, to obtain a given degree of gratification, the proud man must regard himself in possession of a quantity of it greater than what would suffice to append the same degree of gratification to the vain man.

This being the case, the state of the proud man's mind is commonly a state of dissatisfaction: a dissatisfaction which very commonly makes itself manifest in and by his countenance.

Melancholy and malevolence, one or both, in more or less proportion may accordingly be stated as constant concomitants or accompaniments of pride: whether in the character of causes or in the character of effects seems not very easy to distinguish: probably, very commonly in both characters.

Hilarity, in a proportion more or less considerable, is in the same way a very frequent, not to say a constant, accompaniment of vanity: hilarity and not unfrequently benevolence. From small manifestations of esteem vanity, in proportion to its intensity, receives large gratification: the smaller the more easily had: the more easily had the more frequently, and the more frequently the more frequent the causes of exhilaration.

CHAPTER 7

Value of a Pain or Pleasure[1]

1. Of whatever nature a pleasure be; a pleasure of the body, or a pleasure of the mind; a pleasure of enjoyment, a pleasure of possession, or a pleasure of expectation; a pleasure of the concupscible appetites or a pleasure of the irascible; what we shall have to say of any pleasure in the present chapter will be found equally to belong to all: and so it is with pains.

2. A pleasure may be more or less intense, hence we come to speak of its intensity: when this intensity is at a high degree, we say (preserving the same expression) that it is intense, when at a low degree we call it faint or slight.

3. The time it lasts, is either long or short; hence we have to speak of its duration.

4. This is the case with everything that is called pleasure; to exist it must possess two qualities: it must possess intensity; it must possess duration. They constantly belong to it; they are essential to it: it cannot be conceived without them.

5. Body, to exist, must in like manner possess three things: length, breadth and thickness. They constantly belong to it: it cannot be conceived without them. Of them it is said in a certain sense to be composed. Under them it is said to be comprised. By them it is measured. Mathematicians call them its 'dimensions'. 'Dimensions' comes from '*dimetior*': 'dimetior' is 'to measure'.

6. Of mathematicians then let us borrow the appellation and let us begin with saying; pleasure is comprised under two dimensions intensity and duration.

7. It is in respect to the aggregate of these its three dimensions that body is said to be great or small: it is of them that its magnitude is composed: its magnitude is the product of all of them together. Of pleasure the same may be said in respect of these its two dimensions. Its magnitude is the product of one of them by the other.[a]

[a] This expression, common as it is, being a loose and abbreviated

8. Thus much concerning a pleasure considered at the time of its being present: but a pleasure may be distant. When distant, it is either past or future. When past, there is an end of it: we have nothing more to do with it. We have no occasion to concern ourselves about it. When future, it then is the object of our concern; it concerns us to know its value.

9. The perception of a pleasure is an event (may be considered as coming under the catalogue of events). An event that is yet to come, may be at the highest degree of certainty or at any lower: when at the highest degree, it is said simply to be certain: when at a high degree but not the highest, probable: when at a low degree, improbable: when at any degree short of the highest, probable or improbable, it is said to be contingent.

10. Certain or contingent, the period of its arrival may be more or less remote. The non-arrival of an event before a given time may be certain, and its arrival at that time certain; or else its non-arrival at all times before may be certain, and its arrival even then, contingent. That given time may be more or less remote. Hence with respect to all pleasures, as well certain, as well as contingent, we have to speak of their proximity.

11. Presence may be considered as constituting the highest degree as well of certainty as of proximity. The value of a pleasure present of which the proximity and certainty are otherwise given, is as its magnitude.

---

one is apt not to be clearly understood. Length, breadth and thickness are dimensions, elements of body. Intensity and duration are qualities (elements) of pleasure. But it is not body that is multiplied by body: it is not quality that is multiplied by quality; it is number always that is multiplied by number. A product is a number resulting from the multiplication of either of two numbers by the other. The term 'product' therefore is directly applicable to numbers only. When applied to things other than numbers, an imaginary division of them is supposed, by which they are, as it were, resolved into numbers. They are, each of them, supposed to be divided into a certain number of parts or degrees: parts if they are substances: degrees if they are qualities. This done, the number of the parts of one of them taken as many times as there are units in the number of the parts of the other, is that third number that is called the product.

15. The truth of these propositions is testified by universal practice. An article of property, an estate, is valuable: it has a value on what account? As a fund of pleasures. Now the value of an estate, as everyone knows, increases and decreases, according to settled rules in the above proportions.

16. Thus much concerning pleasure in a single person: but we are to consider it in a society: in a State; a State consists of a number of persons. Hence, in speaking of pleasure in a State, to the four considerations above mentioned we must add a fifth; that of number, namely of the persons that are partakers of the pleasure.

17. Pleasure referred to a State, that is to a State taken in its totality, will no longer bear that name: it takes the name of Happiness. We say 'the pleasure' as well as 'the happiness' of a *man*: we seldom say the pleasure, we almost always say the happiness, of a *State*. What in a man therefore is called a pleasure, in a *State* may be called a lot of happiness.

18. A lot of happiness, in proportion to the number pf persons that partake of it, may be said to extend itself through a State. Hence in taking account of the number of persons that are partakers of it we may speak of its extent. In the extent, thus explained, of a lot of happiness we have a fifth ingredient in the value of it and a fifth dimension.

19. Of these five ingredients the two qualities of certainty and proximity do neither of them enter essentially into the consideration of all pleasures: nor therefore of every lot of happiness . . . [3] It can be conceived without them, for it subsists without them when it is present. Extent *is* essential. A lot of happiness cannot be conceived without it. A lot of happiness cannot be conceived to exist in a State, without extending through a certain number, one at least, of the persons in it. Extent on this account may be spoken of as a third dimension of a lot of happiness.

20. Thus much concerning pleasures: and what has been said hitherto concerning pleasures may be said equally of pains.

21. A lot of unhappiness is to a pain, what a lot of happiness is to a pleasure.

22. If the nature of the mind were such, that pleasures and pains started up in it without connexion; if no one sensation were the natural consequance of any other, the qualities above mentioned are

all we should have occasion to notice in them: what has been said is all we should have to say of them. Not that that, or anything else we should say would, on such a supposition, be of any use to us. But this is not the case. Sensations are connected one of them with another; connected by things that are instruments, by actions that are the causes of them both.[b] It may therefore be of use to speak of them, because it may be of use to know how to act concerning them, because they are often in our power: they are

---

[b] It has already been seen what an instrument is. By a cause, I mean not the instrument itself, but the action of the instrument. An instrument is a substance. A cause is a mode of the same substance. It is to this sense alone I would wish to see it restricted. Unhappily, hitherto the usage has been to apply it indifferently to both: to the substance, as well as to the mode. This usage has a bad effect, since it confounds two things that require often to be distinguished: and it is not necessary, since the term 'instrument' is a term that would be full as expressive as any other can be, for the substance, without being liable to be suspected of being intended to express the mode. This distinction therefore between cause and instrument I would wish to see adopted and that generally. It is useful as giving precision to speculations of which precision is the life and soul. It is useful wherever it can be applied: wherever the idea of causality introduces itself, that is, in a manner everywhere. Let us take an example from natural philosophy. 'The pressure of the air,' we say, 'is the cause of the quicksilver's rising in the barometer.' The air itself we are at the same time very apt to speak of as being 'the cause' of the quicksilver's 'rising in the barometer'. Here by the air we mean the substance acting as an instrument on the quicksilver. By the pressure of the air we mean a mode, *viz*: a motion, of that substance. Compare then these two expressions and it cannot but be seen that in one or other of them there is something wrong. The same appellation 'cause', is given in the former of them to the air itself, as by the latter to the pressure of the air. The air a substance, and the pressure of the air a mode, a motion of that same substance, are compounded under the same term. In the latter case therefore to the air itself, I would give the name of instrument. 'The air,' I would say, 'is the instrument the action of which is the cause of the quicksilver's rising in the barometer.' The term 'cause' I would confine to denote, as in the first case, the action of that instrument, the pressure of the air. There is the more reason for this in that to the quicksilver the substance acted on by that

often in our power, because the causes of them are often in our power. The same action that is the cause of the pleasure we would enjoy, is often the cause of the pain we would avoid. The pleasure coming along with the cause, and the pain after it, hence the pain is the consequence of the pleasure. It concerns us to know than this is the case. The cause being in our power, we may forbear producing it. By forbearing to produce it, we may avoid producing the consequence. By forbearing to perform the action that produces the pleasure, we shall it is true forbear producing the pleasure, but we shall at the same time avoid producing the pain. It is our business to forebear producing the pleasure, when the pain thus connected with it is (we are not to say simply greater, since that would be to take into consideration two only out of the five ingredients in its value, but) preponderant in value or importance.[c]

23. A sensation thus connected with one of an opposite nature coming after it, may be styled alloyed or dissimilarly fruitful: a pleasure with a pain after it, an alloyed pleasure: a pain with a pleasure after it, an alloyed pain. In this sense we may have to speak of the purity of a sensation: of the purity of a pain or of a pleasure.[d] And this gives us a sixth ingredient in the value of a pain or pleasure.

---

instrument, the substance acted on by the air, we never apply the term 'effect': a term the sense of what one expects to find universally opposite and correspondent to that of the term *cause*. It is the *rise*, the *motion*, of the quicksilver, and never the quicksilver itself that we speak of as being the *effect* of that *cause*, which we mean when we speak of 'the pressure of the air'.

---

[c] The expression 'value of a pain' may to some appear rather a harsh one. The term 'value' it is not usual to apply to objects other than what are supposed to produce pleasure: to objects other than what are desirable. But either this we must have for objects that are the contrary or none at all: for there is no other that corresponds to it applicable to them. The license of using it in this sense is therefore a license justified by necessity: nor is it by any means an unexampled one. Mathematicians speak without scruple of the values of their x and y: tho' x and y are often made to signify debts; objects as anyone can witness not at all desirable. Perhaps the word importance might be made to answer the same purpose; at least in many cases.

24. For a pair of sensations thus connected it will be of use to provide, in order to distinguish them, a pair of appellations that may serve to indicate the order in which we find them. Let the sensation then which comes first in such a pair be styled antecedent: its opposite that comes afterwards, the consequent.

25. Continuing the allusion the consequent may then be styled the alloy to the antecedent.

26. A sensation is more or less pure in the proportion it bears in value to the sensation that is its consequent. The proportion of its value to that of the consequent is the measure of its purity.

27. As a pleasure may be followed by a pain issuing from the same cause so may it by another pleasure: and so it is with pain. When this is the case with a pleasure or with a pain, we may give it the epithet of prolific: and to this purpose we may speak of its fecundity. And lastly in this we have a seventh ingredient in the value of a pain or pleasure.

Measurement[4]

One of the Roman Emperors, Nero I think it is, is said to have offered a reward to (him who should be) the inventor [of] a new pleasure. (There are moralists who are more scandalised at this idea of the tyrant than at all his cruelties.) A proposition thus calculated to promote the happiness of mankind excites more horror in moralists of a certain stamp than the worst of these cruelties which destroy it. They will answer you nay: for that the pleasures that a sensualist had in view were indubitably impure. But either the word impure had with them no meaning (that was anything to the purpose) or it meant—the only determinate sense it is capable of—a pleasure of such a nature as to be more frequently than not attended or followed by pains more than equivalent to it. But this was certainly no part of the proposal. To a consistent reasoner the

---

[d] I am hungry: I eat: I feel a pleasure. Afterwards comes an indigestion: I then feel plain: my pleasure is alloyed.

I have an indigestion: I am in pain. I take physic. For some time this puts me to intenser pain. But it relieves me from the first. To be relieved from pain is pleasure. The pain it gave me was therefore an alloyed pain.

quality of a pleasure independent of its quantity is of no account. Every thing that produces pleasure is *prima facie* good: if it is to be reputed bad, it can only be in virtue of some pain which produces more than equivalent to such pleasure. The pleasure being incontestable, in order to prove the cause of it to be an evil, it lies upon any one to prove that it is productive of such attendant pain.

Every thing that produces pleasure is good in proportion to the *clear* pleasure it produces: and till it can be shown to produce pain, all the pleasure it is seen to produce ought to be reputed *clear*. This must be eternally true in spite of all prejudices and all declamations to the contrary. Neither Newton's Laws of nature, nor Euclid's axioms are more incontestable.

Under the article of *value*, every observation that can be made with regard to pleasure, applies equally to pain: after this notice, to save words, I shall all along make mention only of pleasure.

The limit of the quantity of a pleasure in respect of intensity on the (this) side of diminution is a state of indifference (insensibility): the degree of intensity possessed by that pleasure which is the faintest of any that can be distinguished to be pleasure, may be represented by unity: such a degree of intensity is in every day's experience. According as any pleasures are perceived to be more and more intense they may be represented by higher and higher numbers: but there is no fixing upon any particular degree of intensity as being the highest of which a pleasure is susceptible.

The limit of the quantity of a pleasure in respect of duration is the least portion of duration that can be distinguished: suppose a moment. If then a moment be taken for the least portion of time that is distinguishable, it is certain that no pleasure, to exist at all, can last for less than a moment. Such a degree of duration for a pleasure is within every day's experience. But there is no fixing upon any particular number of moments as being the greatest during which any pleasure can continue.

The quantum of the value of a pleasure in point of proximity has for its limit on the side of increase actual presence. No pleasure can be nearer, no pleasure can, on the score of proximity, be more valuable, than one that is actually present. Pleasures that are actually present are within every day's experience. But there is no fixing upon any number of moments, months or years that shall constitute the greatest interval which can subsist between any present time, and the time at which the event of a pleasure's being enjoyed is to take place. The greatest possible duration of a man's life, were it determined, might indeed determine the greatest degree of remoteness of a pleasure as far as a single person were concerned: but in the first place the greatest possible duration of a man's life is a quantity that never can be determined; in the next place it often becomes material to consider the pleasure not of a single person only but of many persons in succession.

The quantum of the value of a pleasure in point of certainty, as it is more convenient to call it on the present occasion, has for its limit on the side of increase that absolute certainty which cannot be denied to take place where the pleasure is actually present. No pleasure can be more certain than one that is actually present. But there is no fixing upon any number of chances which shall be the greatest there can be against the event of any pleasure's taking place.

Now then, whole numbers increase continually from a fixed point (unity): fractional numbers decrease continually from the same fixed point. Hence it appears, I imagine pretty plainly, why the degrees of intensity and duration must be expressed by whole numbers: that of proximity and that of certainty by fractions.

So much for the circumstances that are ingredients in the value of a pleasure as far as concerns a single individual: when a whole community, that is, a multitude of individuals is considered as being concerned in it, the value of it is to be multiplied by the number of such individuals. The total value of the stock of pleasure belonging to the whole community is to be obtained by multiplying the number expressing the value of it as respecting any one person, by the number expressing the multitude of such individuals. The accession it, a pleasure, receives in value by this circumstance may be denominated its extent.

A pleasure considered as extending itself in this manner through a whole community would hardly in common language be termed a pleasure: it would rather be termed a lot of happiness.

So much for the value of a pleasure considered by itself. Considered with reference to other sensations that may result from the same causes, the value of it may be regarded as susceptible of two other ingredients, fecundity and purity: fecundity in as far as those causes may be productive of pleasures: sensations of the same kind, to wit, purity in as far as they may be exempt from producing sensations of the opposite kind; to wit pains.

It is evident that the more pleasures in number and value any given pleasure is followed by, the greater will be its value: and the more pains, the less.

Of the four other ingredients in the value of a pleasure there will be perpetual occasion to make mention under their respective names: the whole system of the ensuing disquisitions in a manner turns upon them. Of these two last there will hardly be equal occasion to make mention, at least under these names. For in taking an account of the physiological effects of any mode of conduct the more simple way is to consider the several pleasures and pains it is productive of by themselves, (setting the sum of the pleasures on one side of the account, and on the other, that of the pains) instead of bringing in all the subsequent pleasures and pains in the lump, by way of appendages to the first. For each of them in order to the obtaining a true estimate of its value, must be considered under the same four heads under which the value of the first was taken.

The idea of considering happiness as resolvable into a number of individual pleasures, I took from Helvetius: before whose time it can scarcely be said to have had a meaning. (This is directly contrary to the doctrines laid down in Cicero's Tusculan disputations: which book, like most of the other philosophical writings of that great master of language, is nothing but a heap of nonsense.) The idea of estimating the value of each sensation by analysing it into these four ingredients, I took from M. Beccaria: gleaning up those several articles from different places in which I saw them made use of in estimating the force and utility of punishments. Considering that punishment is but pain applied to a certain purpose, that the value of a pleasure is composed of the same articles and that pains and pleasures, and actions in as far as they had a tendency to produce or prevent the one and the other were all that morals and politics, or so much as was of any use or meaning in those sciences, had in view, it seemed to me that such an analysis was the very thing that was wanted as the foundation for a complete system of moral science. I had already proceeded some length in building upon that foundation when Maupertuis' Essay on Moral Philosophy fell into my hands. That ingenious philosopher whose work is of a date some years prior to that of M. Beccaria, proceeds upon the same idea of making such an analysis for his groundwork. He had however pursued it but by halves, not taking any account of the two articles of proximity and certainty. Besides this omission, he fell into a very melancholy [and] fundamental error, by the wrong turn he gave to his definition of the word pleasure. This led him into a variety of conclusions as false as they are melancholy which seem to have been the reason of his book having been still less noticed than it deserves. The definition he gives of (the word) pleasure, is so construed as to exclude from any title to that appellation, every degree of pleasure that falls short of being the highest.

The business of the legislator is to augment the sum of happiness in a state as much as possible. If the sum of happiness be on any occasion increased, it must be by increasing the sum of pleasures or diminishing that of pains. This may be done in either of three ways: 1. by introducing a pleasure instead of a pain; 2. by introducing a less pain instead of a greater pain; 3. by introducing a greater pleasure in the room of a lesser pleasure. These effects then are brought about sometimes by applying pain, sometimes by applying pleasure. Now, as to pain, the legislator has many modes and those very certain in their operation of applying it at all times directly to the object. With pleasure this is not the case: whenever it were to be applied some individual period must be fixed for the operation to be performed: and were even the object a given person, there is no operation whatever which the legislator could be certain would at any fixed period give him pleasure; produce pleasure in such object.

To produce pleasure therefore the legislator has but one course to take, which is to lay in a man's way some *instrument* of pleasure, and leave the application of it to himself. By instrument of pleasure we are here to understand anything that goes under the name of a *possession*: whether that possession be a real or fictitious entity. Possessions that are real entities are all of them to be found among the several bodies that surround us: the value whereof, that is their aptitude of producing pleasure is measured by that one sort of them which being the pledge and representative of almost all the rest is a means of acquiring them at any time. I mean *money*. Possessions that are fictitious entities, are (either) power (condition) (or) and reputation. Money is also, directly or indirectly a means of acquiring even these.

Now, then, of these three possessions, money, power and reputation, it is only in small quantities to a few persons and on particular occasions that the two latter are at the disposal of the legislator. Suppose a fund of money once collected, no matter by what means, and every individual in the state may be made to profit by a distribution of it:[e] such individuals may be *rich* with respect to the individuals of another state; but if any of them are rendered *powerful* or *honourable* by their own government, they must be *powerful* or *honourable* in comparison of one another and therefore at the expense of, one another. Money therefore is the only current possession, the only current instrument of pleasure. When a legislator then has occasion to apply pleasure, the only method he has of doing it, ordinarily speaking, is by giving money. Now, then, money being the current instrument of pleasure, it is plain by uncontroverted experience that the quantity of actual pleasure follows in every instance in some proportion or other the quantity of money. As to the law of that proportion, nothing can be more indeterminate. It depends upon a great variety of circumstances, which however I shall endeavour to collect in due time.[f] Thus much however is true in general, that the more money a man has given him the more pleasure. There are, it is true, some men to whom the same sum would give more pleasure than to others: to the same man likewise the same sum would give more pleasure at one *time* than at another: and even with respect to the same man and at the same time it is not true where the disproportion is very large between two sums that the proportion between the two pleasures would follow exactly the proportion between the sums. *One Guinea*, suppose, gives a man (a certain

---

[e] See Hume's *Essays*. Contra what Mr Hume says he must be understood with this allowance.

[f] See the next chapter. [Not included here. Ed.]

quantity no matter what, call it)[5] *one degree* of pleasure: it is not true by any means that a *million* of guineas given to the same man at the same time would give him a *million* of such degrees of pleasure. Perhaps not a thousand, perhaps not a hundred: who can say? Perhaps not fifty. In large sums the ratio of pleasure to pleasure is in this way less than a ratio of money to money. There is no limit beyond which the quantity of money cannot go: but there are limits, and those comparatively narrow beyond which pleasure can not go. There are men whose pleasure the acquisition of a hundred guineas would carry to this utmost limit:[6] a hundred thousand could not carry it beyond. Here then is the quantity of money increased a thousandfold, and that of pleasure not at all. For all this it is true enough for practice with respect to such small quantities as ordinarily occur, that *caeteris paribus* the proportion between pleasure and pleasure is the same as that between sum and sum: so much is strictly true that the ratios between the two pairs of quantities are nearer to that of equality than to any other ratio that can be assigned. Men will therefore stand a better chance of being right by supposing them equal than by supposing them to be any otherwise than equal. They ought therefore, in every case in which no particular reason can be given to the contrary, to be supposed equal, and spoken of as such.

Speaking then in general we may therefore truly say, that in small quantities the pleasures produced by two sums, are *as* the sums producing them. But money is capable of being measured: any sum of it considered as a whole is capable of being divided into parts, the ratio of which parts one to another may be made evident to the senses to the utmost degree that can be required; to wit in respect of bulk and weight. Now to these parts correspond so many degrees of pleasure: and thus it is that under the restrictions above specified we may measure with the utmost exactness any such pleasure as is producible by money, that is, any such pleasure as in general it lies within the province of the legislator to bestow.

As pleasure is given by giving money, so is pain by taking it away. This latter fact stands equally uncontroverted, and is equally matter of experience with the former. For correspondent reasons and under correspond[ing] restrictions (it is right to say that) *caeteris paribus* the (quantity of) money is the direct and proper measure, and the only proper measure, of that sort of pain which is produced by means of money. Now money, as has been said, is the only current and universal means in the hands of the legislator of producing pleasure. At the same time it is not by any means the only current and universal means of producing pain. With respect to pain it is not an universal means in itself: nor is it even so general as other means which the nature of mankind affords. For to any man money may be given. But from whom who has no money, no money can be taken. At the same time of producing pain there is another means which is strictly universal: for every man has a body.

Of such pleasure then as is produced by the bestowal of money, and of such pain as is produced by the taking away of money money is the direct and proper measure: being not only the measure, but the producing instrument or cause. But of a pleasure or a pain produced by any other cause, money though not the cause may be the measure; if not the direct one, yet an exact and proper one, and the only one such pain or pleasure will admit of.

If of two pleasures a man knowing what they are would as lief enjoy the one as the other, they must be reputed equal. There is a reason for supposing them equal, and there is none for supposing them unequal. If of two pains a man had as lief escape the one as the other, such two pains must be reputed equal. If of two sensations, a pain and a pleasure, a man had as lief enjoy the pleasure and suffer the pain, as not enjoy the one and not suffer the latter, such pleasure and pain must be reputed *equal*, or as we may say in this case, *equivalent*.

If then between two pleasures, the one produced by the possession of money, the other not, a man had as lief enjoy the one as the other, such pleasures are to be reputed equal. But the pleasure produced by the possession of money is *as* the quantity of money that produces it: money is therefore the measure of this pleasure. But the other pleasure is equal to this: the other pleasure thereof is as the money that produces this: therefore money is also the measure of that other pleasure. It is the same between pain and pain; as also between pain and pleasure.

The use of a common measure is to enable the person who speaks to communicate to any one he is speaking to the same idea of the quantity of any thing he is speaking of as he himself conceives. A common measure must therefore be some instrument the name of which suggests upon being mentioned to both parties an idea of the same quantity. You tell me St Paul's is bigger than the Pantheon: I agree with you that it is so. This agreement does not hinder our ideas of the proportion of those two bodies from being very different. You may think St Paul's ten times as big as the other building: I may think it not more than half as big again: You now tell me that St Paul's contains two millions of cubic feet; the Pantheon but half a million. If I agree with you in this our ideas of the bigness of the respective buildings are now the same. We have found a common measure for them *viz*: a foot ruler an instrument the use of which is familiar to both of us, and which through the medium of our senses presents us with such ideas of quantity as by experience we always find to be alike. In the same manner if you say it was hotter yesterday at noon than it was today at the same hour (and I agree with you), our ideas of the heat of the weather at those periods respectively may notwithstanding be very different. But if you say the thermometer stood at 60 yesterday and fell today to 50 and I agree with you, our ideas of the heat in this case must be alike.

If then, speaking of the respective quantities of various pains and pleasure [*sic*] and agreeing in the same propositions concerning them we would annex the same ideas to these propositions, that is, if we would understand one another, we must make use of some common measure. The only common measure the nature of things affords is money. How much money would you give to purchase such pleasure? 5 Pounds and no more. How much money would you give to purchase such another pleasure? 5 Pounds and no more. The two pleasures must as to you be reputed equal. How much money would you give to purchase immediately such a pleasure? 5 Pounds and no more. How much money would you give to exempt yourself immediately from such a pain? 5 pounds and no more. The pleasure and the pain must be reputed equivalent.

From what source such pleasures or such pains may issue, whether the pleasure consist in drinking so many bottles of wine, in enjoying the favours of such a woman, in possessing the respect or good will of such a man, in relieving such an object in distress, in doing such a service to one's country or to mankind in general, in revenging one's self in such a manner upon such a person; whether the pleasure be in its consequences productive of pleasure, or of pain or of neither: the pain of pain or of pleasure or of neither (in a word whether they be fruitful, pure, or insulated) are circumstances which so long as the pains or pleasures in question be considered *in themselves* and without regard to consequences make no difference with respect to the propriety of speaking of them, as being in money of such a value. If I having a crown in my pocket and not being adry, hesitate whether I shall buy a bottle of claret with it for my own drinking or lay it out in providing sustenance for a family I see about to perish for want of my assistance, so much the worse for me at the long run: but it is plain that so long as I continued hesitating the two pleasures of sensuality in the one case, of sympathy in the other, were exactly worth to me five shillings: to me they were exactly equal.

I beg a truce here of our men of sentiment and feeling: while from necessity and it is only from necessity, I speak and prompt mankind to speak a mercenary language. The thermometer is the instrument for measuring the heat of the weather: the barometer the instrument for measuring the pressure of the air. Those who are not satisfied with the accuracy of these instruments must find out others that shall be more accurate, or bid *adieu* to Natural Philosophy. Money is the instrument for measuring the quantity of pain or pleasure. Those who are not satisfied with the accuracy of this instrument must find out some other that shall be more accurate, or bid *adieu* to Politics and Morals.

Let no man therefore be either surprised or scandalised if he finds me in the course of this work valuing every thing in money. 'Tis in this way only we can get aliquot parts to measure by. If we must not say of a pain or a pleasure that it is worth so much money, it is in vain in point of quantity to say any thing at all about it. There is neither proportion nor disproportion between punishments and crimes.

In conformity to this method of considering the subject, it will be proper to settle the import of several expressions we shall have occasion to make use of. The *pleasure* resulting from any act to the agent may be stiled the *profit of* that act. The *pain* resulting from it, the *loss by* that act. According to the different kinds of pleasures and pains, we may distinguish therefore so many different kinds of profits and losses. Profit accordingly might be distinguished into the sensual kind and the mental: in the latter class we should find pecuniary which includes all that is meant by the word profit in that confined and narrow sense of it which is rather the most common.

It imports a legislator as well as every private man to know how to measure the *value* of a pain or pleasure: to know on what circumstances belonging to it the value of it depends. For the more in number the pleasures are which a man is about to enjoy within a given time, and the greater each of them is in value, the number and value of the pains he is about to enjoy within that time being deducted, the greater for that time will be his happiness.

The circumstances on which the value of a pleasure depends when considered by itself are these four: *viz.* 1. Intensity; 2. Duration; 3. Proximity or remoteness; 4. Degree of certainty, that is of certainty, probability or improbability.

The circumstances of intensity and duration belong necessarily and at all times to all pleasures: every pleasure must be more or less *intense*: every pleasure must last for such or such a *time*. These two circumstances taken together constitute what may be properly termed the magnitude of a pleasure. It is indeed common enough to speak of the magnitude of a pleasure when nothing more than the intensity of it is in view. But then the duration of it is either neglected, or supposed to be already settled. Of two pleasures, that is actually greater than the other which is more intense for the time that they both last. We may accordingly proceed to lay down the following axioms: 1. Of two pleasures, equal in intensity, the magnitude is as the duration. 2 Of two pleasures equal in duration, the magnitude is as the intensity. 3. The magnitude of any given pleasure is as its intensity multiplied by its duration.[7]

Next, with regard to the circumstances of proximity and certainty. A pleasure, like any thing else, must be either past, present, or future. If past, its value is at an end. (As such there can be no further occasion to consider it.) Present, any one single pleasure can be only for a very short space of time, without the interruption of indifference, of pains, or of other pleasures, how long soever any thing may continue that is a fund of pleasures. Future, it may be for an indefinite length of time; accordingly there is much more occasion to consider pleasures as future than as present. When once a pleasure is present, no speculations concerning either its remoteness or its uncertainty can have place. It can be in no degree either remote or uncertain. So long as it is yet to come, it must be in some degree remote, and it may be in a greater or less degree uncertain. Presence therefore is the limit at once of remoteness and uncertainty.

The value of a pleasure is the less, the more remote it is. Its remoteness is measured by the number of moments or other greater parts of time that are to elapse between the time with reference to which the pleasure is considered as being remote, and the time at which it is to be enjoyed. The value of a pleasure considered as present being represented by unity, the value of it considered as remote must be represented by a fraction.

When a pleasure is remote, the value of it will again be less, the less certain it is: or to speak at full length, the less certain the event is of its happening. When such an event is not absolutely certain, the degree of its uncertainty, like that of the certainty of any other event, is measured by the ratio of the number of the chances there are for its happening, to that of the number of chances there are for its not happening.

Concerning the magnitude of the value of a pleasure we may therefore proceed to lay down the following axioms: 1. Of two pleasures equal in magnitude and not both of them present, the value is as the proximity. 2. Of two pleasures equal in magnitude and proximity, and not both of them certain, the value is as the degree of certainty.

The value of any given pleasure is as the intensity, duration, proximity and certainty multiplied together.[g]

The numbers representing the *intensity* and *duration* of a pleasure, should be whole numbers: those representing its remoteness and degree of certainty, fractions; and for this reason. The quantities of intensity and duration of which a pleasure is susceptible have each of them a fixed limit on the side of diminution: they have none

---

[g] At full length thus: the value of any (given) pleasure is to the value of any other pleasure as the product of the numbers representing the intensity, duration, proximity and degree of certainty of the *one* when multiplied together, is to the product of the numbers representing the intensity, duration, proximity and degree of certainty of the *other* when multiplied together.

on the side of increase. On the other hand the quantities of proximity and degree of certainty of which it [is] susceptible have each of them a fixed limit on the side of increase; they have none on the side of diminution.

I am aware that the remoteness of the latter part of the greater pleasure during its continuance is a circumstance that diminishes its value: insomuch that a pleasure which spread out, if one may say, in point of duration, could not be quite so valuable as a pleasure of the same magnitude that spread out in point of intensity. (But the influence of the circumstance is too trifling to be here insisted on.) Accordingly a hundred a year for *thirty* years, come when it will, is not so valuable as a thousand [a] year (commencing from the same time) for *three* years.

As to the proportion in which the value of a pleasure is diminished by its remoteness, this will be rather difficult to ascertain. The proportion in which the value of a sum of money, that is, of a fund of pleasures is diminished by this circumstance is different in different countries, according to the rate of interest.

What has been observed concerning the manner in which the value of a pleasure is affected by the circumstances of remoteness and uncertainty, is far from being a matter of mere speculation. It is exemplified and verified by every day's experience. The value of a sum of money is affected exactly in this manner: and how else is it that a sum of money can be valuable but as a fund of pleasures or what comes to the same thing of the means of averting pains?[8]

The numbers expressive of the intensity of a pleasure and those expressive of its duration, are to be multiplied together, not merely added. For supposing the pleasure to continue all along at the same degree of intensity, every degree of intensity it possesses is carried through every degree of duration: and *vice versa* every degree of duration is extended over every degree of intensity. Accordingly if of two pleasures, the one be *three* times as intense as the other, and likewise continues three times as long, it is not six times only as great, but nine times. The first pleasure (suppose) has three degrees of intensity, and likewise three minutes of duration: the second but one degree of intensity and one minute of duration. The first then during the first minute has three degrees of intensity, that is three times as many as the second: during the second minute it has the same three degrees of intensity over again: which makes it already six times as great as the other pleasure: during the third minute it has the same three degrees of intensity still; which makes it nine times as great.

In like manner the numbers expressive of its magnitude and those expressive of its proximity must be multiplied together and not barely added. The magnitude of the first pleasure is 27, that of the other, 3. At the same time the degree of proximity or remoteness of the first is such as makes its value less by one-third only than it would have been had the pleasure been present: leaving it equal to two-thirds of that of a present pleasure of the same magnitude;[9] while the degree of remoteness of the other pleasure is such as makes it less by two-thirds than it would have been had the pleasure been present: leaving it equal to one-third only of that of a present pleasure of the same magnitude. To multiply a whole number by a fraction is to multiply it by the *numerator* of the fraction, and divide the product of that multiplication by the *denominator*; 27 then multiplied by two-thirds or in other words two-thirds of 27 is 18: and 3 multiplied by one-third, or in other words one-third of 3 is 1. The value then of the greater pleasure will be to that of the lesser, as 18 is to 1. The number expressive of the magnitude of the pleasure supposing it to be present must be magnified by the fraction expressing what it loses in value on the score of its remoteness, not simply added: for the deduction to be made on this account applies equally to every particle of it. If the fraction expressive of the alteration made in its value, by this circumstance instead of being multiplied into the number expressive of its magnitude were added to it, the value of it would be increased by this circumstance instead of lessened: the value of the greater pleasure would be 27 and two-thirds instead of 18: that of the lesser 3 and one-third instead of 1.

After the same manner it may be shown that the number expressive of the magnitude of the pleasure is to be multiplied by the fraction expressive of its degree of certainty, not added to it.

CHAPTER 8

The Idea of a Political Society[1]

1.[2] The idea of a natural society is a negative one. The idea of a political society is a positive one. It is with the latter, therefore, we should begin.

When a number of persons (whom we may style subjects) are supposed to be in the habit of paying obedience to a person, or an assemblage of persons, of a known and certain description (whom we may call governor or governors) such persons altogether (subjects and governors) are said to be in a state of political society.[a]

2. The idea of a state of natural society is, as we have said, a negative one. When a number of persons are supposed to be in the habit of conversing with each other, at the same time that they are not in any such habit as mentioned above, they are said to be in a state of natural society.

3. If we reflect a little, we shall perceive, that, between these two states, there is not that explicit separation which these names, and these definitions, might teach one, at first sight, to expect. It is with them as with light and darkness: however distinct the ideas may be that are, at first mention, suggested by those names, the things themselves have no determinate bound to separate them. The circumstance that has been spoken of as constituting the difference between these two states, is the presence or absence of an habit of obedience. This habit, accordingly, has been spoken of simply as present (that is, as being perfectly present) or, in other words, we have spoken as if there were a perfect habit of obedience, in the one case: it has been spoken of simply as absent (that is, as being perfectly absent) or, in other words, we have spoken as if there were no habit of obedience at all, in the other. But neither of these manners of speaking, perhaps, is strictly just. Few, in fact, if any,

---

[a] *Vide infra*, par. 3, note (a).

are the instances of this habit being perfectly absent; certainly none at all, of its being perfectly present. Governments, accordingly, in proportion as the habit of obedience is more perfect, recede from; in proportion as it is less perfect, approach to, a state of nature: and instances may present themselves, in which it shall be difficult to say whether a habit, perfect, in the degree in which, to constitute a government, it is deemed necessary it should be perfect, does subsist or not.[b]

---

[b] 1. A habit is but an assemblage of acts: under which name I would also include, for the present, voluntary forbearances.

2. A habit of obedience, then, is an assemblage of acts of obedience.

3. An act of obedience is any act done in pursuance of an expression of will on the part of some superior.

4. An act of political obedience (which is what is here meant) is any act done in pursuance of an expression of will on the part of a person governing.

5. An expression of will is either parole or tacit.

6. A parole expression of will is that which is conveyed by the signs called words.

7. A tacit expression of will is that which is conveyed by any other signs whatsoever: among which none are so efficacious as acts of punishment, annexed in time past, to the non-performance of acts of the same sort with those that are the objects of the will that is in question.

8. A parole expression of the will of a superior is a command.

9. When a tacit expression of the will of a superior is supposed to have been uttered, it may be styled a fictitious command.

10. Were we at liberty to coin words after the manner of the Roman lawyers, we might say a quasi-command.

11. The Statute law is composed of commands: the Common law, of quasi-commands.

12. An act which is the object of a command actual or fictitious; such an act, considered before it is performed, is styled a duty or a point of duty.

13. These definitions premised, we are now in a condition to give such an idea of what is meant by the perfection or imperfection of a habit of obedience in a society as may prove tolerably precise.

14. A period in the duration of the society; the number of persons it is composed of during that period; and the number of points of duty incumbent on each person being given; the habit

4. On these considerations, the suppositions of a perfect state of nature, or, as it may be termed, a state of society perfectly natural, may, perhaps, be justly pronounced what our Author for the moment seemed to think of it, an extravagant supposition: but then, that of a government in this sense perfect, or, as it may be termed, a state of society perfectly political, a state of perfect political union,

---

of obedience will be more or less perfect, in the ratio of the number of acts of obedience to those of disobedience.

15. The habit of obedience in this country appears to have been more perfect in the time of the Saxons than in that of the Britons; unquestionably it is more so now than in the time of the Saxons. It is not yet so perfect, as well contrived and well digested laws in time, it is to be hoped, may render it: but absolutely perfect, till man ceases to be man, it never can be.

A very ingenious and instructive view of the progress of nations, from the least perfect states of political union to that highly perfect state of it in which we live, may be found in Lord Kames' Historical Law Tracts.

16. For the convenience and accuracy of discourse, it may be of use, in this place, to settle the signification of a few other expressions relative to the same subject. Persons who, with respect to each other, are in a state of political society, may be said also to be in a state of political union or connexion.

17. Such of them as are subjects may, accordingly, be said to be in a state of submission, or of subjection, with respect to governors: such as are governors, in a state of authority with respect to subjects.

18. When the subordination is considered as resulting originally from the will, or (it may be more proper to say) the pleasure of the party governed, we rather use the word 'submission'; when from that of the party governing, the word 'subjection'. On this account is that the term can scarcely be used without apology, unless with a note of disapprobation: especially in this country, where the habit of considering the consent of the persons governed as being in some sense or other involved in the notion of all lawful, that is, all commendable government, has gained so firm a ground. It is, on this account, then, that the term 'subjection', excluding as it does, or, at least, not including such consent, is used commonly in what is called a *bad* sense: that is, in such a sense as, together with the idea of the object in question, conveys the accessory idea of disapprobation. This accessory idea, however, annexed as it is to the abstract term 'subjection', does not extend itself to the concrete term 'subjects'—a kind of inconsistency of which there are many instances in language.

a state of perfect submission in the subject, of perfect authority in the governor, is no less so.[c]

5. A remark there is, which, for the more thoroughly clearing up of our notions on this subject, it may be proper here to make. To some ears, the phrases, 'state of nature', 'state of political society', may carry the appearance of being absolute in their signification: as if the condition of a man, or a company of men, in one of these states, or in the other, were a matter that depended altogether upon

---

[c] It is true that every person must, for some time at least after his birth, necessarily be in a state of subjection with respect to his parents, or those who stand in the place of parents to him; and that a perfect one, or at least as near to being a perfect one, as any that we see. But for all this, the sort of society that is constituted by a state of subjection thus circumstanced, does not come up to the idea that, I believe, is generally entertained by those who speak of a political society. To constitute what is meant in general by that phrase, a greater number of members is required, or, at least, a duration capable of a longer continuance. Indeed, for this purpose, nothing less, I take it, than an indefinite duration is required. A society, to come within the notion of what is ordinarily meant by a political one, must be such as, in its nature, is not incapable of continuing for ever in virtue of the principles which gave it birth. This, it is plain, is not the case with such a family society, of which a parent, or a pair of parents, are at the head. In such a society, the only principle of union which is certain and uniform in its operation, is the natural weakness of those of its members that are in a state of subjection; that is, the children: a principle which has but a short and limited continuance. I question whether it be the case even with a family society, subsisting in virtue of collateral consanguinity; and that for the like reason. Not but that even in this case a habit of obedience, as perfect as any we see examples of, may subsist for a time; to wit, in virtue of the same moral principles which may protract a habit of filial obedience beyond the continuance of the physical ones which gave birth to it: I mean affection, gratitude, awe, the force of habit, and the like. But it is not long, even in this case, before the bond of connexion must either become imperceptible, or lose its influence by being too extended.

These considerations, therefore, it will be proper to bear in mind in applying the definition of political society above given (in par. 1) and in order to reconcile it with what is said further on [in par. 8].

themselves. But this is not the case. To the expression, 'state of nature', no more than to the expression, 'state of political society', can any precise meaning be annexed, without reference to a party different from that one who is spoken of as being in the state in question. This will readily be perceived. The difference between the two states lies, as we have observed, in the habit of obedience. With respect, then, to a habit of obedience, it can neither be understood as subsisting, in any person, nor as not subsisting, but with reference to some other person. For one party to obey, there must be another party that is obeyed. But this party who is obeyed, may at different times be different. Hence may one and the same party be conceived to obey and not to obey at the same time, so as it be with respect to different persons, or, as we may say, to different objects of obedience. Hence it is, then, that one and the same party may be said to be in a state of nature, and not to be in a state of nature, and that at one and the same time, according as it is this of that party that is taken for the other object of comparison. The case is, that in common speech, when no particular object of comparison is specified, all persons in general are intended: so that when a number of persons are said simply to be in a state of nature, what is understood is, that they are so as well with reference to one another, as to all the world.

6. In the same manner we may understand, how the same man, who is governor with respect to one man or set of men, may be subject with respect to another: how among governors some may be in a perfect state of nature with respect to each other: as the Kings of France and Spain; others, again, in a state of perfect subjection; as the Hospodars of Wallachia and Moldavia with respect to the Grand Signior; others, again, in a state of manifest but imperfect subjection; as the German States with respect to the Emperor; others, again, in such a state in which it may be difficult to determine whether they are in a state of imperfect subjection or in a perfect state of nature; as the King of Naples with respect to the Pope.[d]

---

[d] The kingdom of Naples is feudatory to the Papal See: and in token of fealty, the King, at his accession, presents the Holy Father with a white horse. The royal vassal sometimes treats his lord but cavalierly: but always sends him his white horse.

7. In the same manner, also, it may be conceived, without entering into details, how any single person, born, as all persons are born, into a perfect subjection to his parents,[e] that is, into a state of perfect political society with respect to his parents, may from thence pass into a perfect state of nature; and from thence successively into any number of different states of political society, more or less perfect, by passing into different societies.

8. In the same manner, also, it may be conceived how, in any political society, the same man may, with respect to the same individuals, be, at different periods, and on different occasions, alternately in the state of governor and subject: today concurring, perhaps active, in the business of issuing a general command for the observance of the whole society, amongst the rest of another man in quality of Judge: tomorrow, punished, perhaps, by a particular command of that same Judge, for not obeying the general command which he himself (I mean the person acting in character of governor) had issued. I need scarce remind the reader how happily this alternate state of authority and submission is exemplified among ourselves.

9. Here might be a place to state the different shares which different persons may have in the issuing the same command: to explain the nature of corporate action; to enumerate and distinguish half a dozen or more different modes in which subordination between the same parties may subsist: to distinguish and explain the different senses of the words 'consent', 'representation', and others of connected import; consent and representation, those interesting but perplexing words, sources of so much debate, and sources or pretexts of so much animosity. But the limits of the present design will by no means admit of such protracted and intricate discussions.

10. In the same manner, also, it may be conceived, how the same set of men, considered among themselves, may at one time be in a state of nature; at another time in a state of government. For the habit of obedience, in whatever degree of perfection it be necessary it should subsist in order to constitute a government, may be conceived, it is plain, to suffer interruptions. At different junctures, it may take place and cease.

---

[e] *Vide supra*, par. 4, note (b).

11. Instances of this state of things appear not to be unfrequent. The sort of society that has been observed to subsist among the American Indians may afford us one. According to the accounts we have of those people, in most of their tribes, if not in all, the habit we are speaking of appears to be taken up only in time of war: it ceases again in time of peace. The necessity of acting in concert against a common enemy, subjects a whole tribe to the orders of a common Chief. On the return of peace, each warrior resumes his pristine independence.

12. One difficulty there is that still sticks by us. It has been started, indeed but not solved. This is to find a note of distinction— a characteristic mark, whereby to distinguish a society in which there is a habit of obedience, and that at the degree of perfection which is necessary to constitute a state of government, from a society in which there is not: a mark, I mean, which shall have a visible determinate commencement; insomuch that the instance of its first appearance shall be distinguishable from the last at which it had not as yet appeared. It is only by the help of such a mark that we can be in a condition to determine, at any given time, whether any given society is in a state of government, or in a state of nature. I can find no such mark, I must confess, any where, unless it be this: the establishment of names of office: the appearance of a certain man, or set of men, with a certain name, serving to mark them out as objects of obedience; such as King, Sachem, Cacique, Senator, Burgomaster, and the like. This, I think, may serve tolerably well to distinguish a set of men in a state of political union among themselves, from the same set of men not yet in such a state.

13. But suppose an incontestible political society, and that a large one, formed; and from that a smaller body to break off: by this breach, the smaller body ceases to be in a state of political union with respect to the larger; and has thereby placed itself, with respect to that larger body, in a state of nature—what means shall we find of ascertaining the precise juncture at which this change took place? What shall be taken for the characteristic mark in this case? The appointment, it may be said, of new governors with new names. But no such appointment, suppose, takes place. The subordinate governors, from whom alone the people at large were in use to receive their commands under the old government, are

the same from whom they receive them under the new one. The habit of obedience which these subordinate governors were in with respect to that single person, we will say, who was the supreme governor of the whole, is broken off insensibly and by degrees. The old names by which these subordinate governors were characterised, while they were subordinate, are continued, now they are supreme. In this case it seems rather difficult to answer.

14. If an example be required, we may take that of the Dutch provinces with respect to Spain. These provinces were once branches of the Spanish monarchy. They have now, for a long time, been universally spoken of as independent states; independent as well of that of Spain as of every other. They are now in a state of nature with respect to Spain. They were once in a state of political union with respect to Spain: namely, in a state of subjection to a single governor, a King, who was King of Spain. At what precise juncture did the dissolution of this political union take place? At what precise time did these provinces cease to be subject to the King of Spain? This, I doubt, will be rather difficult to agree upon.[f]

15. Suppose the defection to have begun, not by entire provinces, as in the instance just mentioned, but by a handful of fugitives, this augmented by the accession of other fugitives, and so, by degrees, to a body of men too strong to be reduced, the difficulty will be increased still farther. At what precise juncture was it that ancient Rome, or that modern Venice, became an independent state?

16. In general then, at what precise juncture is it, that persons subject to a government, become, by disobedience, with respect to that government, in a state of nature? When is it, in short, that a revolt shall be deemed to have taken place; and when, again, is it, that that revolt shall be deemed to such a degree successful, as to have settled into independence?

17. As it is the obedience of individuals that constitutes a state of submission, so is it their disobedience that must constitute a state of revolt. Is it, then, every act of disobedience that will do as much? The affirmative, certainly, is what can never be maintained: for

---

[f] Upon recollection, I have some doubt whether this example would be found historically exact. If not, that of the defection of the Nabobs of Indostan may answer the purpose. My first choice fell upon the former; supposing it to be rather better known.

then would there no such thing as government to be found any where. Here, then, a distinction or two obviously presents itself. Disobedience may be distinguished into conscious, or unconscious; and that with respect as well to the law as to the fact.[g] Disobedience that is unconscious with respect to either, will readily, I suppose, be acknowledged not to be a revolt. Disobedience, again, that is conscious with respect to both, may be distinguished into secret and open; or, in other words, into fraudulent and forcible.[h] Disobedience that is only fraudulent, will likewise, I suppose, be readily acknowledged not to amount to a revolt.

18. The difficulty that will remain, will concern such disobedience only as is both conscious (and that as well with respect to law as fact) and forcible. This disobedience, it should seem, is to be determined neither by numbers altogether (that is, of the persons supposed to be disobedient) nor by acts, nor by intentions: all three may be fit to be taken into consideration. But having brought the difficulty to this point, at this point I must be content to leave it. To proceed any farther in the endeavour to solve it, would be to enter into a discussion of particular local jurisprudence. It would be entering upon the definition of treason, as distinguished from

---

[g] 1. Disobedience may be said to be unconscious with respect to the fact, when the party is ignorant either of his having done the act itself, which is forbidden by the law, or else of his having done it in those circumstances, in which alone it is forbidden.

2. Disobedience may be said to be unconscious with respect to the law, when, although he may know of his having done the act that is in reality forbidden, and that under the circumstances in which it is forbidden, he knows not of its being forbidden, or at least of its being forbidden in these circumstances.

3. So long as the business of spreading abroad the knowledge of the law continues to lie in the neglect in which it has lain hitherto, instances of disobedience unconscious with respect to the law can never be otherwise than abundant.

[h] If examples be thought necessary, theft may serve for an example of fraudulent disobedience; robbery of forcible. In theft, the person of the disobedient party, and the act of disobedience, are both endeavoured to be kept secret. In robbery, the act of disobedience, at least, if not the person of him who disobeys, is manifest and avowed.

murder, robbery, riot, and other such crimes, as, in comparison with treason, are spoken of as being of a more private nature. Suppose the definition of treason settled, and the commission of an act of treason is, as far as regards the person committing it, the characteristic mark we are in search of.

19. These remarks it were easy to extend to a much greater length. Indeed, it is what would be necessary, in order to give them a proper fulness, and method, and precision. But that could not be done without exceeding the limits of the present design. As they are, they may serve as hints to such as shall be disposed to give the subject a more exact and regular examination.

CHAPTER 9

Of subjects, or of the personal extent of the Dominion of the Laws[1]

Coextensive to dominion is jurisdiction: dominion the right of the sovereign; jurisdiction of the judge. Not that it is necessary that there should be any one judge or set of judges whose jurisdiction should be coextensive with the dominion of the sovereign; only that for every particle of dominion there should be a correspondent particle of jurisdiction in the hands of some judge or other: correspondent to one field of dominion there may be many fields of jurisdiction.

What is dominion? It is either the power of contrectation, or else that of imperation, for there are no others. But power of contrectation is a sort of power which, in a settled government, it scarcely ever becomes either necessary or agreeable to the sovereign, as such, to exercise; so that under the head of the power of imperation is comprised all the power which the sovereign is in use to exercise. And the same observation may be applied to the power of the judge.

Of the power of imperation, or the power of issuing mandates, the amplitude will be as the amplitude of the mandates which may be issued in virtue of it. The amplitude and quality of the mandates will be as the amplitude and quality of the persons who are their agible subjects, and the persons who are their passible subjects and the things, if any, which are their passible subjects, and the acts which are their objects in place and time.

The persons who are their agible subjects are the persons whose acts are in question—the persons whose acts are the objects of the mandate.

A sovereign is styled such, in the first instance, in respect of the persons whom he has the right or power to command. Now, the right or legal power to command may be coextensive with the physical power of giving force and effect to the command; that is, by the physical power of hurting; the power to hyper-physical contrectation employed for the purpose of hurting. But by possibility every sovereign may have the power of hurting any or every person whatsoever, and that not at different times only, but even at one and the same time. According to this criterion, then, the sphere of possible jurisdiction is to every person the same. But the problem is to determine what persons ought to be considered as being under the dominion of one sovereign, and what (others) under the dominion of another; in other words, what persons ought to be considered as the subjects of one sovereign, and what as the subjects of another.

The object of the present chapter is to determine, upon the principle of utility, what persons ought in the several cases that may present themselves, to be considered as the subjects of the law of the political state in question, as subject to the contrectative or imperative power of that law.

Proceeding as usual upon the exhaustive plan, I shall examine:

1. Over what persons the law can in point of possibility exercise dominion; what persons in point of possibility may be the subject of it; what persons in point of possibility it may treat as upon the footing of its subjects with effect; over what persons the law has possible dominion and jurisdiction; over what persons the law may have dominion and jurisdiction in point of force.

2. Over other persons than these, it is plain that it can never be right to say, the law ought upon the principle of utility to exercise jurisdiction. Why? Because it is idle to say of the lawgiver, as of anybody else, that he ought to do that which by the supposition is impossible.

The next inquiry is, then, the persons over whom the law may in point of possibility exercise dominion being given, over what sort of persons in that number ought the law in point of utility to exercise dominion (jurisdiction); what persons of that number ought to be looked upon as subject to it? Over what persons of that number it has jurisdiction in point of right taking general utility as the measure of right as usual, where positive law is out of the question.

3. It will then be another, and that a distinct question, over what sort of persons, and in what cases, the law in any given state does actually exercise dominion; and over what sort of persons, and in what cases, the law has dominion in point of exercise.

Dominion, then, may be distinguished into: 1. Dominion potential, or in point of force; 2. Dominion actual, or dominion in point of exercise; 3. Jurisdiction rightful or rather approveable, or jurisdiction in point of moral right.

Our object is to determine in what cases, if actual dominion were established, it would be rightful: in other words, in what cases it is the moral right, and at the same time the moral duty, in what cases the moral right without being the moral duty, of the given sovereign, as towards other sovereigns, to cause jurisdiction to be exercised over persons who are subject to his physical power. How far, and in what points, sovereigns, in the jurisdiction which they cause to be exercised over such persons as are within their reach, ought to yield or be aiding to each other?

An individual can be subject to a sovereign no farther than the physical power which that sovereign has of hurting him, or his afflictive power, as it may be called, extends. The question is, the cases in which the sovereign has the power of hurting him being given, in which of them ought he, upon the principle of utility, to exercise that power? In which of them ought other sovereigns, who may think their power concerned, to acquiesce in his exercising such power?

In every state, there are certain persons who are in all events, throughout their lives, and in all places, subject to the sovereign of that state; it is their obedience that constitutes the essence of his sovereignty. These may be styled the standing or ordinary subjects of the sovereign or the state; and the dominion he has over them may be styled fixed or regular. There are others who are subject to him only in certain events, for a certain time while they are at a certain place: the obedience of these constitutes only an accidental appendage to his sovereignty: these may be termed his occasional or extraordinary subjects, or subjects *pro re nata*; and the dominion he has over them may be styled occasional.[a]

His afflictive power being the limit of his actual as well as of his rightful dominion, his standing subjects will be those over whom he has the most afflictive power, over whom his afflictive power is the

---

[a] Country allegiance, sovereignty and subjection, may therefore be either fixed and regular, or occasional.

strongest; over his occasional subjects, his afflictive power will not be so strong. Now the points in which a man can be hurt are all [of them] comprised, as we have seen, under these four, *viz.* his person, his reputation, his property, and his condition. Of these four points, that in respect of which he can be made to suffer most is his person: since that includes not only his liberty, but his life. The highest jurisdiction therefore, is that of which the subject is a man's person. According to this criterion, then, the standing subjects of a sovereign should be those individuals whose persons are in his power.

This criterion would be a perfectly clear and eligible one, were the case such that in the ordinary tenor of human affairs, the persons of the same individuals were constantly under the physical power, or, as we say, within the reach of the same sovereign. But this is not the case. The different interests and concerns of the subject, the interest even of the sovereign himself, require the subject to transport himself necessarily to various places, where, according to the above criterion, he would respectively become the subject of so many sovereigns. But the question is, to what sovereign a given individual is subject, in a sense in which he is not subject to any other. This question, it is plain, can never be determined by a criterion which determines him to be the subject of one sovereign, in the same sense in which he may be subject to any number of other sovereigns. According to this criterion, a sovereign might have millions of subjects one day, and none at all the next.

Some circumstances, therefore, more constant and less precarious, must be found to ground a claim of standing dominion upon, than that of the present facility of exercising an afflictive power over the person of the supposed subject: a facility which, in truth, is no more than might be possessed not only by an established sovereign but by the most insignificant oppressor. Any man may, at times, have the power of hurting any other man. The circumstances of territorial dominion, dominion over land, possesses the properties desired. It can seldom happen that two sovereigns can, each of them, with equal facility, the other being unwilling, traverse the same tract of land. That sovereign then who has the physical power of occupying and traversing a given tract of land, insomuch that he can effectually and safely traverse it in any direction at pleasure, at the same time, that against his will another sovereign cannot traverse the same land with equal facility and effect, can be more certain of coming at the individual in question than such other sovereign can be, and therefore may be pronounced to have the afflictive power over all such persons as are to be found upon that land, and that a higher afflictive power than any other sovereign can have. And hence the maxim, dominion over person depends upon dominion over land.

But even this indicium, this mark, is not a ground of sufficient permanence whereon to found the definition of standing sovereignty: for the same individual who is one day on land which is under the dominion of a given sovereign, may another day be on land which is not under his dominion: from this circumstance, therefore, no permanent relation can be derived. But that the relation should be a permanent one is requisite on various grounds upon the principle of utility—that each subject may know what sovereign to resort to (principally) for protection; that each sovereign may know what subjects to depend upon for obedience; and that each sovereign may know when to insist, and when to yield, in any contest which he might have with any other sovereign who might lay a claim to the obedience of the same subject.

The circumstance, then, which is taken for the indicium of sovereignty on the one part, and subjection on the other, should be not a situation which at any time may change, but an event. This event should be one which must have happened once, which cannot have happened more than once, and which, having happened once, cannot be in the condition of one which has not happened; in a word, an event which is past, necessary and unrecurrent. Such an event is that found in the event of a man's birth: which must happen for the man to exist, which must have happened in some district of the earth, which can not happen a second time, and which, being over, cannot but have happened. At that period he must have been within the physical power of the sovereign within whose territory he was born.

Yet still it is not birth that is the immediate ground of jurisdiction: the immediate ground is presence, presence with reference to the locus of the territorial dominion; if birth be the ground of dominion, it is only in virtue of the presumption which it affords of the other circumstance. In every state, almost, there are some who emigrate out of the dominion within which they were born. But in every state almost, it is otherwise with by far the greater number. In civilised nations the greater part of mankind are *glebae ascriptitii*, fixtures to the soil on which they are born. With nations of hunters and shepherds, with tribes of American savages, and hordes of Tartars or Arabians, it is otherwise. But with these we have no business here.

Thus it is that dominion over the soil confers dominion *de facto* over the greater part of the natives, its inhabitants; in such manner that such inhabitants are treated as owing a permanent allegiance to the sovereign of that soil. And in general there seems no reason why it should not be deemed to do so, even *de jure*, judging upon the principle of utility. On the one hand, the sovereign, on his part, naturally expects to possess the obedience of persons who stand in this sort of relation to him: possessing it at first, he naturally expects to possess it—he is accustomed to reckon upon it: were he to cease to possess it, it might be a disappointment to him. Any other sovereign having even begun to possess the allegiance of the same subject, has not the same cause for expecting to possess it; not entertaining any such expectation, the not possessing it is no disappointment: for subjects, in as far as their obedience is a matter of private benefit to the sovereign, may, without any real impropriety (*absit verbo invidia*), be considered as subjects of his property. They may be considered as his property, just as any individual who owes another a service of any kind, may, *pro tanto*, be considered as his property. We speak of the service as being his property (such is the turn of the language), that is, as being the object of his property; but a service being but a fictitious entity can be but a fictitious object of property; the real, and only real object, is the person from whom the service is due.

On the other hand, let us consider the state of mind and expectations of the subject. The subject having been accustomed from his birth to look upon the sovereign as his sovereign, continues all along to look upon him in the same light: to be obedient is as natural as to be obedient to his own father. He lives, and has all along been accustomed to live under his laws. He has some intimation (I wish the universal negligence of sovereigns, in the matter of promulgation, would permit me to say anything more than a very inaccurate and general intimation), some intimation he has, however, of the nature of them. When occasion happens, he is accustomed to obey them. He finds it no hardship to obey them, none at least in comparison with what it would be were they altogether new to him; whereas, those of another sovereign, were they in themselves more easy, might, merely on account of their novelty, appear, and therefore be, harder upon the whole.

Thus much for the more usual case where a man continues to inhabit, as his parents did before him, the country in which he was born. But what if his parents, being inhabitants of another country, were sojourners only, or mere travellers in the country in which he was born, and he, immediately after his birth, carried out of it never to see it again? The manners and customs, the religion, the way of thinking, the laws, of the one country opposite to those of the other? The sovereign of the one, at war with the sovereign of the other? If regard be paid to birth, something surely is due to lineage: an Englishwoman, travelling with her husband from Italy through France, is delivered of a son in France: shall the son, when he grows up, be punished as a traitor, if taken in battle when fighting against the King of France? Or, on the other hand, supposing it to be right and politic for the King of France to refuse to strangers born out of his dominion any of the rights enjoyed by his native subjects, would it be right that this man who has never looked upon the French as his countrymen, nor the King of France as his sovereign, should partake of privileges which are denied to the subjects of the most favoured foreign nation? Shall the offspring of English Protestants, born at Cadiz, be reclaimed as a fugitive from the Inquisition, or the offspring of Spanish Catholics, born in London, undergo the severity of the English laws, for being reconciled to the Church of Rome? Shall the Mahometan, born at Gibraltar, be punished for polygamy or wine drinking?

Nor would it, it should seem, be an adequate remedy to these inconveniences to take the birth-place of the parents, or, in case of their birth-places being different, that of the father, for example, as the indicium, to determine the allegiance of the child: the circumstances of their birth might have been accompanied by a similar irregularity. During a man's education, his parents may have lived half their time in one country, half in another; what external mark can there be to determine to which of the two countries, if to either, his affections are attached?

The best way, therefore, seems to be to refer the solution of the question to those alone who are in a condition to give it; and to refer the option of his country, in the first instance, to the parents or guardian provisionally, while the child is incapable of judging for himself; afterwards to himself, as soon as he is judged capable; so that when he comes to a certain age he shall take his choice.

CHAPTER 10

What a Law Is

1. We all know what volition is: it is what we are all practising almost continually. The idea we have of it is a simple one: the term is not to be defined.

2. The object of volition is always some event. We understand tolerably well what an event means. Such a motion or assemblage of motions as we take notice of, among things that we take notice of, or the stoppage of such motion or motions, we style an event. The idea we have of motion is a simple one. The idea we have of stoppage of it is so too. The terms are not to be defined.

3. An event may be said to be an object of our will: our will to be directed to that event, when we will, or in other words, when our will is that that event should happen.[a]

4. An event, in the production of which a being capable of volition is instrumental, we style an action.

5. The intellectual instrument of an action, that instrument or

---

[a] 'The will is a faculty'; 'Volition is the exercise of that faculty'; 'The will exercises acts of volition'. Such has been the language. Not that there is really any such thing as a little being that under the name of will gets into men's heads, and exercises acts of volition, or any other acts—as some appear almost to have imagined. But it is man that exercises these various acts, that perceives these various emotions: it is man that wills, that exercises acts of volition: that perceives, that exercises perception: that remembers, that exercises memory: that imagines, that exercises imagination: that judges, that exercises judgment: howsoever it may be found convenient for many purposes to say that the will does so and so, rather than that man wills in this or in that manner. It varies the discourse, saves words and marks out the different operations more distinctly. This conceit, if seriously entertained, would not be absolutely without a parallel. The ancient physicians at least could have made no difficulties about it. The womb, according to them, was of itself an animal: insomuch that every female consisted of two animals one within another.

as some would say, cause of it, that is in the mind, is styled a motive.

6. A motive is an idea: it is the idea of some pleasure or some pain: the pleasure conceived as about to exist, or the pain as about not to exist, in consequence of our action.

7. Cessation of pain may be spoken of as pleasure. The pleasure then whereof the idea becomes a motive, is styled an end. It is also styled an object. It may be styled either way: thither the mind's prospect is directed there it terminates.

9. Acts are either of the body, or of the mind. An act of the body is styled an exterior or external act: an act of the mind is styled an interior or internal one.

10. Forbearance is the privation of action: it is to action what rest in general is to motion in general. We may say a forbearance, where rest is the object of volition, as we say an action, where motion is the object of volition.

11. An article of conduct is a middle[b] expression that may be employed to signify indifferently an action or a forbearance.

12. A mode of conduct may be used to signify indifferently one article of conduct, or several. A course of conduct may be used for an assemblage of articles of conduct in succession.

13. A restrictive is to forbearance, what a motive is to action.

14. A determination is a middle expression, capable of signifying indifferently a motion or a restrictive.[c]

---

[b] I use the word 'middle' here in the sense in which it is used by grammarians, when applied to that voice in verbs which in the Greek is capable of occupying the place sometimes of the active, sometimes of the passive mode and a substance. For the difference between mode and substance see Locke's *Essay*.

[c] The term forbearance with the article *a* before it, is not very common. The terms restrictive and determinative are not more so. Action is used in its proper sense and that of forbearance: the same term to denote two contraries. Motive, in like manner, is used in its own sense and that of restrictive; as command is and that of prohibition. And so it is in many other instances. So then it must be. There is no help for it. We must submit to usage, and in great measure be content to take language as we find it: nor attempt throughout to make a new one; lest we find none willing to be at the pains to understand it but ourselves. It may be of use, however, to have registered these distinctions, in order to refer to them in case of need.

15. The end of an action may be distant and ill-defined: but no man acts without an end: no man acts without a motive. Every action has its end; its motive.

16. A volition, whereof the object is an article of conduct of that person himself who wills, is styled, when the article of conduct is conceived to be in his power, a resolution. Such an act may, in reference to the resolution, be styled, the act (article of conduct) resolved on.

17. A volition whereof the object is an act of the person himself who wills, but not conceived to be absolutely in his power; or an event at large, or an act of a person other than he himself who wills, is styled a wish. Such an event may, in reference to the wish, be styled the event wished for.

18. A wish, when the object of it is an article of conduct of another person, must, in order to produce its object, be communicated to that other person. For it to be communicated to him, two ideas must be excited in his mind. First the idea of the article of conduct (act wished for), second the idea of the act of volition in him who wishes it. It is this latter that is to furnish him with the motive.

19. The means and only means whereby a wish or any other act of the mind can be communicated must be some external actions. These actions are said to be signs of the wish or other act of the mind they serve, to communicate.

20. The signs most frequently employed for this purpose are such actions as produce certain particular sounds. These sounds are styled words spoken, or by a collective appellation, speech: and from their connection with the signs do, when put together after a certain mode of assemblage just mentioned, become signs themselves.

21. Sounds address the sense but for an instant: that instant over, they are gone. Visible marks remain: they are substance: masses of matter or interruptions: masses of matter disposed in a certain order. On this account among others it is found convenient to employ visible marks as the signs of sounds. These marks put together after a certain mode of assemblages are styled words written: or by a collective appellation, writing.

22. A wish communicated takes a different name according to the

relation which the party whose wish it is, is conceived as standing in to the party whose action is the object of it; that of an inferior, that of an equal or that of a superior: if that of an inferior, a prayer, an entreaty, a petition, a request: if that of an equal, a requisition, a demand: if that of a superior, an injunction, an order, a command. But of many of these the import is apt to fluctuate.

23. Inferiority, equality, superiority are attributed to one, with reference to another, in various respects. The import of these terms in all cases is not easy perhaps to settle; but for the present purpose it may be said: an inferior is one who is supposed not able to occasion so much pain or pleasure to another as that other is to him: an equal, as much but not more: a superior, more.

24. A command, of which the object is a forbearance, that is a command not to do an act, is styled a prohibition, a forbiddal. *Vide* note C². Such act may with reference to the *prohibition*, the *forbiddal*, be styled the *act prohibited*, the *act forbidden*.

25(i)³. We are come now then to a law. A law is a command. It is a species of command. Thus much we must conceive of it on all occasions, to conceive clearly. Everything that is not a command therefore is not a law.

25(ii). A motion of an inanimate being is not a law: no more are ten thousand such motions of ten thousand such beings: no more is any uniformity we see or fancy among such motions, no more is the unknown and unostensible cause of such motions and of their uniformity. For an inanimate being is a being *not* endued with mind. But a command is an act of a being that *is* endued with mind. It is an act of the mind. And a law is a command.

26. This stone, placed in certain circumstances, moves towards the earth. This motion is not a law. Ten thousand stones, placed in similar circumstances move also towards the earth. Neither is here a law. There is a certain uniformity observable in the motions of all these stones. But neither is this uniformity a law. Finding that other motions have their cause, and concluding that this must have one too, we give a name beforehand to that cause, not professing to know anything of its nature. We call it attraction: it is in virtue of attraction, we say, that stones move towards the earth. But it is not in virtue of any law, that stones move towards the earth. Attraction is not a law. For what a law is, we know. But of

attraction we know nothing, beyond the name. And thus we are cleared of one branch of the pretended laws of nature.[d]

27. An exterior act of an animated being, an exterior act of a man is not a law. No more are ten thousand such acts: no more is any uniformity we observe among such acts. For a command is an act interior. No more is any interior act that is not a command; nor any assemblage of such acts; nor any uniformity among such an assemblage. A custom therefore is not a law. For a custom is an assemblage of acts in some respect or other uniform: or else it is the uniformity there is between those acts. But a law is a *command*.

28. All men within the Manor of Dale carry their corn to be ground at John Trott's mill: they have done so this year: they did so last year: they have done so every year: it has been their *custom*. The successive assemblage of resembling acts here spoken of is not a *law*. For to be one of many who for a length of time have without *commanding* carried their corn to John Trott's mill is one thing: to *command* them there to carry it, or to *command* anyone to punish them for not carrying it is another.[e]

---

[d] Of this stamp are the laws of motion, as they are called; laws concerning the motions of bodies in general: the laws of mechanics; laws concerning the motions of bodies solid; the laws of hydrostatics, laws concerning the motions of bodies fluid; the laws of pneumatics, laws concerning the motions of bodies in the state of vapour; the laws of optics, laws concerning the motions of the particles of light, the laws of vegetation, laws concerning the motions of particles solid, fluid and vaporous in such bodies as we call plants. By the word law in all these instances, is meant either some point of uniformity among the individual motions or things moving that are in question: or else some proposition asserting it. In all these instances the meaning of the word law is plainly figurative; and as such may in this case be tolerated with little or no inconvenience. Why it may in this case and not in another we shall see presently.

[e] Of this stamp or something like it, are Montesquieu's four laws of nature. Placed he says in a state of nature, men would do four things. First they would run away from one another; secondly they would eat; thirdly they would propagate their kind; fourthly they would seek society. These are Montesquieu's laws of nature. All this he sees men do: and this therefore is what, in a state which he imagines, he imagines they *would be disposed* to do. A disposition, a

29. Utility is not a law. For utility is but a quality, a property: a property an act has of increasing happiness; that is of averting pains or increasing pleasures. Utility is a quality of many kinds of acts. But a command is one particular kind of act itself. And a law is a command.

30. A dictate of utility is not a law.ᶠ For a dictate of utility is

---

propensity, is Montesquieu's law of nature: or he leaves you to imagine a cause for it; and it is this cause that is to be the law of nature.

I am sorry for a great man to whom the science is under many signal obligations: who has polished the garb of it: enriched it with many useful truths; and taught it to address itself to the heart. I am sorry for him: but his method and his general principles, as witness this specimen, are such as no man alive can profit from. He has met lately with two formidable antagonists in his friends, Helvetius and Voltaire. These two philosophers have displayed in a spirited manner the falsehood, or to speak more properly, the inanity of many of his notions.

ᶠ A dictate of utility *is* *not* a law: but it *is* a reason, however, for a law, as it is for any other *article of conduct*, and the only sort of reason that deserves the name: all else is but empty declamation.

When a man takes upon him to *blame* or *approve* a mode of conduct, and can give a reason for it, his reason is always of this sort. His reason then is an aportion of a general matter of fact; the truth of which rests upon experience. When I say the custom in parents of providing sustenance for their children is a useful custom, when I blame the not observing it, and give the utility of it as a reason for observing it, or what comes to the same thing, when I give the mischief of not observing it as a reason for blaming the non-observance of it, I allege a matter of fact. I put in essence a set of facts, and call in experience to witness. I allege the existence of certain pains and pleasures in the case I speak of: pleasures, the customary consequences of the mode of conduct I approve of: pains, the consequences of its opposite: pains and pleasures such as men have felt in themselves, or recognized in others: pains and pleasures felt not by any new-discovered moral sense, sole property of the discoverers: but by the old stock of senses, such as all men (are acquainted with) have, and all men know of. Of this sort then are a man's *reasons*, if he has any. When a man chooses the pleasure of deciding, but does not choose the trouble of finding reasons, there are various contrivances for avoiding it. One says he has an but someone's opinion that there is utility in a certain mode of conduct; that is that the mode of conduct in question is likely upon

---

understanding, and his understanding without the trouble of hearing *pro* and *con* pronounces an action to be right or to be wrong: and so there is a law of nature for it or against it. This is the way Dr Price makes laws of nature. Another says he has a sense on purpose: and it is this sense that pronounces what is right and what is wrong. This is the way that Lord Shaftesbury, Dr Hutchinson, and the triumvirate of doctors lately slaughtered, not to say butchered, by Dr Priestly make laws of nature. For though, as Euclid told King Ptolemy, there is no short cut, no *royal road* to geometry; there are these two it seems to morals. I know not whether even these philosophers do not consider themselves sometimes as giving reasons, and whether you are not expected to take the following as a reason; for instance, against your doing an act: *viz.* that your *understanding*, or your *moral sense* (whichever is the word) tells you that you ought not. If so the distinguishing property of these reasons is to be of sovereign efficacy wheresoever they are not wanted. If your understanding does not happen to tell you precisely the same things as Dr Price's, or your sense as Dr Hutchinson's, you have not got the reason: if it does, you have it without their giving it. The wonder is that man should have said so much to prove that nothing is to be said about the matter. What reason a man, in any of these ways of thinking, could find to give himself for saying anything about the matter to any other manner,[4] is more than I can find. The reasons he might find for saying nothing seem obvious and unanswerable. "Those who are with me are wise without study: to them all I could say would be unnecessary. Those who are against me are foolish without remedy: to them all I could say would be unavailing." It is but putting an *action* instead of a *person* and one short epigram of Martial's will better express the system of these philosophers than all the volumes they have given or can ever give us.

> *Non amo te, Sabide; nec possum dicere quare*
> *Hoc tantum possum dicere, non amo te.*

It[5] may be the ground of a law: it may be that consideration which *determines* those, whose concern it is, to make a law: as any act of the judgment may be that which serves to *determine* any act of the will. It may be the ground of a law. But it is not itself a law, or any part of one.

the whole to be productive of more pleasure (good) than it is of pain (evil). An opinion is an act of the understanding. But a *command* is an *act* of the *will*. And a law is a command. And thus we are cleared of another branch of the pretended law of nature.

31. Parents provide sustenance for their young. It is their *custom*. In this *custom*, I say, there is *utility*: it is a useful one. The several acts of which it consists are acts which taken together, make the mass of happiness that is in the world greater than it would be without them. This is what I say, this is my opinion: and my opinion further is, that most other men, if asked, would be of the same. But it is not my saying so, not their saying so that is a law: no, tho' I were Puffendorf: no, tho' I were a legislator. For to say that it is useful for men to do thus and thus, is one thing: to command them to do so, is another.

32. Two very different things, two very different *acts* of the mind are current under the common name of *resolution*: one which may be termed a *resolution of judgement* or *opinion*: and another which may be termed a *resolution of volition*: but it is not either of them that is a *law*. A *resolution of opinion* is not a law: for a resolution of opinion is an act of the understanding: but a command is an act of the will: and a law is a command.

33. "Resolved that general warrants are illegal." This resolution was not a law: though it was an *act* of one of the three branches of the body which makes laws. It would not have been a law though it had been the *act* of all three. For an opinion that an act is already among *acts* forbidden, is one thing; a *command* forbidding it is another.

34. A resolution of volition is not a law. For a resolution of volition is such an act of the will as has an act of the party himself whose will it is for that object. But a command is such an act of the will as has for its object the act not of the person whose will it is, but of some other person. And a law is command.

35. 'Resolved that this House will on Friday next resolve itself into a committee to consider of the "loyalty of General Warrants".' This resolution was not a law: though it was an act of one of the three branches of the body which makes laws. It would not have been, though it had been the act of all the three. For a discourse serving to communicate an intention of doing an act one's self, is

one thing: a discourse serving to communicate such a wish as shall cause other persons to do it, is another.

36. A promise is not a law. For a promise is but the expression of a resolution of volition (intentionally communicated).[g] But a law is a command.

37. 'Lewis, my people shall be at peace with thine.' This is not a law. For the expression of a resolution to do those acts, to issue those commands, which shall make the people of him who speaks at peace with those of Lewis who is spoken to, the expression, I say, of such a resolution is one thing. But the act itself that is resolved on, is another.

38. A compact is not a law. For a compact is but a pair of promises reciprocal.[h] But a law is a command.

39. 'Lewis, my people shall be at peace with thine, upon condition that thy people be at peace with mine.' 'George, my people shall be at peace with thine, upon condition that thy people be at peace with mine.' All this together is not a law. For it is but a pair of promises: and it is not a thousand pair of promises that can constitute a command.

41.[6] A law then is a command. Nor yet is everything that is a command a law. Commands there are that in common speech do not go by the name of laws. If then a command is not a law;

---

[g] A promise may be thus defined at length. In every promise there are two persons at least, concerned: one *by* whom it is communicated; the promiser: another, *to* whom it is communicated; the promisee. A promise, then, is a sign or assemblage of signs uttered to the end that a certain belief may be produced in the mind of a promisee: *viz*: a belief that a certain resolution subsists in the mind of the promiser. The act which it is designed should be believed by the promisee to be the act resolved on, is the act promised.

[h] A compact may be thus defined at length. A compact is a pair of promises by two parties mutually (reciprocally) given, the one of them in consideration of the other.

One promise is said to be the consideration of another or in other words, given in consideration of another, when (the resolution expressed by the one promise is the condition of the resolution expressed by the other promise) the one party's having been made or resolved to make the one promise is the condition of the resolution expressed by the other party in his promise.

it is on account of one or other of three particulars, in which the sort of command that is a law is understood to differ from those that are not. These are, its source, its substance, and (or) its formalities.

42. By the source of a law, I mean the person or body of persons whose command it is.

43. A body of persons, styled commonly for shortness sake, a body, is an assemblage of persons acting in a body. An assemblage of persons are said to act in a body, when every act they do is first willed by the greater number of them, the wills of the lesser number being ineffective.

44. By the substance of a law, I mean the sign or assemblage of signs, viz: the words expressing the command, and the act or assemblage of acts that is the object of it.

45. By the formalities of a law, I mean those transactions or other circumstances extrinsic to the law itself, on which depends, whether it shall be taken to have issued from that source, from which in itself it purports to have issued.

46. But here we must make a pause. In order to do what yet remains to distinguish a law from the several sort of things that are liable to be confounded with it, in order to show by which of the three particulars just mentioned it stands distinguished from other sorts of commands, there are a set of terms and expressions standing in relation to it that will require to be explained. Nor is this discoursing in a circle, as at first might be suspected. To explain them, the import they have will indeed be referred to the import of the term law: but for this purpose nothing more need be understood of it, than that it signifies a command issuing from the requisite source, and accompanied by the requisite formalities to constitute it a law. What is that source, of what nature are those formalities, will be more commodiously explained afterwards.

47. A law in the first place may be distinguished into first, a primary law; secondly a secondary law.

48. By a primary law, I mean any law that may be understood of itself, without reference to another. 'Steal not,' may be taken for the example of such a law.

49. By a secondary law, I mean a law that is not of itself to be understood (that would not of itself have been framed) nor without reference to some such law as that just mentioned. By a secondary

law (penal command) I mean a law commanding punishment to be applied for an offence; that is, to be applied on him who shall have committed an offence; against a primary one. '*Whosoever shall have stolen, hang him*', may serve for an example of a secondary law: a law subservient to the primary law before instanced '*steal not*'.[7]

50. I have mentioned offence. I have mentioned punishment. An offence is a mode of conduct contrary to the mode of conduct commanded by a law: a forbearance, when the mode of conduct commanded by the law is action; an action, when the mode of conduct commanded by the law as in the example, is forbearance.

51. Punishment is nothing but pain inflicted by or by command of a superior for or, in other words, on account of an act done.[i]

52. An act of disobedience is synonymous to an offence.[8]

53. An act of obedience is the opposite to an offence. It is a mode of conduct conformable to the mode of conduct commanded by the law. An action where the mode of conduct commanded by the law is action: a forbearance, where the mode of conduct commanded (by the law) is forbearance.

---

[i] I stop here. I do not go on and say 'by that inferior' because that would exclude the sort of punishment that is called vicarious.

CHAPTER 11

Source of a Law[1]

1. Considered in this point of view, the will of which it[2] is the expression must, as the definition intimates, be the will of the sovereign in *a* state. Now by a sovereign I mean any person or assemblage of persons to whose will a whole political community are (no matter on what account) supposed to be in a disposition to pay obedience:[a] and that in preference to the will of any other person.[b] Suppose the will in question not to be the will of *a* sovereign,

---

[a] I do not say in all cases: cases in which the sovereign shall not make any law, acts which he shall neither command nor prohibit, laws already subsisting which he shall not alter, *may* be settled in a variety of ways: by the original compact where any such thing has taken place (See *Fragm. on Govt.* Ch. 4 par. 34.), by subsequent compacts and engagements such as we see entered into by sovereigns every day: as in the cases of conquest, capitulation, cession, exchange, succession, and so on. I speak all along as to what is practicable: as to the matter of expediency, that is not in question here (Ibid., para 37).

[b] It may happen that one person or set of persons shall be sovereign in some cases while another is as completely so in other cases. (See Ch. 16, Division, xvii*n*, *Introduction to the Principles of Morals and Legislation.*) On this supposition they may be considered as composing all together but one sovereign. The truth of these propositions, which perhaps may[3] be found not very conformable to the most current notions, may presently be made appear. Power over persons is either power over their passive faculties merely, or power over their active faculties: which latter may be termed *power of imperation*. Now in point of fact not to meddle at present with the point of right (or to speak more intelligibly with the point of utility or expediency, since right independently of law and of utility is unintelligible) in point of fact, I say, the ultimate efficient cause of all power of imperation over persons is a disposition on the part of those persons to obey: the efficient cause then of the power of the sovereign is neither more nor less than the disposition to

footnote continiued.

obedience on the part of the people. Now this disposition it is obvious may admit of innumerable modifications—and that even while it is constant; besides that it may change from day to day. The people may be disposed to obey the commands of one man against all the world in relation to one sort of act, those of another man in relation to another sort of act, else what are we to think of the constitutional laws of the Germanic body: those of one man in one place, those of another man in another place, as we see all the world over: those of one man (for instance the dictator at Rome) at one time, those of another man or set of men (for instance the assembly of the governing part of the Roman people) at another: they may be disposed to obey a man if he *commands* a given sort of act: they may be disposed not to obey[4] him if he *forbids* it and vice versa. In some of these cases, sharp, one should think, must be the eye that can detect encroachments, and resolute the hand that can bear up against them, and that can say to the torrent of sovereign power, thus far shalt thou go and no farther. But there is nothing of this sort which religion cannot do at any time: in the purest monarchies as well as in the freest commonwealths. The Jews would have done every[5] thing else for Antiochus, but they would not eat his pork. The exiled Protestants would have done anything else for Lewis, but they would not go to Mass: the Catholics of Great Britain would obey any other law of the Parliament of Great Britain but they will not stay away from Mass. In all other points they will obey the temporal sovereign for the time being: in this point alone they choose to obey the commands of departed sovereigns or of the Pope, or what comes to the same thing, what to them appear to be the dictates of the religious sanction. Why might not this (in point of practicability I mean) be settled by law, as well as by an inward determination which bids defiance to the law? Does not the Briton when in France obey the sovereign of France? Does not the Frenchman when in Great Britain obey the sovereign of Great Britain? And do not the Briton and the Frenchman both when at Rome do as they do at Rome? Let it be observed once more I consider here not what is most eligible, but only what is possible.

One great difficulty is to draw the boundary line betwixt act and act, betwixt such classes of acts as the sovereign may, and such as he may not, take for the objects of his law, and to distinguish it by marks so clear as not to be in danger of being mistaken: especially when religion and the *acumen* and pertinacity which that principle inspires, are out of the question. The plainest marks are those which are made by *place* and *time*. By place: for this is all that there is to that is of some sovereign or other; in such case, if it come backed with motives of a coercive nature, it is not a law, but an illegal mandate: and the act of issuing it is an offence.[c]

2. If the person of whose will it is the expression be a sovereign, but a sovereign to whose power in the case in question a person of the description in question happens not to be subject, it is a law, which as to that person indeed has no force, yet[8] still it is a law.[d] The law having no force, the not obeying it is either no offence or

---

distinguish the power of any one sovereign from that of another. By time: accordingly at Rome, even in a rude age, a man could[6] be absolute for six months without any hope or chance of protracting his power a day longer: so in regencies, as we see every day, though the minority be ever so long. As to *place*, where the circumstance is the mark, the law is the stronger, in as much as the physical power terminates in great measure with the political. But to examine these matters in detail belongs to the particular head of constitutional law.

[c] If the mandate (being a command) comes to be obeyed, the act of issuing it is an act of *simple injurious restrainment*, or *simple injurious compulsion*, according as the command is positive or negative (see *infra*, Ch. 12) if not obeyed, it is an attempt to commit the one or the other of those offences: at any rate, as also if it be a countermand, it is a *disturbance*, or if on pretense of title an *usurpation*, of some branch of power beneficial or fiduciary, private or public. (See Ch. 16, Division, liv. n., p. 287. *Introduction to the Principles*.)[7]

[d] It is evident that in point of fact (for to that point I still exclusively adhere) sovereignty over any given individual is a matter which is liable to much diversity and continual fluctuation. Subjection depends for its commencement upon birth: but for its continuance it depends upon a thousand accidents. In point of fact a man is subject to any and to every sovereign who can make him suffer: whether it be in person (that is in body or in mind) in reputation, in property, or in condition. (Ch. 16, Division, xi and B.I. tit., Persons Subject, *Introduction to the Principles*.) In body he can be subject to but one at a time: but in mind in reputation and in property he may be subject to multitudes at once. Every Catholic for example, or if there be any difference, every Papist who is so at heart, whatever nation he belong to, is in a certain sense subject to the Pope, in virtue of those pains of the religious sanction (See Ch. 5, Pleasures and Pains ix, *Introduction to the Principles*) which the head of the Catholic church has it in his power to inflict upon minds whose religious biases (Ch. 6, Sensibility, xix, *Introduction to*

an offence which cannot be punished. Yet still it cannot here be said that the issuing of it is an offence: because the person from whom it issues is one whose act, as such, cannot be invested with the character of an offence. Were the Lord High Treasurer of Great Britain to issue of his own authority an order for levying[9] a tax on all the inhabitants of Great Britain the issuing of that order would indeed be an offence: since the Lord High Treasurer of Great Britain is no more a sovereign in Great Britain than he is anywhere else. But were the King of France to issue an order to the same effect addressed to the same persons, such law would indeed be of no force, but yet it would hardly be looked upon as coming under the name of an offence: why? Because the King of France, though not the sovereign in Great Britain is sovereign elsewhere; to wit in France: on his part then it would be an act not of delinquency but of hostility.

3. Now a given will or mandate may be the will or mandate of a given person in either of two ways: in the way of *conception* as it may be called (that is of original conception) or in the way of *adoption*. A will or mandate may be said to belong to a sovereign in the way of conception when it was he himself who issued it and who first issued it, in the words or other signs in which it stands expressed: it may be said to belong to him by adoption when the person from whom it immediately comes is not the sovereign himself (meaning the sovereign for the time being) but some other person: insomuch that all the concern which he to whom it belongs by adoption has in the matter is the being known to entertain a will that in case such or such another person should have expressed or should come to have expressed a will concerning the act or sort of act in question, such will should be observed and looked upon as his.[e]

4. Where a mandate appertains to the sovereign only by adoption,

---

the Principles) prepare them for such impressions: pains the infliction of which, were it an offence, would come under the head of simple mental injuries. (Ch. 16, Division xxxiii, *Introduction to the Principles*.)

---

[e] In this there is no mystery: the names perhaps are new, but the distinction itself is constantly exemplified, and that in the most ordinary concerns of life. You are giving orders to your servant:

such adoption may be distinguished in several respects: in respect of the *time* in which the mandate adopted appears with reference to that of the adopting mandate: 2. in respect of the persons whose mandates are thus adopted. 3. in respect of the *degree* in which the adoption is performed: fourthly in respect of the *form* of expression by which it may be performed.

First then, with regard to *time*, the mandate which the sovereign in question is supposed to adopt may be either already issued, or not: in the former case it may be said to be his by *susception*; in the latter by *pre-adoption*. Where the sovereign holds himself thus in readiness to adopt the mandates of another person when so ever they shall happen to have been issued, he may thereby be said to invest that person with a certain species of power, which may be termed a *power of imperation*. Examples of this distinction we shall see immediately.

5. As to the *persons* whose mandates the sovereign may have occasion to adopt, it would be to little purpose here, and indeed it would be premature, to attempt reducing the enumeration of them to an analytic method. In the way of susception, the sovereign for the time being adopts as well the mandates of former sovereigns as those of subordinate *powerholders*:[t] in the way of pre-adoption, he can adopt the last mentioned mandates only: for to pre-adopt the mandates of subsequent sovereigns would be nugatory, since whatever actual force there is in sovereignty rests in the sovereign for the time being: in the living, not in the dead. As the propensity to obedience may admit of every imaginable modification, it is just conceivable indeed that the people should in certain points obey the mandates of a deceased sovereign in preference to those of his living successor. Lycurgus, if the story be a true one, found means

---

this it is plain you may do in either of two ways: by saying to him, 'Go and do so and so,' mentioning what: or by saying to him, 'Go and do what Mr such-an-one bids you'. One of these ways is just as familiar as the other: the order you yourself give in the former case, is yours by conception: the order Mr such-an-one gives in the latter case is yours by adoption.

---

[t] *Power-holders:* So I will take leave to term those who stand invested with a power: the term is analogous in its formation to the words *landholder, freeholder, householder.*

by a trick, thus to reign after his death: but it is a trick that would hardly succeed a second time: and the necessity he found himself under of having recourse to that expedient would be a sufficient proof, if there required any, how little need the sovereign who is recognised as such for the time being has to be beholden for his power to his departed predecessors.

6. As to the subordinate power-holders whose mandates the sovereign pre-adopts, these are of course as many and as various as the classes of persons to whom the law gives either *powers of imperation* or the contrary *powers of de-imperation*, if such is the name that may be given to the power of undoing what by imperation has been done. These powers it may give to the power-holder on his own account, in which case the power is beneficial; or on that of another, in which case it is fiduciary: and in this latter case, on account of an individual, or on account of the public at large; in which latter case again the power is of the public or constitutional kind. It is thus that every mandate that is issued within the limits of the sovereignty and that is not illegal, is in one sense or the other the mandate of the sovereign. Take any mandate whatsoever, either it is of the number of those which he allows or it is not: there is no medium: if it is, it is his; by adoption at least, if not by original conception: if not, it is illegal, and the issuing it an offence. Trivial or important makes no difference: if the former are not his, then neither are the latter. The mandates of the master, the father, the husband, the guardian, are all of them the mandates of the sovereign: if not, then neither are those of the general nor of the judge. Not a cook is bid to dress a dinner, a nurse to feed a child, an usher to whip a school boy, an executioner to hang a thief, an officer to drive the enemy from a post, but it is by his orders. If anyone should find a difficulty in conceiving this, he has only to suppose the several mandates in question to meet with resistance: in one case as well as in another the business of enforcing them must rest ultimately with the sovereign.[10] Nor is there anything of fiction in all this: if there were, this is the last place in which it should be found.[11]

To continue the laws of preceding sovereigns, and the powers of the various classes of magistrates, domestic as well as civil, is (in every tolerably well settled commonwealth at least) a matter of course. To suffer either of those systems of institutions to perish, and not to establish anything in their stead, would be to suffer the whole machine of government to drop to pieces. The one course no sovereign was ever yet mad enough, the other none was ever yet industrious enough, to pursue. If the adoption be not declared in words, it is because the fact is so notorious, that any express form of words to signify it would be unnecessary. It is manifested by means not less significant than words, by every act of government, by which the enforcement of the mandates in question is provided for. If it be alleged that the trivial transactions that pass in the interior of a family are not specifically in the contemplation of the sovereign: (trivial as they may be termed when individually considered, though in their totality they are the stuff that human life is made of) the same may be said of the transactions of fleets and armies: of those which become the objects of the mandates issued by the general or the judge. The same may even be said of those laws which emane[12] directly from the very presence of the sovereign. It is only by the general tenor of their effects and not by any direct specification that individual acts of any kind can be comprised under extensive and general descriptions.

It is in this very way that conveyances and covenants[13] acquire all the validity they can possess, all the connection they have with the system of the laws: adopted by the sovereign, they are converted into mandates. If you give your coat to a man, and the gift is valid, and nobody else has a right to meddle with your coat, it is because a mandate subsists on the part of the sovereign, commanding all persons whatever to refrain from meddling with it, he to whom you gave it alone excepted, upon the event of your declaring such to be your pleasure. If a man engages or covenants to mend your coat for you, and such an engagement is valid, it is because a mandate on the part of the sovereign[14] hath been issued, commanding any person upon the event of his entering into any engagement, (exceptions excepted) and thereby that particular person in consequence of his having entered into that particular engagement, (it not being within the exceptions) to perform it: in other words to render you that particular service which is rendered to you by performance of the act which he has engaged for.

Thus then in all cases stands the distinction between the laws which belong to the legislator in the way of conception, and those which belong to him in the way of pre-adoption. The former are the work of the legislator solely: the latter that of the legislator and the subordinate power-holder conjunctively, the legislator sketching out a sort of imperfect mandate which he leaves it to the subordinate power-holder to fill up.[g] In the first case there are no other mandates in the case than those which emane[15] from the legislator *immediate*: in the latter case whatever mandates there are emane[16] from the subordinate power-hodler *immediate*, and whenever they happen to be issued can only be said to emane[17] *potestative* from the legislator. In the former case there are mandates from the first that exist *in actu*: in the latter issued by the subordinate power-holder, whatever mandates there may be conceived to be exist only *in potentia*. In the former case the law will more readily than in the other be perceived to be occupied in issuing or repeating commands: in the other case it will be apt to appear as if it were employed solely in giving descriptions; for example of the *persons* by whom powers shall be possessed; of the *things* over which, or persons over whom, such power shall be possessed; of the *acts* to which such power shall extend, that is of which the performance shall be deemed an exercise of such power; of the *place* in which and the *time* during which such powers shall be exercised, and so on. Yet still such descriptions have so much in them of the nature of a command or what stands opposed to it, that whenever the power which they confer or limit comes to be exercised, the expression of will whereby it is exercised may, without any alteration made in the import of it, be translated into the form and language of a mandate: of a mandate issuing from the mouth of the lawgiver himself.[h]

8. Next as to the degrees in which the mandate of a subordinate power-holder may be adopted by the sovereign: or in other words

---

[g] This is one way among innumerable others in which as will be seen hereafter, the complete power of imperation or de-imperation may be broken into shares, see Ch. 11, Generality [Ch. IX in Hart].

[h] The fundamental law of those by which conveyances of property in things corporeal are adopted is that which corresponds to and prohibits the offence of, wrongful occupation of property: that by which covenants are adopted, is that which corresponds to and prohibits the offence of wrongful withholding of services. (See Ch. 16, Division, *Introduction to the Principles*.)

the degree of force which such mandate acquires by the adoption. Take any single manifestation of the sovereign's will, and all the assistance that the mandate of a subordinate power-holder can receive from it consists in a bare permission: this is the first step that the sovereign takes towards the giving validity to subordinate mandates: the first and least degree of assistance or rather countenance that the inferior can receive from the superior: the not being made the subject of a law commanding him not to issue the subordinate mandate which is in question. The part thus far taken by the sovereign is, we see, merely a negative one. Nor would it be worthwhile, or indeed proper, to notice him as taking any part at all, since it is no more than what is taken by every the merest stranger, were it not for its lying so much in his way to take the contrary part; a part which he actually does take in relation to the greater number of the other members of the community. If any further degree of countenance is shewn it must be by another law or set of laws: a law permitting the subordinate power-holder to punish with his own hand the party who is made subject to the mandate in case of disobedience, by a law permitting others to assist in the administering such punishment, by a law commanding others to assist; and so on. Such ulterior corroborative laws however are not to be reckoned as exclusively necessary to the particular business of adoption: for a set of subsidiary laws like these are equally necessary, as will be seen hereafter, to the giving *force* and efficacy to such laws as issue from the sovereign himself in the most immediate manner.[1]

9. Next as to the form or manner in which the adoption may be performed. We have already intimated that it may be done by permission: that is by a legislative permission: but it may also be done by mandate, by a legislative mandate: by a permission addressed in the first instance to the power-holder; a permission to issue the mandates which it is proposed to adopt; or by a mandate addressed immediately to those whom it is sent to subject to his power; a mandate commanding them to obey such and such mandates whensoever if at all, he shall have thought fit to issue them. In the former case the mandate of the subordinate power-holder whenever it

---

[1] V. *infra*, Ch. 13, Force [Ch. XI in Hart op. cit.].

comes to be issued, is a *primordial* one: in the latter case it is *superventitious*, the mandate of the sovereign being the primordial one, of which this which is superventious is *reiterative*. These terms should they appear obscure, will hereafter be explained.[j] Whichever be the form, it comes exactly to the same thing: and the difference lies rather in the manner in which we may conceive the inclination of the sovereign to be expressed, than in the inclination itself. In both cases the mandate depends for its force upon a further set of mandates, as hath been already intimated and will be shewn more particularly further on. Whether these subsidiary mandates be annexed to a mandate on the part of the sovereign *ab initio*, or to the mandates of the subsidiary power-holder when they arise, is a matter of indifference.

10. I shall conclude this section with the analytical recapitulation promised in the last. A mandate is either referable to the sovereign or it is not: in the latter case it is illegal, and what we have nothing to do with here.

A legal mandate then is either private or domestic, or public or civil: a domestic mandate is one that emanes from a person having power in virtue of his being invested with a condition of the domestic kind, and is addressed to the person who stands invested with the correlative condition: a civil or public mandate is either sovereign or subordinate. If sovereign either it is *suâ naturâ* permanent or it is not: in the former case it is a sovereign law at any rate: in the latter, if it proceesd from a number of persons possessing the sovereignty in conjunction, it is still a sovereign law as before; if from a single person possessing the sovereignty in severalty, it is a sovereign order. If the authority from which it immediately emanes be subordinate, it is issued either on the occasion of a suit, or independently of any such occasion: in the former case it is a judicial order or mandate, and may be styled an order *litis causa* or *propter quid*: in the latter case it may be styled a subordinate legislative mandate *ex mero motu*. In this latter case again if it is susceptible of perpetuity it may be styled a *subordinate law* or *by-law*: if not, it may be styled an *executive order*.

---

[j] *Infra*, Ch. 12, Aspect [Ch. X in Hart].

CHAPTER 12

Force of a Law[1]

1. . . . . with respect to the *force* of the law: that is, with respect to the motives it relies upon for enabling it to produce the effects it aims at. Motives of some sort or other to trust to it evidently must have: for without a cause no such thing as an effect: without a motive no such thing as action. What then are motives? We have seen that they are but the expectations of so many lots of pain and pleasure, as connected in a particular manner in the way of causality[a] with the actions with reference to which they are termed *motives*.[b] When it is in the shape of pleasure they apply, they may be termed *alluring* motives: when in the shape of pain, *coercive*.[c] It is when those of the alluring kind are held up as being connected with an act, that a *reward* is said to be offered: it is when those of the coercive kind are thus held up, that a *punishment* is said to be denounced.

2. The next question is from what source these motives may issue. Now it has already been observed, that of the four sources from whence pain and pleasure may be said to take their rise, there are three which are under the influence of intelligent and voluntary agents; *viz*: the political, the moral, and the religious sanctions. The legislator then may, in the view of giving efficacy to his laws, take either of two courses: he may trust altogether to the auxiliary force of the two foreign sanctions, or he may have recourse to motives drawn from that fund which is of his own creation. The former of these courses is what has sometimes been taken with success:[d] there seem even to be cases in which it is to be preferred

---

[a] Ch. 7, Actions, *Introduction to the Principles of Morals and Legislation*.

[b] Ch. 10, Motives, *Introduction to the Principles*.

[c] Ch. 16, Division, *Introduction to the Principles*.

[d] See Ch. 18, Indirect Legislation. [*Works of Jeremy Bentham*, Vol. I, pp. 533–80. In his explanatory note on 'indirect legislation' on p. 63 Hart refers to vol. II of Bowring's edition of Bentham's works. The reference should be to vol. I not vol. II.]

to any other. These cases however are in comparison but rare. For the most part it is to some pleasure or some pain drawn from the political sanction itself, but more particularly, as we shall see presently, to pain that the legislator trusts for the effectuation of his will.

3. This punishment then, or this reward, whichever it be, in order to produce its effect must in some manner or other be announced: notice of it must in some way or other be given, in order to produce an expectation of it, on the part of the people whose conduct it is meant to influence. This notice may either be given by the legislator himself in the text of the law itself, or it may be left to be given, in the way of customary law by the judge: the legislator, commanding you for example to do an act: the judge in his own way and according to his own measure punishing you in case of your doing it. As to the particular nature of customary law, more will be said of it by and by.

4. But the most eligible and indeed the most common method of giving notice is by inserting a clause on purpose: by subjoining to that part of the law which is expressive of the legislator's will, another part the office of which is to indicate the motive he furnishes you with for complying with such will.

In this case the law may plainly enough be distinguished into two parts: the one serving to make known to you what the inclination of the legislator is: the other serving to make known to you what motive the legislator has furnished you with for complying with that inclination: the one addressed more particularly to your understanding; the other, to your will. The former of these parts may be termed the directive: the other, the sanctional or *incitative*.

5. As to the incitative this it is evident may be of two kinds: when the motive furnished is of the nature of punishment, it may be termed the *comminative* part, or *commination*: when it is of the nature of reward, the *invitative* part, or *invitation*.

6. Of the above two methods of influencing the will, that in which punishment is employed is that with which we are chiefly concerned at present. It is that indeed of which we hear the most and of which the greatest use is made. So great indeed is the use that is made of it, and so little in comparison is that which is made of reward, that

the only names which are in current use for expressing the different aspects of which a will is suspectible are such as suppose punishment to be[2] the motive. Command, prohibition, and permission, all of them point at punishment: hence the impropriety we were obliged to set out with, for want of words to remedy it.

7. The case is, that for ordinary use, punishment is beyond comparison the most efficacious upon the whole. By punishment alone it seems not impossible but that the whole business of government might be carried on: though certainly not so well carried on as by a mixture of that and reward together. But by reward alone it is most certain that no material part of that business could ever be carried on for half an hour.[e]

----

[e] The reasons why the principal part of the business of government cannot be carried on any otherwise than by punishment are various: among which there are several which would each of them be abundantly sufficient of itself:

1. In the first place, any man can at any time be much surer of administering pain than pleasure.

2. The law (that is the set of persons employed for this purpose by the legislator) has it still less in its power to make sure of administering pleasure than particular persons have: since the power of administering pleasure depends upon the particular and ever-changing circumstances of the individual to whom it is to be applied: (See Ch. 6, Sensibility, *Introduction to the Principles*, of which circumstances the law is not in any way of being apprised.) In short the law seems to have no means of administering pleasure to any man by its own immediate operation: all it can do is to put the instrument in his way, and leave him at liberty to apply it himself for that purpose if he thinks proper: this is accordingly what the law does when it is said to give a man a pecuniary reward.

3. The scale of pleasure supposing it actually applied is very short and limited: the scale of pain is in comparison unlimited.

4. The sources of pleasure are few and soon exhausted: the sources of pain are innumerable and inexhaustible. It has already been observed that the only means the law has of administering pleasure to a man is by placing the instruments of it within his reach. But the number and value of these instruments is extremely limited. Any object in nature may be converted into an instrument of pain: few in comparison and rare are those which are calculated to serve as instruments of pleasure.

The sense of mankind on this head is so strong and general, however confused and ill developed, that where the motives presented to the inclination of him whose conduct it is proposed to influence are of no other than the alluring kind, it might appear doubtful perhaps whether the expression of the will of which such conduct is the object could properly be styled a law. The motives which the law trusts to being[3] in most cases of a coercive nature: hence the idea of coercion shall in their minds have become inseparably connected with that of a law. Being then an invitation, that is an expression of will trusting for its efficacy to motives not

---

5. The law has no means of producing pleasure without producing pain at the same time: which pleasure and which pain being considered by themselves apart from their effects, the pain is more than equivalent to the pleasure. For, an instrument of pleasure before it can be given to one man must have been taken from another: and since *caeteris paribus* it is more painful to lose a given sum than it is pleasurable to gain it, the pain produced by the *taking* is upon an average always more than equivalent to the pleasure produced by the *giving*.

6. The insufficiency of rewards is more particularly conspicuous when applied to acts of the negative kind. The acts of a positive kind of which it is necessary to enjoin the performance are always made referable to some definite possible subject, and included within a definite portion of time: such as to pay money on a certain occasion to a certain person: to lend a hand to the repair of a certain road for such a number of days; and so forth. But acts of a negative kind are commonly comprised under no such limitations. Take for instance the not stealing, and the not doing damage to the roads. Now by not stealing is meant the not stealing from any person any stealable articles at any time: but persons are numerous, stealable articles still more so, and time indefinitely divisible. If then Paul for example were to be rewarded for not stealing it must be in some such way as this: for not stealing from Peter a farthing at 12 o'clock, one shilling: for not stealing another farthing from the same Peter at the same time, another shilling: for not stealing another farthing from the same Peter at a moment after 12, another shilling: for not stealing from John a farthing at such a place at 12 o'clock, another shilling: the same sums to be given also to Peter and John for not stealing from Paul: and so on for everlasting.

coercive, they will conclude that it can not with propriety be styled a law.[t]

9. The conclusion however seems not to be a necessary one. For as these invitations are as much the expressions of the will of a lawgiver as commands themselves are, as they issue from the same source, tend to the same ends, are susceptible of the same aspects, applicable to the same objects, and recorded indiscriminately in the same volumes with those expressions of will which beyond dispute are entitled to the appellation of a law, it should seem that without any great incongruity, they might be established in the possession of the same name. To distinguish however, a law of this particular kind from the other, it should never be mentioned but under some particular name, such as that of an *invitative* or *praemiary* law, or it might be styled a *legislative invitation*, or a bounty.

10. As the law may have sometimes a penal sanction to back it, sometimes a sanction of the praemiary kind, so may it (as is obvious) be provided with two opposite sanctions, one of the one kind, the other of the other. A law thus provided may be styled *a law with an alternative sanction*. In this case the mode of conduct with which the one of these sanctions is connected is the opposite to that with which the other is connected. If the one sanction is connected with the positive act, the other sanction is connected with the correspondent negative act. Take the following example. Whosoever comes to know that a robbery has been committed, let him declare it to the Judge: if he declares it accordingly, he shall receive such or such a reward: if he fails to declare it, he shall suffer such or such a punishment.

---

[t] In the nomenclature as well as in the practice of the law, it is upon punishment that every thing turns: nothing upon reward. Try, for instance, the words *obligation, duty, right, power, title, possession,* and *conveyance.* Take away the idea of punishment, and you deprive them of all meaning. A set of fictitious entities analogous to these might indeed be conceived to be generated by reward. But they would evidently be of a very flimsy consistence in comparison of the objects men have hitherto been accustomed to call to mind upon the mention of those names. The obligation would be a cobweb; the duty, a feather; the right, power, title, possession, conveyance not worth a straw.

11. We are now arrived at the notion of an object which might in a certain sense admit of the appellation of a law. It may even be looked upon as constituting a law and something more: since there are to be found in it two distinguishable parts: the directive part, which must of itself be a complete expression of will, and an article of a different nature, a *prediction*.[g] But nothing hath as yet been brought to view by which the efficacy of the directive part, or the verity of the predictive can have been established upon any solid footing. Let the law stop here, and let the influence of the two auxiliary sanctions be for a moment set aside, what has been done by the law as yet amounts to nothing: as an expression of will, it is impotent; as a prediction, it is false. The will of the legislator concerning the matter in question has indeed been declared: and punishment has been threatened in the case of non-compliance with such will: but as to the means of carrying such threats into execution, nothing of this sort hath as yet been made appear.

What course then can the legislator take? There is but one, which is to go on commanding as before: for as to taking upon himself the infliction of the punishment with his own hands, this, were it practicable in every case which it manifestly can not be, would be overstepping the bounds of his own function and exercising a different sort of power.[4] All he can do then in his capacity of legislator is to issue a second law, requiring some person to verify the prediction that accompanied the first. This secondary law being issued in aid of the primary may with reference thereto be termed the *subsidiary* law: with reference to which the primary law may on the other hand be termed the *principal*.

12. To whom is it then this subsidiary law should be addressed? It can never be the same person to whom the principal law was addressed: for a man *can* not reward himself; nor *will* he punish himself. It must therefore be to some other person: a circumstance which of itself is sufficient to show that the principal and subsidiary are two distinct laws, and not parts of one and the same

---

[g] A prediction is the expression of an act of the understanding, whereby a man declares it to be his opinion or belief that such or such an event is certain or more or less likely to happen in time future.

law. It may be any other person indefinitely. Commonly however it
is to some particular class of persons, who, occupying some particular station or civil condition instituted for the purpose, such as
that of Judge, are presumed on the one hand to be properly qualified,
on the other hand to be previously disposed, to execute or cause to be,
executed any such commands when issued by the legislature.

13. But neither can the hand nor the eye of the judge reach everywhere: to be in a condition to discharge his functions he must be
provided with a variety of assistants: which assistants must for
various[5] purposes be of various ranks and[6] occupations and descriptions: witnesses, registers, court-keepers, jail-keepers, bailiffs,
executioners, and so forth. Of these there are many who must
begin to act in their respective characters even before the matter is
submitted to his cognizance: consequently before they can be in a
way to receive any commands from him. On this and other accounts
they too must have their duties prescribed to them by the law itself:
and hence the occasion for so many more subsidiary laws or sets of
subsidiary laws, of which they are respectively the agible subjects,
and their acts the objects.

14. It is evident that the number and nature of the subsidiary
laws of this stamp will be determined by the number and nature of
the different sorts of acts which on the part either of the same
person or of different persons it is thought proper should be
performed or abstained from in the course of the *procedure*. Now by
the procedure is meant on the present occasion[h] the suite of steps
which are required to be taken in the view of ascertaining whether
a man has or has not done an act of the number of those which
stand prohibited by some principal law: and thereby of ascertaining whether he is or is not of the number of those persons, on
whom a punishment of the sort denounced by the principal
law in question is required to be inflicted.

15. Amidst this various train of laws subsidiary, that which is

---

[h] All judiciary or contentious procedure as there will be occasion
to show hereafter (*Infra*, Ch. 20) is divisible into procedure *delictu
causa* and procedure *petitionis causa*. The former comes nearest to
what is commonly meant by penal procedure, the latter to what is
meant by civil procedure. The former is that with which we are
concerned at present.

addressed to the judge and contains the command to punish, may for distinction's sake be termed the punitive or *punitory* law: and with reference to the rest the *proximate* subsidiary law: the rest may indiscriminately be termed *remote*. Where the principal law is of the praemiary kind, the proximate subsidiary law may be termed *remunerative*.

16. Now it is evident that in like manner as a principal law must have its subsidiary laws, so also must each of those subsidiary laws have a train of subsidiary laws to itself, and that for the same reason. This is a circumstance that belongs alike to every law which takes its support from the political sanction. A. commits an offence: it is thereupon rendered the duty of B. to contribute in such or such a way to the bringing of him to punishment in the event of his proving guilty: and a particular process is appointed to be carried on for ascertaining whether he be or no. In the course of that process such and such steps are required to be taken by C. in such and such contingencies: such and such others by D. and E. and F. and so on, indefinitely. But what if B. also proved refractory? a similar process must thereupon be carried on and a similar provision made by the law for the bringing of him also to punishment: and so on if any failure should arise on the part of D. or E. or F. In this way must commands follow upon commands: if the first person called does not obey, the second may: if the second should not, yet a third may: if even the third should fail, yet there may be hopes of a fourth. If it is not expected that anyone will obey, the law is plainly impotent and falls to the ground: but let obedience be but expected from any one of the persons addressed, at whatever distance he stands from him who was addressed first, this expectation may prove sufficient to keep all the intermediate persons to their duty. If an offence then be committed, until obedience takes place on the part of some one[7] or other of the persons thus connected, the law is as it were asleep, and the whole machine of government is at a stand: but let any one law in the whole penal train meet with obedience, let punishment take place in any quarter, the law awakens out of its trance, and the whole machine is set agoing again: the influence of that law which has met with obedience flows back as it were through all the intermediate laws till it comes to that principal one to which they are all alike subsidiary.

CHAPTER 13

Power and Right[1]

3. . . . As yet there is no law in the land. The legislator has not yet entered upon his office. As yet he has neither commanded nor prohibited any act. As yet all acts therefore are free: all persons as against the law are at liberty. Restraint, constraint, compulsion, coercion, duty, obligation, those species I mean of each which issue from the law are things unknown. As against the law all persons possess as great a measure of this great blessing of liberty as it is possible for persons to possess: and in a greater measure than it is possible for men to possess it in any other state of things. This is the first day of the political creation (creation of the political world): the state is without form and void. As yet then you and I and everyone are at liberty. Understand always, as against the law: for as against one another this may be far from being the case. Legal restraint, legal constraint and so forth are indeed unknown: but legal protection is unknown also. You and your neighbour, suppose, have quarrelled: he has bound you hand and foot (or has fastened you to a tree): in this case you are certainly not at liberty as against him: on the contrary he has deprived you of your liberty: and it is on account of what you have been made [to] suffer by the operation which deprives you of it that the legislator steps in and takes an active part in your behalf. Since the legislator then takes an active part, how is it that he must demean himself? He must either command or prohibit, for there is nothing else that he can do: he therefore cuts off on the one side or the other a portion of the subject's liberty. Liberty then is of two or even more sorts, according to the number of quarters from whence coercion, which it is the absence of, may come: liberty as against the law, and liberty as against those who first in consideration of the effect of their conduct upon the happiness of society, and afterwards in consideration of the course taken against them by the law, may be styled *wrongdoers*.

These two sorts of liberty are directly opposed to one another: and in as far as it is in favour of an individual, that the law exercises its authority over another, the generation of the one sort is, as far as it extends, the destruction of the other. In the same proportion in which[2] and by the same cause by which, the one is increased, the other is diminished.

4. The law, after certain exceptions made (of which hereafter), prohibits in me[3] and in others all such acts as it thinks advisable to prevent in consideration of their being liable to produce on your part either bodily imperfection (the source of future pain or of[4] loss of future pleasure) or actual pain of body or actual pain of mind not[5] proceeding from any of the specific sources which are here mentioned: in other words all such acts as come under the denomination of simple corporal injuries, irreparable corporal injuries, homicide, menacement, or simple mental injuries. What then is the result? To me and the rest of the community, restraint: to you, personal security and protection. To speak more at length, it takes measures for affording you personal security, it makes provision for the security of your person: it affords you its[6] protection for your person against those injuries: and (to introduce the word right) it gives you, when corroborated by the requisite apparatus of subsidiary laws, a right of being protected by the hands of its ministers against the endeavours of any who would inflict on you such injuries.

5. After certain exceptions as before, it prohibits in me and in others all such acts as it thinks advisable to prevent in consideration of their being liable to restrain you from doing such acts, from the doing of which it is a prejudice to you to be by such means restrained, or to constrain you to do acts which it is a prejudice to you to be constrained to do: in other words, it prohibits all such acts as come under the denomination of simple injurious restrainment, simple injurious compulsion, wrongful confinement, and wrongful banishment. What is the result now? To you, liberty: to me restraint as before. Personal liberty is accordingly either liberty of behaviour in general or liberty of loco-motion. Liberty of behaviour again is either the absence of restraint or the absence of constraint: and liberty of loco-motion either the absence of confinement or the absence of banishment.

6. After the like exceptions as before it prohibits in one and in others all such acts as it thinks advisable to prevent in consideration of the tendency they appear to have to diminish your reputation. What is the result? To me and the rest of the community another species of restraint: to you another species of protection.

7. Thus far we have been treading on plain ground. As to the fictitious entities which are the result of the processes whereby offences against property and offences against reputation are created, these and the processes by which they are produced are of a more various and more complicated nature. To begin with property. Now property before it can be offended against must be created: and the creation of it is the work of law. To show how the several modifications of it are created by law we may thus proceed. Conceive any material thing at pleasure: a piece of land for instance. The law issues no mandate at all to me or anyone with respect to that piece of land: on the one hand it does not command us, or any of us, to exercise any act upon the land: on the other hand neither does it command us to forbear exercising such act. It does nothing at all in short in relation to the land: and of course, nothing in your favour. What is the result? On all sides liberty as before. Moreover, considering that it might have commanded us all, you and me and others, not to exercise any acts[7] upon that land, and that such are the commands which to you, to me and to everybody but one or a few it actually does give with respect to by far the greatest part of the land under its dominion, it is on that account frequently spoken of as if it had done something in favour of those whom it has left thus at liberty: it is spoken of as having given them or rather left them a *power over* the land: it may also be said to have left them a *property in* the land. As this same sort of property is given not to you only, but to me and everybody else, no restraint with respect to the use of the land being laid on anybody, that which is given to you may on that account be styled *inexclusive*: an inexclusive power over the land: an inexclusive property in the land. The land in this case is said to be the common property of us all: and each of us is said to have a property in it in common with the rest: and each man may even be said to have *the* property of it, so as this phrase be added '*in common with the rest*'.

8. Again. The law prohibits me and certain others from exercising

any act upon the land: leaving you and certain others at liberty as before. In this case it gives you a power or property which, according to the persons with reference to whom it is spoken of, is at once inexclusive and exclusive. It is inexclusive with reference to your own associates: it is exclusive with reference to me and mine. You and they have each of you a power over, a property, an estate, an interest, in the land: we have not any of us any such property or power, nor for anything that appears any interest or estate in it.

9. The law forbids everybody but you from exercising any act upon the land. In this case it gives you alone a power over the land: it makes the land your property, your estate: it makes you sole owner, the proprietor of the land: it gives you not only *an* estate, an interest, in the land in severalty, but *the* property *of* the land, *the* estate *of* the land, both also in severalty.

10. As to this case it would be found upon examination[8] that in reality it is never completely verified[9] under any system of law: some occasions there are in which for the carrying on of government it is necessary that any man's ownership over any object of property should[10] be liable to be suspended: as if for instance there were need to make use of the land in question for the encampment of an army. But when these periods are not long, and the commencement of them is casual only and contingent, as in the case just stated, such slight exceptions are not in common speech considered as derogating from the general rule.

11. The law having left you a power over the land, no matter whether in severalty or in common, prohibits me and others from doing such and such acts in consideration of the tendency which they appear to have to annihilate or at least to diminish the benefit which you might otherwise reap from the exercise of your power over the land. It forbids me for instance not only from walking on it, or carrying away turf or stone from it, but also from making a wet ditch all round in[11] it though on the outside, or building a wall close to the windows of a house which you have built on it. In this case the law not only permits you to exercise such power over the land as without its interference you were enabled to enjoy, but interferes itself in your favour, and takes an active part in your favour in securing to you the exercise of that power by taking measures for averting such obstacles as might be opposed to the exercise of it

by the enterprises of other men. The power or liberty you had before, as against the law, may now be said to be corroborated or assisted by the law: corroborated by the mandate it issues to other persons, prohibiting them from exercising[12] such acts as it thinks fit to prevent in the consideration above mentioned. The acts thus prohibited it will be proper to specify. In general they will be any acts whatever which appear to possess the tendency above mentioned. But the catalogue of them will require various exceptions, as well in favour of the general interests of the community as in favour of the liberty and property of other persons whose interests may interfere with those which you have in the occupation of that land.

12. It has been seen that there are acts which interfere with your enjoyment of a piece of land without being acts exercised upon that very piece of land. But among the acts which may interfere with such[13] enjoyment, there are few which are so likely to interfere with it as any acts of another person when exercised upon the same land. At Athens there were certain spots which were the common property of the whole Athenian people: such were their amphitheatres or places which among them answered the purpose of an amphitheatre. It is evident that the right which was enjoyed by particular persons in choosing the best station in such an amphitheatre, the *prohedria* as it was called, was a right which in general would contribute more materially to narrow and impede the right which another Athenian citizen possessed of fixing[14] himself in the same station than the right of opposing any of those indirect impediments that have been exemplified above. It appears therefore that rendering the power which a man has over a thing exclusive is one way though not the only way in which the law may corroborate that power. Exclusive power and inexclusive power are both capable of being corroborated, and that without altering their nature: but a power when exclusive is already corroborated in some degree by being exclusive: and a power which is as yet but inexclusive can scarcely by any means be so materially corroborated as by being rendered exclusive. Powers (property and so forth) when thus corroborated whether exclusive or inexclusive, may be said to be corroborated by *prohibition of disturbance*, or simply, by *prohibition*.

13. All this is not enough: in order to give you the complete enjoyment of the land which is made your property, something

more effectual should be provided than the precarious expedient of a
legal mandate. In order to give a further degree of corroboration to
a power over things, there are two other powers that have been
provided. It is intended you should have the complete enjoyment
of your land, it is necessary therefore that[15] if any impediments to
that enjoyment should arise such impediments be removed. Now
the causes, or constraints rather, from which such impediments
may arise must be either *things* or persons. Hence the occasion for
two other sorts of powers, the one over other things; the other, over
persons. These additional powers may be styled by the common
appellation of *subservient* powers: in contradistinction to the power
you have over the land itself: which again, in contradistinction to
these may be styled the *principal* power.

14. First with regard to (the subservient power over) things.
The things which[16] may be the objects[17] of this power are any things
which happen to be in such a situation as to prevent[18] or impede your
exercising the power you have over the principal thing, the piece of
land, in question. You have a power of travelling over a road: a man
sets up a fence across the road: in corroboration of the power which
he is thus impeding, the law permits you to beat down and remove
the fence. In this way it is that the law creates a subservient
power over impeding things in corroboration of a principal power
already given.

15. It is obvious that this subservient power may in the same
manner as that to which it is subservient be corroborated by prohibition of disturbance. The only point in which it is essentially
distinguished from the principal one is that of constancy. The power
you have over the land, the power of travelling over it may either be
immediate and uninterrupted, or may be constituted so as to be
brought to appear or disappear by any variety of events of any sort:
on the contrary with regard to the power you have over the things
which may happen to stand in the way of your exercising the power
you have over the land; such former power if subservient to the
latter can be only occasional. Upon all other occasions perhaps the
only power possessed by anybody over the wood of which the fence
is composed would have been possessed by your antagonist: no
power at least would be possessed over it by you: it is only upon the
occasion of its being so situated as to prove an impediment to the

exercise of the power you have over the land, that the law gives you this power over the wood which is upon it.

16. Next with regard to the subservient power over such *persons* as may chance to be circumstanced in a manner to impede the exercise of the principal one. This application of power over persons must be explained in its turn as well as any other: but as this is but one among a great variety of applications and modifications of which that branch of power is susceptible, it will first be proper to give a general explanation of the whole together.

To understand the nature and possible modifications of that sort of fictitious entity which is called a power over persons it will be necessary to make a distinction between the corporeal, or purely passive faculties, of man and his mental or active faculties. By the first I mean those which are common to man's body with the rest of matter: by the second I mean those which are common to him with other sentient beings only, and which either belong to or constitute his[19] mind. By the first he is assimilated to the legal class of *things*: it is by the second only that he stands distinguished from that class. Of the power which may be exercised over his passive faculties we have therefore in effect been already speaking: That which may be exercised over his active faculties requires a further consideration.

17. In the former case in order for the power to be exercised there[20] needs but one person to act, to wit the person by whom the power is said[21] to be exercised, and one act to be performed, to wit the act of that person: in[22] the latter case there must be two persons who act, and two acts to be performed. In the first place, on the part of the person by whom the power is exercised there must be one act; in the next place, on the part of the person over whom the power is exercised, there must be another: the first of these when spoken of with reference to the power may be styled its *subservient* or *instrumental* object: the latter its *ultimate* or *final* object. The first may be spoken of as the means by which the power operates: the latter is the end in which it terminates. The latter[23] may be termed an act of power, the former an act of compliance. From each of these acts a source of distinction may be derived. From each of these acts a source of distinction may be derived. From the nature of the act of compliance, the power may be either *productive* or

preventive: it may be styled productive if that act be of the positive kind: preventive, if of the negative kind. (As to the act of power it may be of a nature to produce a change in the condition of the body of the party from whom the compliance is sought, without affecting his will, or by means of its influence on his will.) As to the means whereby the power may operate, these may be either of a *physical* or of[24] a *mental*, in which latter case it may otherwise be said to be of a *moral* nature: those may be said to be of a physical nature which tend to produce the effect by the influence they exert over his body or the adjacent bodies, independent of any which they may exercise on his will: those may be said to be of a mental or moral[25] nature which tend to produce the effect no otherwise than by the influence they exert upon his will. Now for acting upon the will of a sentient being there are but two sorts of means, the prospect of pain and that of pleasure: those which act by holding out the prospect of pain may be termed *coercive* motives, those which act by holding out the prospect of pleasure may be termed *alluring* motives. When the means by which a[26] power of the sort in question operates are such motives of the coercive kind as persons in general are prohibited from applying, in so much that were it not for the creation of such power in favour of the person in question[27] the application of them would be an offence, the power (whether it be of production or of[28] prevention) may be said to act by the *power of punishment*: when they are such motives of the coercive kind as persons in general are not prohibited from applying, it may be said to enforce itself by *coercive influence*: when they are of the alluring kind, by *alluring influence*. And in particular when the motives which are applied are of the nature of those which result from a change made in the condition of the body, the power may be said to enforce itself by the *power of corporal punishment*.

18. It may be observed that of[29] the two sorts of acts which must be performed in order for a power of this sort to have been exercised the performance of the former stands upon the whole on a much higher footing in respect of certainty than that of the latter. This footing will again be different according as the act which is the final object of the power is of the positive kind or of the negative. For causing a man to forbear exercising acts which it is intended he should abstain from there are very effectual expedients: physical

means have their application here: and the efficacy of those operations which apply themselves directly to the body is much more certain than of those which before they can produce any change in the condition of the body are forced to make their way to it through the mind. The law can be much more certain of giving birth to an [act]30 which has its termination in the person of any man, than of giving birth to an act which takes its commencement from that person. Indeed properly speaking it is the power of giving birth to the act which is the instrumental object which is all the power that the law can be said to confer upon a man: the power of giving birth to the act which is the final object of the productive or preventive power 31, it can no otherwise give him than by giving him the power before mentioned. The truth of this observation will be perceived when we come to give an account of the several operations by which the several modifications of power are created and confirmed.

19. In the general mandate above mentioned, the law has prohibited you from doing any such act to the body of any person as that person does not like. It now takes a certain person in particular under consideration, and in derogation of that general mandate permits you to exercise certain acts on his body whether it be his pleasure they should be exercised or no. In this case it gives you a power over the body or in other words over the passive faculties[32] of that person. This power being constituted by bare[33] permission is as yet uncorroborated. As all other persons but you are excluded from exercising the acts in question upon the person in question, the power is exclusive and so entirely exclusive as to belong to you in severalty. It is plain enough that if the general mandate of which this particular permission is an exception had never been established, every other person in the community would have had the same power over the person in question: as on the other hand so would that person over every other.

20. The law having given you the power above mentioned, prohibits me and others from doing such and such acts in consideration of the tendency which they appear to have to annihilate or at least diminish the benefit which you might otherwise reap from the exercise of your power over the person in question. By this means the uncorroborated power you had before is now corroborated: corroborated exactly in the manner of a power over things, by

prohibition of disturbance. What is the result? To you a species of liberty as well as of power: the liberty of exercising such acts upon such persons, in other words a property in the use of his body: to others restraint. As to the person himself on whom the power is to be exercised, on his part nothing ensues: his personal security, insofar as your power over him extends, is diminished, but his liberty as against the law remains on the same footing as before: you are left at liberty to exercise the acts in question upon his person: but he is left at liberty to resist you.

21. But now then the law addresses itself to the person himself over whom the power is to be exercised and includes him under a prohibition similar in its design to that just mentioned to have been addressed to other persons. By this means your power secures a further degree of corroboration: it may be said to be corroborated by prohibition of noncompliance, or which comes to the same thing, by command of submission.

22. It may have been observed that in giving you a power over the passive faculty of a man the same operation gave you virtually a power over the active faculties of the same person. Of this latter power the amplitude, as far as depends upon that act of yours which is the instrumentary object of it, is in proportion to the uneasiness which can be produced on your part by the acts in which the exercise of the power you have over the passive faculties of the person consists: as far as concerns that act of his which is the final object of the former power the amplitude of it depends upon the nature of the acts which he can be brought to perform by the apprehension of such uneasiness. On the other hand the converse of this proposition does not hold good. It is not true that a power over the active faculties of a person involves in it of necessity a power over his passive faculties. This may have been inferred already from the analytical sketch that has been given above: and it will unavoidably be made appear in a more particular manner by the statement of the several operations by which a power over the active faculties of a person may be given in other ways.

23. Of the number of the sorts of acts which tend to produce uneasiness in a person by the influence they have on his person, reputation, property or condition in life, the law leaves you still at liberty to perform such articles as in affording him its protection

in those several points it left unprohibited. In so doing it gives you such and so much power over his active faculties as is constituted by what may be called coercive influence: or more at length, the liberty of applying coercive influence: the liberty of endeavouring to determine him to perform or not to perform such and such actions by the application of coercive influence to his will.[a]

24. The law (after such exceptions as it thinks proper), leaves you at liberty to perform what acts you please of the number of those which are attended with such effects as are of a nature to prove agreeable to him. In so doing, it gives you that sort of power over his active faculties which is constituted by what may be termed alluring influence. Of this and that last mentioned permission, what is the result? To you, liberty of behaviour as before; to the person over whom the power is given and to others, nothing.

25. Upon considering these two last species of power it will be observed that they are neither more nor less than what every man in proportion to his physical faculties possesses of course over every other. Accordingly they do not either of them constitute any species of what is commonly called property: any more than would any power over things while it remained inexclusive and uncorroborated except in virtue of the contrast which the condition a thing is in which a man has this sort of power over makes with the condition of the thing over which no power is left him by the law.

---

[a] It may here[34] be wondered what acts of the nature above specified can upon the principle of utility remain unprohibited? The answer is certainly not many, in comparison at least with those which ought to be prohibited. Of the number of those which affect a man in his person, perhaps none: of those which affect him in his reputation almost all, provided there be no mixture of falsehood in the proceeding. The like may be observed with respect to such as affect him in respect of his property or in respect of his condition in life, but no otherwise than in virtue of the tendency they may have to intercept some benefit which might otherwise devolve on him. Let the law have done everything for you which it ought to do, every man will still be left at liberty to endeavour to persuade your customers not to deal with you, your mistress not to give you her hand, or your electors not to give you the place you wish for, so long as neither force nor falsehood, nor in the last-mentioned case bribery, be employed.

26. It would have been an omission however not to have mentioned them under the head of power: they are commonly comprised under that name: they make as much figure in the world nearly as any other sort of power:[b] and although it requires no express and positive operation on the part of the law to constitute or confer them, yet by the law they may be, and in many instances are, taken away.[c]

27. Let us return to power over things: we are now prepared for obtaining a clear[35] idea of the manner in which it may be corroborated by an occasional power over persons. As to mere influence whether coercive or alluring this as hath been already observed is no more than every[36] man, unless it be expressly taken from him, possesses of course upon all occasions: it is therefore what every man has of course to corroborate any share that may have been given him of power over things: to give it him therefore on the present occasion requires no express operation or aspect of the law. There remain power over the passive faculty, and power of punishment.

28. First with regard to power over the passive faculty. The persons who may be the objects of this power are any persons who happen to be in such a situation as to prevent or impede your exercising the power you have over the thing in question: the occasion of its accruing to you is the time at which they are thus em-

---

[b] In Great Britain for example the greatest and most effective part of the King's power is of these two kinds: nor is the efficacy of it thought in general to be too little. The King of Great Britain has abundance of places to put a man into, such as men love to be put into; but he has no Bastilles. Possessing this power he is the object of a constant and not unsalutary jealousy: without it, he would be a cipher.

It may be said that he has this power from the law: since he possesses it in virtue of his possessing the power of appointment to these offices (a particular species of property of which hereafter) which is given him by the law. True but it is not by any separate operation on the part of the law: the same operation which gives him those powers gives him this unavoidably and of course.

[c] For example when the influence, assuming the shape of *Bribery* or other species of *Corruption*, tends to produce a breach or abuse of trust: or when in the shape of *subordination*, it tends to give birth to any offence at large.

ployed.[d] You have a[37] power of travelling over a piece of land. A man,[38] designing to prevent you, watches the moment when you are making your way through a narrow pass and plants himself in your way: the law permits you hereupon to push him aside. In this way it is that the law gives a power over the passive faculty impeding persons in corroboration of a power over things.

29. Next with regard to a power of punishment over persons. A man is obstructing you as in the case just mentioned: the law permits you to threaten to beat him for example, or doing[39] him some other harm which, were it not for this particular occasion, it would be an offence in you to bring upon him: and in case the threat proves ineffectual the law permits you to carry it into execution. In this way it is that the law may give you a power of punishment in corroboration of a power over things.

30. Thus far the corroboration that has been given to powers by powers, whether over persons or over things, has been given by operations of which the parties only have been the immediate objects:[e] by permission given to the party favoured: by prohibition denounced to the party restrained. But the resources of the law are not yet exhausted. Against the attack of a number of invaders or even of a single invader the force of a single person taken at random will often be insufficient, and as to the force of the law,[40] the force of which the application is implied in the act of prohibition, it can seldom be applied till after the mischief has been incurred. In most cases if not in all it will be requisite to make provision for affording further assistance to him whom it is meant to favour: to wit such assistance as is to be met with on the spot, and is[41] in the way to be applied at the very time at which alone assistance can be of use: this assistance may be afforded of whichever nature the impediment is which it is requisite to overcome: whether in the first instance it arises from a person or a thing. In either case the force of the corroboration is susceptible as it were of two degrees: it may apply itself in the way either of simple permission, or of positive command. The occasional powers which persons are permitted to exert in

[d] See *supra* para 18 [p. 263 in Hart].

[e] On these as on other occasions in the giving powers over persons various precautions will be requisite: but to enter into such details suits not the present purpose.

corroboration of a principal power may themselves receive a further degree of corroboration: in the first place by a power given to third persons to render their assistance: in the next place by a command given to the same purpose: in the first case the power in question may be said to be corroborated by permission of assistance: in the other case by command of assistance.

31. We come now to speak of right to services. In order to have given you by means of the power of punishment a power over my active faculties, the legislator should have permitted you of your accord to perform in a certain contingency certain acts of the number of those which on account of the prejudice which it is in the nature of them to impart to me (in respect either of my person, my property, my reputation, or my condition in life) he is disposed in general to prohibit. Instead of this he reserves this power in his own hands. He causes me to perform certain acts for your benefit, that is, for the sake of the benefit which such acts seem calculated to produce to you: but he leaves not the motives by which you are to be induced to perform these acts, nor the time of applying those motives, to your choice. He intends for example that I should plough your field for you; and that I should be caused to do it whether I like to do it or not. As a means of causing me to do it he intends accordingly that upon the contingency of my not doing it I should be turned out of a field of my own or kept in confinement. But he intends not to leave me exposed to as much suffering as I should be exposed to were you permitted to judge in every case in the first instance whether I had failed or not in doing what I ought to do in the way of ploughing it or to determine the time during which I should be kept out of the possession of my field, or the time during which or place at which I should be kept under confinement. He therefore reserves these points to the determination of the magistrates who in cases like this are specially commissioned to execute his will. Accordingly he either of himself commands me at once to perform the acts in question, or shows himself to be in readiness to adopt any command issued on your part to the same effect in case of your thinking fit to issue such command: reserving in his own hands in either case the enforcement of such command. In so doing he gives you a right to my services in the behalf in question: a right to certain services on my part. Wherein consists the exercise of such

a right? In the demanding of the services only or in the demanding and receiving them accordingly?

The varieties of proprietary interest are not yet exhausted. In what manner and by what operations powers are created, whether over things or over persons, has been already shewn. But powers are not the only things of which property may consist. It may consist also of rights, a sort of fictitious objects which in some cases indeed coincide with powers, but in other cases are essentially distinct from them. In order to give you a power over a thing the law permitted you to exercise certain acts having their determination in that thing: and that, at any time, without waiting for the consent of any one. To give you a right to a thing, or to the use of a thing, the law takes a different course. It does not permit you to exercise any act on it in the first instance: it however shews itself resolved that upon the happening of a certain event, or the performance of a certain act on the part of some other person, it will thereupon immediately give you such permission: and in the meantime it commands that person to perform that act. As soon then as he performs that act you have a power over the thing: till he performs it, you have none. Or (which is but to express the same meaning in other words) if before he has performed that act you should take upon you to meddle with the thing, you would be liable to be punished: as soon as he has performed it, you are exempt from being punished on that score.[f] This is in effect to command him to execute, in your favour, an act of investitive power over that thing: which power we shall have occasion to explain more particularly a little further on. It is also giving you a right to a service on his part: to

---

[f] I ow'd you yesterday ten guineas. I have just been paying you with ten pieces of that name. I took them out of my pocket and counted them into your hand: or I laid them down on the table and bid you take them up. You now have a power over those pieces; you have the property of the pieces. But before I performed those acts in virtue of which I am deemed to have paid you (that is to have invested you with that power) you had no such power: you had only a right to any such pieces of money amounting to that value, as I might think fit to give you. Had you taken the pieces in question off the table before I bid you, and gone off with them, you would have committed an offence.

wit the service which consists in his performing in your favour the act just mentioned: another sort of right which will be considered immediately after the present. But as the service to be performed is referrable solely to no other object than this particular thing, and is no otherwise of importance than in virtue of its having the effect of giving you a power over this thing, it will be convenient to consider the right in question in the class of a right to things, then in that of a right to a service: for it will be convenient to have a class of rights to things in order to contrast with the class of rights to services.

32. Now an act, we may remember, may either be of the positive or of the negative stamp: services may accordingly be either active services or services of forbearance. When the legislator in order to procure you a benefit commands me to do certain acts, the services on my part to which he thereby gives you a right are of the active stamp: when in the same view he commands me not to do such or such an act the services to which he thereby gives you a right are services of forbearance. He commands me to plough your field for you as before: it is thereby that he gives you a right to active services: he commands me not to cut certain trees which though growing on my own land are of use to you in[42] affording shelter for your field: he thereby gives you a right to services of forbearance.

33. Services may be considered again in two other points of view: according to the faculties by which they are performed; and according to the object on which they are performed. With regard to the first of these points it is plain enough that being the result of the active faculty, there is no sort of service in the rendering of which the mind must not be concerned as well as the body. Although the acts in which they consist should have originated in the mind, yet these acts, before they can have been productive of any effect beneficial or otherwise in society must have been communicated to the body. On the other hand, let the concern which the body has in the business be ever so considerable, the production and regulation of its motions must still have originated with the mind. For distinction's sake, however, where the share which the body has in the production of the effect appears the most considerable, they may be referred to the body; where that which the mind has, to the mind. The service for instance which a husbandman renders to his landlord by ploughing his field for him may be referred to the head of

corporal service, notwithstanding the attention which it is necessary
the mind should give to the guidance of the plough: (or on the other
hand) the instruction which is given by the professor to his pupil
may be referred to the head of mental service, notwithstanding the
part which it is necessary the lips or the hand should take in the
communication of it.

34. Secondly as to the object on which the service is to be performed. As the commencement of the act whereby the service is
rendered is determined by the person whose faculties are in question,
so the termination is determined by the object on which the service
is performed. This object must belong of course to the class either
of persons or of things. In the first case the service may be styled as
service *in personam*, in the other case a service *in rem*.[g] The service
render'd by a surgeon is a service *in personam*, that render'd by the
husbandman as above, a service *in rem*. Each of these classes again
may be divided indefinitely according to the nature of the persons
or things on which the acts in question are to be performed, according to the natures[43] and tendencies of those acts which are to be
performed, and according to the occasion or circumstances in which
they are to be performed.

35. Power (and right) considered with respect to the identical
person by whom it is exercised may be distinguished again into
direct and indirect. It may be styled direct, when the acts in which
the exercise of it consists are the acts of the very person by whom the
power is said to be possessed: in this case it may be styled the power
or right of occupation: it may be termed indirect, when those acts
though still taking their origin in some measure from his will, are
not his acts but those of some other person.

36. Indirect power or right may again be divided into investitive
and divestitive. It may be styled investitive power when the will of
the one person is that such or such another should perform the act
in question: divestitive, when the will of the former[44] is that the
latter having exercised them should exercise them no longer: in the
former case we see the acts which result from the will of the[45]

---

[g] The division of services into *personal* and *praedial* as distinguished by the Roman law is ambiguous and inexhaustive. It does
not quadrate with either of those given in the text.

person considered as being in possession of that power are of the positive kind: in the other, of the negative kind. Let us see how these powers are created.

37. The law shews itself resolved that, upon the event of my declaring that such is my will in this behalf it will issue those mandates, that set of permissions, prohibitions, dispensations, and commands by the issuing of which it will have given you a power of occupation over the land in question. It is by so doing that it gives me investitive power over the land in question. By this[46] means it in a manner adopts the expression of your[47] will, and turns it into a law.

38. You are already in possession of the direct power over the land; or what comes to the same thing you are about to possess it. The law shows itself resolved that upon the event of my declaring that such is my will in this behalf it will revoke or forbear to issue those mandates by the issuing of which it gave or would have given you such power of occupation. It is by so doing that it gives me a divestitive power over the land in question.

39. It will be proper to observe that the exercise of either branch of the indirect power is a very different thing from the exercise of the direct power. The act by which a direct power is exercised is an act which terminates in the person or thing which is the object of the power. The act by which the indirect power is exercised is any act which serves as a sign of my entertaining the desire in question.

The exercise of an investitive power is one sort of investitive event: The exercise of the divestitive power one sort of divestitive event: of these two events considered in a general point of view more will be said a little further on.

40. This division into direct and indirect is applicable to un-consummated rights a well as to powers.

41. The law shows itself resolved that upon the event of my declaring it to be my will that upon the event of your declaring it to be your will that a third person should have a direct power over the land it shall happen accordingly. In this way it gives me a sort of indirect power[48] which may be styled an investitive power of the 2d order: and so with respect to the divestitive power. In the same manner it may constitute investitive powers of the third, fourth or fifth orders, and so on.

42. When the law shewed itself resolved to give me the direct power over a thing in the event of my declaring such to be my will, such declaration of will on my part may be considered as a kind of signal which the law waits for, in order to invest me[49] with such power. But in the same manner it might have taken the expression of the last of[50] any number of wills or of any proportion of any such number of wills for the signal. In this case, the investitive power may be considered as residing in the whole number of such persons together,[51] each of them having a joint share in it: or what comes to the same thing a conditional investitive power may be considered as residing in any one of them, each one of the rest having a power of control by non-assent.[h]

43. The law shows itself resolved that in the event of my declaring it to be my will that you should have a direct power over the thing in question, it will at the end of a certain time after such declaration confer on you such power, provided a third person does not within that time declare it to be his will that you should not possess such power. In this case I may be said to have a conditional investitive power over the land in question: and such third person may be said to possess another sort of power of control over the investitive power: a power of control by dissent.

44. It appears then that the investitive and divestitive powers may each of them be possessed either exclusively or inexclusively: when inexclusively each of the sharers may exercise it indiscriminately or in association only, that is not but in conjunction with the rest: if in association, the share he has may either be a power of control by non-assent, or a power of control by dissent.

45. Moreover the persons who share in the power in question may on the occasion of their exercising it be divided into groups, which groups may be indefinitely diversified: but the consideration of these and the other variations that may attend the constitution and operations of corporate bodies is not necessary to the present purpose.

46. A mutual exercise of the investitive power by two persons in

---

[h] This is the sort of power which the members of a corporation possess over the lands and other articles that are the property of the corporation.

7

favour of each other is called buying and selling. Or more fully thus. You have the investitive power over a measure of corn: I have the like power over a measure of wine. You exercise in my favour the investitive power that you have over the corn, in consideration that I exercise in your favour the investitive power I have over the wine: doing thus we may each of us be said to buy and to sell: You buy my wine with your corn: you sell your corn for my wine: I buy your corn with my wine: I sell my wine for your corn.

CHAPTER 14

Leading Principles of a Constitutional Code, for any State[1]

A. Ends aimed at

1. This constitution has for its general end in view, the greatest happiness of the greatest number:[a] namely, of the members of this political state: in other words, the promoting or advancement of their interests. By the universal interest, understand the aggregate of those same interests. This is the all-comprehensive end, to the accomplishment of which, the several arrangements contained in the ensuing code are, all of them, directed.

2. Government cannot be exercised without coercion; nor coercion without producing unhappiness. Of the happiness produced by government, the net amount will be—what remains of the happiness, deduction made of the unhappiness.

3. Of the unhappiness thus produced, is composed, in the account of happiness, the expense of government. Of the happiness

---

[a] If the nature of the case admitted the possibility of any such result, the endeavour of this constitution would be—on each occasion—to maximise the felicity of every one of the individuals, of whose interests the universal interest is composed: on which supposition, the greatest happiness of all, not of the greatest number only, would be the end aimed at.

But, such universality is not possible. For neither in the augmentation given to the gross amount of felicity, can all the individuals in question ever be included; nor can the infelicity, in which the expense consists, be so disposed of, as to be borne in equal amount by all: in particular, such part of that same expense, as consists in the suffering produced by punishment.

Thus it is, that, to provide for the greatest felicity of the greatest number, is the utmost that can be done, towards the maximisation of universal national felicity, in so far as depends on government.

produced by government, the gross amount being given, the net amount will be inversely as this expense.

4. Of the members of this, as of other states in general, the great majority will, naturally, at each given point of time, be composed of the several persons, who, having been born in some part or other of the territory belonging to the state, have all along remained inhabitants of it. But, to these, for the purpose of benefit, of burden, or of both, will be to be added sundry other classes of persons, or whom designation is made in an appropriate part of the ensuing code.

5. Immediately specific, and jointly all-comprehensive, ends of this constitution are—subsistence, abundance, security, and equality; each maximised, in so far as is compatible with the maximisation of the rest.

6. As to subsidence;[b] this speaks for itself.

7. As to abundance; this is an instrument of felicity on two accounts: on its own account, and as an instrument of security for subsistence. In this latter character, its usefulness may be still greater to those who possess it not, than to those who possess it.

8. As to security;[c] this is for good, or against evil. Security for

---

[b] By subsistence—or say matter of subsistence—may be understood every thing, the non-possession of which would be productive of positive physical suffering: that and nothing more. In so far as distinct from, and not comprehended in, the corresponding branch of security, namely, security for subsistence, subsistence itself must be understood as being, in the field of time, limited to a single instant: any instant taken at pleasure.

Accordingly, of the several elements or dimensions of value, to extent alone, as measured by the number of the individuals in question, can maximisation, on this occasion, be applicable.

[c] In the words good and evil, apt additaments being employed, may be seen two appellatives, which—opposite as are the sensations and other objects which they are employed to designate—are, as to no small part of their extent, interconvertible: by ablation of good, evil is produced: by ablation of evil, good. But, on some occasions, the one is the more convenient appellative; on others, the other: on others again, both. Infinite, and in no small degree perhaps irremoveable, are the ambiguity and obscurity, produced at every tune by the imperfections of language: language, that almost

exclusively applicable, though so deplorably inadequate, instrument of human converse.

Of security—considered in so far as it belongs to government to afford it—the several subject-matters, corporeal, incorporeal, or say fictitious, taken together, have been found comprehendible under the five following heads:

1. *Person*: the security afforded in this case, is security against evil, in whatever shape a man's person, body and mind included, stands exposed to it.

2. *Property*: under which denomination, the matter of subsistence and the matter of abundance, as above, are comprehended.

3. *Power*: considered in its two distinguishable branches—the domestic and the political.

4. *Reputation*: a fictitious entity, the value of which, considered in the character of a subject-matter of possession and security, consists in its being a source of respect, or love, or both: and as being, in either case, an eventual source of good offices, or say of services, receivable from other persons, by the person by whom it is possessed. Take away all services, eventual as well as actual, you strip it of all intelligible value.

5. *Condition in life*: a factitious and fictitious entity, compounded of property, power and reputation, in indeterminate and indefinitely diversifiable proportions. In the idea of power, that of right—meaning legal right, as being a particular modification of it—a sort of eventual power is include.

Examples of condition in life are: 1. Those constituted by the several genealogical relations, expressed by the words, husband, wife, son, daughter, father, mother, and so on, throughout the whole genealogical tree. 2. The several distinguishable occupations, profit-seeking ones included; and the several political situations, corresponding to the several offices, with the powers and functions respectively attached to them.

Taken together, the injuries against which security for these five several subject-matters is requisite to happiness, constitute the most obvious, and as it were tangible, portion of the matter of the Penal Code: as does the detailed description of the several cases, in which a man has a right to security against these several injuries, those to property in particular, that of the Civil Code: right to security, that is to say, to the eventual appropriate services, of the several classes of public functionaries—that is to say, judges and their subordinates, by the exercise of whose functions it is afforded.

A distinction—which must here be kept in view, or a conception, as afflictive as it would be erroneous, will be entertained, is—that good, is—either for the matter of subsistence, or for the matter of abundance.

9. Security against evil, is either against evil from calamity,[d] or against evil from hostility.

10. By calamity, understand human suffering, in the case in which, by its magnitude and indeterminateness in respect to extent, it stands distinguished from, and above, the quantity ordinarily produced by one and the same cause.

11. By evil from calamity, understand evil from purely physical agency: by evil from hostility, evil from human agency. But, by purely physical agency, no evil is producible, which may not, from human agency, receive its commencement or its increase.

12. Of calamity, the principal sources are, inundation, conflagration, collapsion, explosion, pestilence, and famine.

13. The evil-doers, against whose hostility, that is to say against whose evil agency, security is requisite, are either external or internal. By the external, understand those adversaries who are commonly called enemies.

---

between a defalcation made from a subject-matter of security (say for example from property), and a defalcation from security itself: in which latter case, in the phrase commonly employed, a shock is spoken of as being given to security. Howsoever the subject-matter of security be lessened, security itself will not be lessened, if by means of the defalcation made from the subject-matter, the probability of retaining what remains of it be not lessened. By any such defalcation made from the subject-matter of security taken in the aggregate, so far is security itself from being necessarily lessened, that without such defalcation it could not have existence. Witness taxation: without which, no where could the business of government be carried on: no where could security against adversaries of any class have place: no where could security against calamity in any shape be afforded by government.

[d] The giving execution and effect, to precautionary arrangements, taken with a view to calamity, belongs to one branch of that part of the business of the Executive department, which in the ensuing code is styled the Preventive service: the giving the like support, to such precautionary arrangements as are taken with a view to hostility at the hands of the unofficial and resistible class of adversaries, belongs to the other branch of that same service.

14. Internal adversaries, against whose evil agency security is requisite, are the unofficial and the official.

15. By the unofficial adversaries, understand those evil-doers, who are ordinarily termed offenders, criminals, malefactors. These are resistible, every where resisted, and mostly with success.

16. The official are those evil-doers, whose means of evil-doing are derived from the share they respectively possess, in the aggregate of the powers of government. Among these, those of the highest grade, and in so far as supported by those of the highest, those of every inferior grade, are every where irresistible.

17. To provide, in favour of the rest of the community, security against evil in all its shapes, at the hands of the above-mentioned internal and—so long as they continue in such their situation— irresistible adversaries, is the appropriate business of the constitutional branch of law, and accordingly of this code.

18. As in difficulty so in importance, this part of the business of law far surpasses every other. Of the danger, to which an assemblage of individuals stand exposed, the magnitude will be in the joint ratio of the intensity of the evil in question on the part of each, the duration of it, the propinquity of it, the probability of it; and, on the part of all, the extent of it; the extent, as measured by the number of those who stand exposed to it. Measuring it in every one of these dimensions—taking into account every one of these elements of value in both cases—minute will be seen to be the danger, to which the other members of the community stand exposed at the hands of those their resistible, in comparison with that to which they stand exposed at the hands of these their irresistible, adversaries. In the first case, it has place on no other than an individual scale; in the other, on a national scale.

19. Inferior even is the danger, to which they stand exposed, at the hands of foreign and declared enemies, in comparison with that, to which they stand exposed, at the hands of their every where professed protectors. Foreign enemies, in the event of their obtaining the object of their hostility, withdraw most commonly from whatever territory they invade, leaving the inhabitants thenceforward unmolested. At the worst, they keep possession of it: and, in that case, from the external and resistible, become the internal and irresistible adversaries, such as those above mentioned.

20. On the texture of the constitutional branch of law, will depend that of every other. For, on this branch of law depends, in all its branches, the relative and appropriate aptitude, of those functionaries, on whose will depends, at all times, the texture of every other branch of law. If, in the framing of this branch of law, the greatest happiness of the greatest number is taken for the end in view, and that object pursued with corresponding success, so will it be in the framing of those other branches: if not, not.

21. Lastly, as to equality. In the instances of subsistence, abundance, and security, the title of the object, to the appellation of an instrument of felicity, is stamped, as it were, upon the face of it: designated by the very name. Not so in the case of equality.

22. In the idea of equality that of distribution is implied. Distribution is either of benefits or of burdens: under one or other of these names, may every possible subject-matter of the operation be comprised. Benefits are distributed by collation made of the instruments of felicity: burdens by the ablation of them, or by the imposition of positive hardship.

23. In proportion as equality is departed from, inequality has place: and in proportion as inequality has place, evil has place. First, as to inequality, in the case where it is in the collation made of those same instruments, that it has place. In this case, it is pregnant with two distinguishable evils. The one may be styled the domestic or civil; the other, the national or constitutional.

24. The domestic evil is, that which has place, in so far as the subject-matter of the distribution is the matter of wealth—matter of subsistence and abundance. It has place in this way. The more remote from equality are the shares possessed by the individuals in question, in the mass of the instruments of felicity, the less is the sum of the felicity, produced by the sum of those same shares.

25. The national or constitutional evil is that which has place, in so far as the subject-matter of the distribution is power. It has place in this way. The greater the quantity of power possessed, the greater the facility and the incitement to the abuse of it. In a direct way, this position applies only to power. But, between power and wealth such is the connexion, that each is an instrument for the acquisition of the other: in this way, therefore, the position applies to wealth likewise.

26. Of inequality as applied to both subjects—and of the evil, with which, in both the above shapes, it is pregnant—the case of monarchy may serve for exemplification: for exemplification, and thereby for proof.

27. Of the maximum of inequality, every monarchy affords an example. Of the matter of wealth, to the monarch is allotted a mass, as great as suffices for the subsistence of from 10,000 to 100,000 of the individuals, from whom, amongst others, after being produced by their labour, it is extorted. Yet does it still remain matter of doubt, whether the quality of felicity, thus produced in the breast of that one, be greater than that which has place, in the breast of one of those same labourers taken on an average: has place, or at least would have had, but for the extortion thus committed.

28. What is certain is that the quantity of felicity habitually experienced by a gloomy, or ill-tempered, or gouty, or otherwse, habitually diseased monarch, is not so great as that habitually experienced by an habitually cheerful, and good-tempered, and healthy, labourer.

29. True it is, that if, *per contra*, by a monarch, maintained at an expense such as the above, good is, by means of that same expense, produced in greater quantity than by a commonwealth chief, whose maintenance will not be a hundredth part of the monarch's; true it is, that on this supposition, the excess of expense, vast as it is, may be not ill-bestowed. But, by whomsoever the existence of any such excess of good is asserted, upon him does it rest to prove or probabilise it.

30. If, in the case of those whose share in the instruments of felicity is greatest, the excess of felicity itself is, on an average, so small—and, in some individuals out of the small number belonging to this class, the non-existence of any such excess certain—still less and less will be the probable amount of the excess of felicity, in the case of those whose share in the instruments of felicity is less and less. And thus it is, that, as in a pure monarchy, the distribution made of the external instruments of felicity is in the highest degree, so, in a pure aristocracy is it in the next highest degree, unfavourable to the maximisation of felicity itself.

31. Hence, throughout the whole population of a state, the less the inequality is, between individual and individual, in respect of

the share, possessed by them, in the aggregate mass or stock, of the instruments of felicity, the greater is the aggregate mass of felicity itself: provided always, that, by no thing that is done towards the removal of the inequality, any shock be given to security: security, namely in respect of the several subjects of possession above mentioned.

B. Principal means, employed for the attainment of the above ends.

1. These means are comprisable, all of them, in one expression: maximisation of appropriate official aptitude, on the part of rulers.

2. Of this aptitude, three branches are distinguishable: 1. Appropriate *moral* aptitude; 2. Appropriate *intellectual* aptitude; 3. Appropriate *active* aptitude.

3. Of appropriate intellectual aptitude there are two distinguishable branches: 1. Appropriate knowledge; 2. Appropriate judgement.

4. By appropriate moral aptitude, understand—disposition to contribute, on all occasions and in all ways, to the greatest happiness of the greatest number: in other words, to the promoting or advancement of the universal interest.

5. If appropriate moral aptitude be to a certain degree deficient, the consequence is that, by abundance of appropriate aptitude in those other shapes, the aggregate of appropriate aptitude will naturally, instead of being increased, be diminished. If hostile to the interests of the greatest number: the more able the functionary, the more mischievous.

6. To the different branches of appropriate official aptitude, apply correspondingly different means. Expressed in the shortest manner, indication may be given of them by the following rules.

I *Means applying to appropriate moral aptitude.*

7. Rule 1. In the hands of those of whose happiness the universal happiness is composed, keep at all times the choice of those agents, by whose operations that happiness is to be promoted.[e]

---

[e] To this arrangement, no objection, wearing the face of a rational one, could ever be made, other than that of impracticability: an objection, formed by the assertion that, consistently with internal peace and security, no such arrangement can have place. But, in the

8. Rule 2. In the hands of each such agent, minimise the power of doing evil.

9. Rule 3. Leave, at the same time, as little diminished as may be, the power of doing good.

10. Rule 4. Minimise the quantity of public money at his disposal.

11. Rule 5. Minimise the time during which it remains at his disposal.

12. Rule 6. Minimise the number of hands, through which it passes, in its way to the hand by which it is received in payment.

13. Rule 7. Extra-reward give none, without proportionable extra-service: extra-service proved, and that by evidence not less conclusive than that which is required to be given of delinquency, with a view to punishment.

14. Rule 8. Maximise each man's responsibility, with respect to the power and the money with which he is entrusted.

15. Rule 9. Means, by which such responsibility is maximised, are—1. Constant dislocability; 2. Eventual punibility.[1]

16. Rule 10. By the several means above mentioned, so order matters, that, in the instance of each such agent, the course, prescribed by his particular interest, shall, on each occasion, coincide, as completely as may be, with that prescribed by his

---

case of the Anglo-American United States, the groundlessness of this objection has been completely demonstrated by experience: demonstrated, by the very first experiment ever made: while, to the purpose of all such persons, as had a new constitution to make— this same arrangement, even on the supposition that the experiments made of it, had, in a considerable number, all of them failed, might still have remained the only eligible one; for, as will be seen below, the above mentioned constitution is one, which, hating irresistible force from without, affords a reasonable promise of everlasting endurance: whereas every other form of government contains in the very essence of it, the seeds of its own dissolution: a dissolution which, sooner or later, cannot but have place.

---

[1] Namely, immediately or unimmediately, at the hands of those by whom the responsible agents in question were chosen: as is the case in the Anglo-American United States. Say—dislocability, immediately; punibility, unimmediately: namely, by the hands of other agents.

duty: which is as much as to say—with that prescribed by his share in the universal interest.

II. *Means applying to appropriate intellectual and active aptitude.*

17. Rule 1. For appropriate intellectual and active aptitude, establish, throughout the whole field of official duty, appropriate preliminary tests and securities. For these, see the code itself.

18. Rule 2. Maximise, throughout, the efficiency of these same tests and securities.

19. Rule 3. Minimise, in the instance of each office, the pecuniary inducements for the acceptance of it.

20. Follow the observations on which rule 3 is grounded. The less the money required by a man for subjecting himself to the obligations attached to the office, the stronger the proof afforded by him of his relish for the occupations.

21. Still stronger, and in a proportionable degree, will be the proof, if, instead of receiving, he is content to give.

22. Every penny, added to whatsoever remuneration is, as above, sufficiently—adds strength to predatory appetites, and to the means of gratifying them.

23. A throne—seat of the most extravagantly fed—is so, every where, of the most invariably insatiable appetites.

24. As to the means, applying, as above, to appropriate moral aptitude—there is not one of them of which an exemplification may not be seen in the constitution of the Anglo-American United States.

25. Under that constitution, in so far as depends on government, has uncontrovertibly been and continues to be enjoyed, a greater quantity of happiness, in proportion to population, than in any other political community, in these or any other times.

26. By that one example, is excluded, and for ever, all ground, for any such apprehension, real or pretended, as that of inaptitude, on the part of the people at large, as to the making choice of their own agents, for conducting the business of government.

27. No where else has such universal satisfaction been manifested: satisfaction with the form of the government, satisfaction with the mode in which, satisfaction with the hands by which, the business of it has been carried on. No other political community is there, or has

there every been, in which, by so large a proportion of the population, so large a part has been constantly taken, in the conduct and examination of the affairs of government. No other, in which the part so taken has been so perfectly unproductive of disorder and suffering in every shape.

28. No other constitution is there, or has there been, under which, in any thing like so small a degree, (slave-purchasing and pertinaciously slave-holding states always excepted) the interest and happiness of the many has been sacrificed to that of the ruling and influential few: no other under which what yet remains of that sinister sacrifice, will, with so little difficulty, and sooner or later with such perfect certainty, be abolished.

29. Thus much, as to the all-comprehensive end of government, in so far as the government is good. As to the several above-mentioned specific ends, the means for compassing them would not here have been in their place. The description of them will be found to be in great measure different, according to the differences between the respective ends: they will form the subject-matter—in the first place of the constitutional, in the next place of the penal and non-penal, codes.

CHAPTER 15

The People

[The *Constitutional Code* from which the following pages are taken was intended to be Bentham's greatest work. It was to encompass the entire range of political thought from the highest general principles to the minutest details of political organisation. Bentham planned it in three volumes. Vol. I was to deal with the ends and forms of government, and the nature, powers and functions of the electorate, public-opinion tribunal; legislature and the prime minister. Vol. II was to deal with the powers and functions of different ministers and 'defensive forces'. Finally, Vol. III was to deal with the judiciary, justice minister, lawyers, and the legislative and executive arrangements at the district and sub-district level. Of the three projected volumes Bentham managed to publish only Vol. I (and ch. I of vol. II) in his lifetime, and that too without an 'Introductory Dissertation' discussing the merits and demerits of different forms of government. He did, however, say in his preface to Vol. I that to the completion of the other two 'very little is now wanting; they are, both of them, in such a state of forwardness that, were the author to drop into his last sleep . . . able hands are not wanting from which the task of laying the work before the public would receive its completion'. (P.V.) Vol. IX of Bowring's collected works includes the whole of Bentham's Vol. I and large parts of Bentham's manuscripts. Excerpt for Vol. I from which the following three chapters are excerpted, I have relied on the mss. In order not to interrupt the flow of the argument, I have not indicated where passages and chapters have been omitted.]

Authorities.

The Authorities, which have place in the state are these:
1. The Constitutive.
2. The Legislative.
3. The Administrative.
4. The Judiciary.

Their relations to one another are as follows:

To the *constitutive* authority it belongs, amongst other things, to depute and *locate*, the members composing the legislative; and eventually, to dislocate them: but not to give direction, either *individual* or *specific*, to their measures, nor therefore to *reward* or *punish* them: except in so far as *relocation* may operate as reward, and *dislocation* as punishment; or, in so far as at the instance of the constitutive, punishment may come to be eventually applied to them, by the hands of succeeding legislatures.

To the *legislative* it belongs, amongst other things, to *locate* the *chiefs* of the two other departments; and eventually to dislocate them: to give—not general only, but upon occasion, *individual direction* to their conduct, as well as to that of all the several functionaries respectively *subordinate* to them; eventually also to punish them, in case of non-compliance with its directions.

To the *administrative* it belongs, amongst other things, to give execution and effect to the ordinances of the legislative, in so far as regards the persons and things placed under its special direction by the legislative: to wit, in so far as *litis*-contestation has not place.

To the *judiciary* it belongs, amongst other things, to give execution and effect to the ordinances of the legislative, in so far as *litis*-contestation has place: to wit, either as to the question of *law*, or as to the question of *fact*.

Taken together, the *legislative* and the *administrative* compose the *Government*; the *administrative* and the *judiciary*, the *executive*; the *legislative* and the *executive*, what may be termed the *operative*, as contra-distinguished from the *constitutive*.

CONSTITUTIVE AUTHORITY

1. *Constitutive what—in whom*

The constitutive authority is that, by which at all times the holders of the several other authorities in this state, are what they are: by it, immediately or interventionally, they have been in such their situations located, and therefrom are eventually dislocable.

The constitutive authority is in the whole body of electors belonging to this state: that is to say, in the whole body of the inhabitants, who, on the several days respectively appointed for the several elections, and the operations thereunto preparatory, are resident on the territory of the state, deduction made of certain classes.

Classes thus deducted, are—1. Females; 2. Males, non-adult: that is to say, who have not attained the age of (21) years. 3. Non-readers: that is to say, those who have not, by reading, given proof of appropriate aptitude. 4. Passengers.

2. *Powers.*

Subordinate to the consecutive authority, as per Section 1, are all other authorities, and thereby all other public functionaries belonging to the state.

Those whom it cannot dislocate in an immediate, it can in an unimmediate or say interventional way; to wit, by dislocating those who, having the power, have failed to dislocate them, in conformity to its sufficiently understood desire.

Exercisible by the constitutive, in relation to them respectively, are the several functions following, with the power therein essentially included. These are:

A. *Locative function*: exercised by locating, in the official situation in question, the individual in question.

B. *Dislocative function*: exercised by dislocating, out of the situation in question, the functionary therein located.

C. *Punifactive function*: exercised by putting, at the time of dislocation, in a way to be punished, but by a different authority, the functionary so dislocated.

A. *Locative function*. Functionaries, in relation to whom this function is exercised by the members of the constitutive authority, are as follows:

1. Their *deputies*, deputed by them to the legislature, to act as members of the supreme legislature, styled collectively *the legislature*. In relation to all these, this power is exercised by the members of whole constitutive body, as divided into the bodies belonging to the several election districts; in each district, the members of the constitutive electing for that district a member of the legislature.[a]

---

[a] [*Deputy.*] Question 1. Why *deputy* rather than *representative*?

footnote continued.

Answer: Reason 1. Because by the word *deputy*, a plain matter of fact is indicated, and *that* the appropriate one.

Reason 2. Because the word *representative* is less apposite, and not exclusively characteristic. In the concerns of individuals, for example, in the field of private right, many are the cases in which it is necessary that one person would act on behalf of another, without having been appointed by him for that purpose: witness guardians of orphans, administrators of the property of intestates, and the like.

3. Under favour of this ambiguous and indeterminate use of the word *representative* in preference to *deputy*, it is—that, in the case of the English form of government, the fictitious and fallacious security for the people against the monarch and the aristocracy, has been imposed upon the people, in the character of a real one. To the members who, in effect, are located—some, by the located and at pleasure dislocable instruments of the monarch, others by individuals possessing an interest opposite to theirs—the appellation of *representative* is habitually applied: applied, and by many whom shame might deter from styling them *deputies*—deputies of the people, belonging to the districts for which they respectively sit. Styled *deputies*, they would be immediately recognized as impostors; obtainers of a share in supreme power on false pretences.

Styled as they are *representatives*, the colours of imposture are not altogether so glaring upon the face of this their common name: and, as to their being *members*, members of the body in question, it is a truth but too incontrovertible: as such, they are admitted to act, nor would any others be admitted in their places, any thing of course they would rather style themselves, than what to the knowledge of every body they are not, to wit, *deputies*.

Question 2. Why, rather than *depute*? Answer. By the word *depute*, the matter of fact would indeed be expressed; and in a manner equally *apposite*: not, however, in a manner equally, because not exclusively, *appropriate*. Of the word *depute*, continual need, as will be seen, has place, for the designation of functionaries in little less than all the several subordinate grades: of functionaries —located, each of them, by no more than a single principal, and with functions wanting little of being altogether identical with his.

The deputy of the prime minister will thus be seen to be styled the *prime minister depute*: the deputy of a minister, the *minister depute*. The election minister, for example, the *election minister depute*: and so on in the case of the *justice minister* and the several judges, and other judiciary functionaries.

In all these instances, the word *depute* is in the adjective form: as

2. The members of the several sublegislatures. In relation to each sub-legislative body, this power is exercised by the members of the constitutive body, belonging to its district, as divided into the bodies belonging to the several subdistricts therein contained; the body belonging to each such subdistrict electing a member of the sub legislature.

B. *Dislocative function.* Functionaries, in relation to whom this function may upon occasion be exercised, are the following:

1. The several members of the legislature.

2. The prime minister.

3. The several ministers belonging to the administrative department.

4. The justice minister.

5. In each judicatory, appellate as well as immediate, the judge and the several other magisterial functionaries.

6. In every such situation, as above, every depute.

7. The several local headmen and local registrars.

8. The several members of the several sub-legislative bodies.

3. *Powers Exercised—how*

A. *Locative Function.* In each subdistrict, immediately after he has voted for a deputy to act as a member of the legislature for the district, each member of the constitutive body will, at the same place, and in the same manner, vote for another deputy to act as a member of the sublegislature of that same district. The arrangements of detail—necessary to adapt, upon the same principles, the mode of ascertaining the election of a member of the legislature, to the case of a member of a sublegislature—are upon the face of the election code, obvious: they will be settled *in terminis* by the legislature.

----

in the case of the functionary, who, in Scottish Law, is styled *sheriff depute*.

To no functionary other than those deputed by the electors of the election districts to the legislature, and of the election subdistricts to the several sublegislatures, is the term *deputy*, in the substantive form, applied in this code: and, by this means, the idea of the highest sort of functionary, styled a *deputy*, and that of the subordinate sort of functionary styled a *depute*, are preserved from being confounded.

B. *Dislocative function*, how exercised by the entire constitutive? On the receipt of a requisition, signed by [one fourth?] of the whole number of the electors of any election district, requiring the dislocation of any functionary, the hereinafter-mentioned election minister will appoint a day or days, as near as may be, on which, in the several districts, the electors shall meet at the several voting offices of the several sub-districts therein respectively contained, in the same manner as on the occasion of an election. The voting cards of those who are *for* the proposed dislocation, will, on the concealed surface, bear the words '*Dislocate him*', of those who are *against* the proposed dislocation, the words '*Retain him*'. In each district, the votation finished, the voting-box will, by the vote clerk, be forthwith transmitted to the election minister's office. By the election minister, as soon as all are received, or the time for receiving them is elapsed, they will, in concert with the legislation minister, be opened in the legislation chamber, at the next sitting of the legislature. The numbers will thereupon be immediately cast up, and the result declared. In case of dislocation, the vacancy produced on this extraordinary occasion will thereupon be forthwith filled up, in the same manner as on any ordinary one.

C. *Punifactive function*, how exercised? If, in addition to *dislocation*, in the case mentioned in B, *punifaction* be required—in this case, together with the pair of voting cards, bearing respectively the words '*Dislocate him*' and '*Retain him*', will be delivered by the vote clerk, another pair, bearing in like manner the words '*Accuse him*' and '*Absolve him*'. Thereupon, in regard to accusation and absolution, the result will be ascertained and declared, in the same manner, as in regard to dislocation and retention, as above.

If the majority be, as above, in favour of accusation, the election minister will make declaration to that effect: in which case, by that same declaration, the function and duty of conducting legal pursuit to that effect, devolves at the instant upon the hereinafter-mentioned government advocate general.

4. *Public Opinion Tribunal*[1]

A. *Composition.* This constitution recognises the *public opinion tribunal*, as an authority essentially belonging to it. Its power is judicial. A functionary belonging to the judiciary, exercises his functions by express location—by commission. A member of the public opinion tribunal exercises his functions without commission; he needs none. Dislocability and puniability of members excepted, the public opinion tribunal is to the supreme constitutive, what the judiciary is to the supreme legislative.

Of the following members may this judiciary be considered as being composed:

1. All individuals, of whom the constitutive body of this state is composed.

2. All those classes, which stand excluded from all participation in such supreme power.

3. Of all other political communities, all such members, to whom it happens to take cognisance of the question, whatever it may be.

Of this judiciary, different classes or assemblages of persons may be considered as constituting so many committees or subcommittees. Examples are as follows:

1. The auditory, at the several sittings of the supreme legislature.

2. The auditory, at the several sittings of the several sub-legislatures.

3. The auditory, at the several sittings of the several judicatories.

4. Persons having business with the several functionaries belonging to the *administrative* department: such business excepted as, for special reasons, shall by law have been consigned to temporary secrecy.

5. At meetings, publicly held for the consideration of any political question, the several individuals present.

6. The auditory, at any dramatic entertainment, at which objects of a political or moral nature are brought upon the stage.

7. All persons, taking, for the subject of their speeches, writings, or reflections, any act or discourse of any public functionary, or body of public functionaries belonging to this state.

Public opinion may be considered as a system of law, emanating from the body of the people. If there be no individually assignable form of words in and by which it stands expressed, it is but upon a par in this particular with that rule of action which, emanating as it does from lawyers, official and professional, and not sanctioned by the legislative authority otherwise than by tacit sufferance, is in England designated by the appellation of *Common Law*. To the pernicious exercise of the power of government it is the only check; to the beneficial, an indispensable supplement. Able rulers lead it; prudent rulers lead or follow it; foolish rulers disregard it. Even at the present stage in the career of civilisation, its dictates coincide, on most points, with those of the *greatest happiness principle*; on some, however, it still deviates from them: but, as its deviations have all along been less and less numerous, and less wide, sooner or later they will cease to be discernible; aberration will vanish, coincidence will be complete.

B. *Functions.* To the several members of the public opinion tribunal, as such, belong the distinguishable functions following; namely:

1. *Statistic* or say *evidence-furnishing function.* Exercise is given to it, in so far as indication is afforded of facts, of a nature to operate, as grounds for judgment, of approbation or disapprobation, in relation to any public institution, ordinance, arrangement, proceeding or measure, past, present, or supposed future contingent, or to any mode of conduct, on the part of any person, functionary or non-functionary, by which the interests of the public at large may be affected.

2. *Censorial function.* Exercise is given to it, in so far as expression is given to any judgment of approbation or diapprobation, in relation to any such object as above.

3. *Executive function.* Exercise is given to it, in so far as, by the performing or withholding of good offices, such as a man is by law warranted in withholding, or by the performing of evil offices, such as a man is by law allowed to perform, addition—whether in consequence of such indication, as above, or otherwise—is made to or defalcation made from, the happiness of the person in question, as above; and as by the thus withholding of good offices the effect of punishment, so by the rendering of them may the effect of reward, be produced.

4. *Melioration-suggestive function.* Exercise is given to it, in so far as, from the observation of what is amiss, or wanting, a conception of something better, having been formed, has as such been held up to the view of those whom it may concern, to the end that, if approved, it may be brought into practice.

On the tutelary influence of the public opinion tribunal, this constitution relies, in a more especial manner, for the efficiency of the securities which it provides, for good conduct, on the part of the several functionaries, belonging to the judiciary department. See in the several chapters the several sections headed by the words *Securities for appropriate aptitude*.

C. *Securities against Legislative, and Judiciary*. To every person, elector, inhabitant, or foreigner—to every individual of the human species, belongs the right of exercising, in relation to the condition of every department of this government, and the conduct of every functionary thereto belonging, the *statistic, executive*, and *melioration suggestive* functions above-mentioned.

So likewise the *censorial*: howstrongsoever the terms, in which the approbation or disapprobation stands expressed. Vituperation, if indecorous, will receive its proportionate punishment at the hands of the public opinion tribunal: defamation, if mendacious or temeracious, at the hands of the Penal Code. Defamation there is none, without intimation given of some illegal or immoral act; intimation individually, or at least specifically, determinate. If, being false, the intimation is temeracious only, and not mendacious, the official situation, of the party defamed, is a ground—not of aggravation, but of extenuation. The military functionary is paid for being shot at. The civil functionary is paid for being spoken and written at. The soldier, who will not face musquetry, is one sort of coward. The civilian who will not endure obloquy, is another. Better he be defamed, though it be ever so unjustly, than that, by a breach of official duty, any sinister profit sought should be reaped. To him who has power, opulence, or reputation, self-defence is, in proportion to his power, opulence, or reputation, more easy than if he had none: defenders cannot be wanting to him, so long as he has patrons, colleagues, or dependants.

By prohibition, restriction or taxation, to throw obstruction in the way of the production or diffusion of political tracts, especially news-papers and other periodical ones, would, on the part of the legislature, be a breach of trust, a violation of its duty to the constitutive; an act of insubordination, obstructing their constitutional super-ordinates in the exercise of their authority, by depriving them of the means of forming correct judgments: an act of partiality and oppression, withholding from one class of men, documents not withholden from another: withholding, from *the many*, benefits, not withholden from the more wealthy *few*: withholding instruction from those, by whom it is most needed. It would be an anti-constitutional act: as such, it would call for marks of disapprobation, at the hands of the members of the supreme constitutive; namely, as well in their character of electors, as in their character of members of the public opinion tribunal.

No such act of insubordination is committed, by punishment judicially inflicted, or demanded, for defamation, when effected or endeavoured at by falsehood, accompanied by criminal *evil-consciousness*, or culpable *temerity of assertion*, as to which see the Penal Code.

Every act, whereby, in the above or any other way, a man seeks to weaken the effective power of the public opinion tribunal, or by falsehood, or (what comes to the same thing) by suppression of truth, to misdirect it, is evidence, of hostility on his part to the greatest happiness of the greatest number: evidence of the worst intentions, generated by the worst motives: evidence which, though but tacit and circumstantial, and though it be ever so unwilling, is not the less conclusive. Every act, whereby a man seeks to diminish the circulation of opinions opposite to those which he professes, is evidence of his consciousness of the rectitude of those which he is combating, and thereby of the insincerity, hypocrisy, tyrannicalness, and selfishness which have taken possession of his mind. Sincere or insincere, he may, without fear of injustice, be numbered among the enemies of the human species.

CHAPTER 16

Legislature

I. *Powers and Duties.*

The Supreme Legislature is omnicompetent. Coextensive with the territory of the state is its local field of service; coextensive with the field of human action is its logical field of service; to its power, there are no limits. In place of limits, it has checks. These checks are applied, by the securities, provided for good conduct on the part of the several members, individually operated upon.

The supreme legislative authority has, for its immediate instrument, the supreme *executive*, composed of the *administrative* and the *judiciary*, acting within their respective spheres. On the will of the supreme constitutive, the supreme legislative is dependent. Absolute and all-comprehensive is this dependence. So also on the will of the legislature, the will of the executive, and the wills of the sublegislatures.

Only by unalterable physical impotence, is the supreme legislature prevented from being its own executive, or from being the sole legislature. The supreme legislature will not, to the neglect of its own duties, take upon itself any of those functions, for the apt exercise of which, when taken in the aggregate, those subordinate authorities alone, can, in respect of disposable time, appropriate knowledge, judgment, and active aptitude, have been provided with sufficient means. But, in case of non-performance, or unapt performance, or well-grounded apprehension of either, to the exercise of no function of the executive or the sublegislative authority can the supreme legislature be incompetent. Unfaithfulness, yes: but to the supreme legislature, neither can usurpation nor encroachment, be imputed.

Separately or collectively, the constituents of a member of the legislature will, at all times, as such, make to such their deputy what communication they think fit: to his cognitive faculty, to his judicative faculty, or even to his will, it may be addressed. But, in so far as the good of the community taken in the aggregate is the paramount object of his care, no obedience will he pay to any such particular will, to the detriment of what appears to him the universal interest. Paramount to his duty to a part is, on every occasion, his duty to the whole. An engagement, exacted of him by a part, would be an act of insubordination as towards the whole. It belongs not to him to judge, until he has seen or heard. His will is commanded by his judgment, not his judgment by his will. Such contrariety may have place, without detriment to moral aptitude on either side. They may have good reason for dislocating him; he for exposing himself to be so dislocated.

If, on this or that particular occasion, in the opinion of Constituents, or in the opinion of their Deputy, a conflict should have place between their particular aggregate interest and the national interest, he will not be considered as violating his duty to the public, by giving his vote in favour of that same particular interest. For, the national interest being nothing more than an aggregate of the several particular interests, if against that which has been regarded as being the national interest, there be a majority, this result will prove that, in the so declared opinion of that same majority, that which had been spoken of as if it were the national interest, was not so: and if, in support of that which, by a *majority* of his *constituents*, is regarded as being their interest, there be *not* a *majority* in the *legislature*, his vote will be of no effect; and, to the national interest, no evil will have been done by it. On the other hand, a practice, which in every case is evil, is *insincerity*: and in this case, by the supposition no good at all, therefore no preponderant good would be produced by it.

Accordingly, if so it should happen, that, after *speaking* in *support* of an arrangement, which, in the opinion of his constituents, is contrary to their particular interest, he gives his vote *against* that same arrangement, in such conduct there is not any real inconsistency. By his *speech*, his duty to the *public* is fulfilled; by his *vote*, his duty to his constituents.

Moreover, what, on an occasion of this sort, may very well happen, is that an arrangement which, in the eyes of constituents, is detrimental to their interest, is not so: and *vice versa*: and, in this case, his speech in support of the opposite arrangement may have the effect of working a change in their opinion; and, on a succeeding occasion, causing them to concur with the arrangement supported by him, instead of opposing it.

2. *Responsibility.*

Of the constitutive authority, the constant will (for such it cannot but be presumed to be) is—that the national felicity, the happiness of the greatest number—be maximised: to this will, on each occasion, it is the duty of the supreme legislature, according to the measure of its ability, to give execution and effect.

If, on any occasion, any ordinance, which to some shall appear repugnant to the principles of this constitution, shall come to have been enaetcd by the legislature, such ordinance is not on that account to be, by any judge, treated or spoken of, as being null and void: not even although its tendency, intended as well as actual, were to appear to him to be to diminish the mass of power hereby reserved to the constitutive authority. But if, of any such act, the tendency be anti-constitutional, as above, it may form an apt ground of an exercise to be given by the electors, to their incidental, dislocative, and punifactive functions, applying them respectively to such members of the legislature, by whom motion, speech, or vote shall have been given in favour of the supposed anti-constitutional arrangement; and, in any judicatory, such, by the judge principal, may any such act, on its coming regularly before him, be in his opinion declared to be.

3. *Attendance.*

Exceptions excepted, the legislature sits every day in the year. Exceptions are vacation days. Vacation days are every seventh day; that is to say, every day of general rest. But urgency declared, sittings have place in vacation days.

A domestic servant is a servant of one: a legislator is a servant of all. No domestic servant absents himself at pleasure, and without leave. The masters of the legislator give no such leave. From non-attendance of a domestic servant, the evil is upon a domestic scale: of a legislator, on a national scale. A legislator is a physician of the body politic. No physician receives pay but in proportion to attendance. The physician has no vacation days.

4. *Attendance and Remuneration—how connected.*

Into the assembly chamber there is but one entrance. The retiring rooms are behind and above. Committee rooms have other entrances.

Each day, on entrance into the assembly chamber, each member receives that day's pay at the hands of the doorkeeper. In his view, and in that of the company in the assembly chamber, is a clock. On delivery of the pay, the doorkeeper stamps, in the *Entrance and Departure Book*, on the page of that day, the member's name, adding the hour and minute.

No member departs without leave of the president, who, on a sign made by the departer, rings, by a string within his reach, a bell hanging near the doorkeeper, who, after stamping in the *Entrance and Departure Book*, on the page of that day, the member's name, with the hour and minute, lets him out. (A retiring place, opening only into the chamber, is of course supposed.)

Sick or well, for no day, on which he does not attend, vacation days excepted, does any *legislator* receive his pay.

If, by sickness, a member has been prevented from attending, he, on the first day of his re-attendance, presents to the doorkeeper a sickness ticket, on which are marked the day or days of non-attendance, with an intimation of the nature of the sickness, authenticated by his name in his own hand-writing, and the attestation of a physician.

To clear a member from the suspicion of employing sickness as a pretence for avoiding to give his vote or speech, questions may be put to him and others, in the face of the assembly, and observations made.

5. *Continuation Committee.*

Lest, by the exit of members, by whom introduction or support has been given to useful arrangements, any such arrangement should, after proposal and acceptance, be lost or deteriorated, as also lest the appropriate intellectual and active aptitude produced by experience should, by such secession, be rendered less than, without prejudice to appropriate moral aptitude—to wit, to length of exposure to corruption from the Executive—it may thus be made to be—each Legislature, antecedently to its outgoing, will elect a Committee, the Members of which—to the number of from (seven) to (twenty-one) or more—will, under the name of the *continuation committee*, under the direction of the legislature, apply their endeavours, collectively or individually, in the next succeeding legislature, to the carrying on of the designs and proceedings of the then next preceding legislature, in an unbroken thread.

Locable in the continuation committee is, in each year, not only every member of the outgoing legislature, but every member of the continuation committee, serving in that same legislature. Thus may any person serve as a continuation committee man for any number of successive years.

A continuation committee man has, for the above purpose, on every occasion, right of argumentation and initiation, or say of speech and motion: but, not having been elected by the people, he has not a vote.

CHAPTER 17

Prime Minister and Ministers

A. *Prime Minister*

To the Prime Minister, exercisable within his logical field of service, belong the functions following: namely,

1. *Executive function.* Exercise is given to it, in so far as, within that same field, he gives execution and effect to any ordinances, emanating, whether immediately or unimmediately, from the legislature: thus giving corresponding execution and effect to the rightly presumed will of the constitutive.

2. *Directive function.* In the exercise of this function, by him is the business of the administrative department conducted: by him, with the assistance of the several ministers and their respective subordinates, performed. Under his direction they all are. In their functions may be seen his functions.

3. *Locative function.* In the exercise of this function, by him are the ministers, all of them, located.

4. Promotion is location: location to wit, in a situation higher than that which, before such promotion, the person so promoted occupied.

5. *Dislocative function.* In the exercise of this function by him are the ministers, all of them, eventually dislocable.

6. *Imperative function.* In the exercise of this function, to him belongs the command in chief of the whole land defensive force.

7. So, of the whole of the sea defensive force.

Relation to the Legislature.

Exceptions excepted, no otherwise than by epistolary discourse to wit, by message, does the prime minister address the legislature.

Exception is if, on some extraordinary occasion, for the purpose of explanation, he has been invited or ordered by the legislature to a personal conference.

Of a prime minister, the term of service is (four) years.

No prime minister is re-eligible, until there are in existence, at the same time, out of whom choice may be made (two or three) *quondam* prime ministers, he being one.[1]

Exceptions excepted, in this office any person, who, in the judgment of the legislative authority, is, in respect of all points of appropriate aptitude taken together, most apt, is locable.

Excepted are: 1. All monarchs, and every person, connected by any known tie of consanguinity, or affinity, with any monarch. 2. Every person, who has not, either in a resident or migratory state, passed at least (   )[2] years, in some part or other of the territory of this state.

Located is this functionary by those to whose will it belongs to him to give execution and effect. He is located by the legislature.

Dislocable is this functionary at any time, by that authority, for the giving execution and effect to whose will, he has been located. He is dislocable by the legislature.

B. *Ministers Collectively*

Under the Prime Minister are the Ministers following: namely,

1. The Election Minister;
2. The Legislation Minister;[3]
3. The Army Minister;
4. The Navy Minister;[4]
5. The Interior Communication Minister;
6. The Preventive Service Minister;[5]
7. The Indigence Relief Minister;
8. The Education Minister;[6]
9. The Domain Minister;[7]
10. The Health Minister;
11. The Foreign Relation Minister;
12. The Trade Minister.

C. *Architectural Arrangements*

Of the thirteen ministers, two, to wit, the election minister and the legislation minister, not being necessarily subject to the direction of the prime minister, remains *eleven* as and for the *number*, of those, in the instance of each of whom, need may have place for an office within the reach of the common superordinate, for the purpose of instantaneous intercommunication with him.

Ministers' offices—say eleven, twelve, or thirteen, as above, disposed in a *crescent*: a *crescent*, or else—what, to the purpose here in question, would serve equally well—instead of any such *fragment* of a circle, one entire circle, or rectilinear *quasi-circle*—a polygon of that same number of sides, circumscribing, or inscribed on, a circle: or an *oval* form correspondently diversifiable. So far as *ventilation* alone is regarded, if protection against violent winds from particular quarters be not regarded as necessary, an *unenclosed* space, such as that covered by a crescent, presents itself as obviously preferable to the above proposed or any other plan, by which a thorough draught of air, sweeping the whole, is excluded. In any case, though not necessarily, yet naturally, is the central situation with reference to the rest would be placed the prime minister's office, from whence directions will have to be continually issued.

In the apartment of the prime minister, from an apt position within reach of the seat occupied by him, issue thirteen *conversation tubes*, terminating in corresponding positions contiguous in like manner to the seats of the several ministers in their several apartments.

From the apartment of each minister to the apartment of every other minister runs in like manner a conversation tube.

As between one and every other of these fourteen administration functionaries—thus is promptitude of oral intercourse maximised.

By these same means, effectual security is afforded, against an imaginable mishap, the realisation of which is not without examples. From office to office, official papers are of course sent in locked boxes. The offices being, many of them, out of sight of one another, and situated at indefinite distance—the bearers of these boxes have been way-laid, and for some sinister political purpose robbed of them.

On the above construction, the messengers, by whom papers are carried to and fro, need never be out of sight of the intercommunicators; by means of wheels within doors, boxes, if it were worth while, might even be borne to and fro, by ropes instead of messengers, at the immediately preceding moment: notice being given by accompanying bells.

CHAPTER 18

Sublegislature and Local Headman[1]

A. *Sublegislature*

In every district is a sublegislature. By sublegislature, understand a political body, exercising, under the authority of the legislature, either as to the whole or as to a part of its logical field of service, functions of the same nature as those of the legislature.

For a member of a sublegislature, the term of service is, in every particular, the same as for a member of the legislature.

To each sublegislature, under the authority of the legislature, belong the several functions following, that is to say:

1. Its ministerial function [i.e. helping in the enforcement of laws].
2. It's institution-rearing function [i.e. establishing public works].
3. Its money-supplying function.
4. Its expenditure-watching function.
5. Its transfer-compelling function [i.e. compelling a man to sell property when in public interest].
6. Its informative or information supplying function.
7. Its publicity-securing function.

Sublegislation Ministers, in each district will be a set of administrative functionaries bearing the same names, and within that local field having, exceptions excepted, the same logical fields of service, as the several ministers of the whole state.

In this case each sublegislature, within its fields of service, local and logical, standing in the place of the legislature, the several single-seated functionaries, its subordinates, will be in every respect on the same footing as those of the legislature: namely, in respect of the several topics treated of in the different sections of Chapter. 17, Ministers Collectively.

Taking the national administrative establishment for the standard of reference, each sublegislature, under the direction of the legislature, will settle with itself, and by appropriate ordinances express, in what particulars, alterations and in what shapes (the difference in respect of extent of local and logical field of service considered) the nature of the case, in such instances, appears to require alteration.

The only instance in which it can be clear beforehand, that in and for a district, no minister correspondent to a national minister can have a place, is that of the foreign relation minister: since it is for all districts collectively, and not for any one in particular, that what is done in the foreign relation department is done.

B. *Local Headman*

For giving effect to the will of government in all its several main branches—legislative, administrative, judicial, sublegislative, not forgetting the constitutive authority, which is superordinate to the government itself—one set of functionaries remains still wanting: functionaries who, with reference to every distinguishable species of political action, shall at all times be as near as possible to the spot. Functionaries of this description are those who, under the name of *local headmen*, are here instituted.

By a *local headman*, understand a functionary, who—in each one of the smallest portions of territory, called *bis-subdistricts* or *tris-subdistricts*, into which, by any all-embracing process of division and subdivision the territory of the state is divided—is, of all public functionaries whose authority is confined within the limit of that same portion of territory, the *head*.

Of the authority of each local headman, the local field is accordingly the *bis-subdistrict*, or *tris-subdistrict*, for, and in which, he serves.

The logical field is marked out by the several functions which in this chapter are allotted to him, together with all such others, as the legislative, or subject to its authority the sublegislative, shall from time to time have added or substituted.

FUNCTIONS

1. *General assistance Function.* In the exercise of this function, at the call of the prime minster, or of any one of the ministers, or of the judge of any immediate judicatory, the local headman of the

8

bis-subdistrict does what depends on him towards giving execution and effect to all such orders, ordinances in relation to which, in conformity to the will of the legislature, it may happen to them to regard the business of their respective departments and sub-departments, as standing in need of such his assistance: and this whether for the purpose of securing *execution* and *effect*, or for the purpose of minimising the amount of *delay, vexation* and *expense*.

2. *Presidential Function.* In the exercise of this function at all meetings of the inhabitants of the bis-subdistrict held for the exercise of any public function, the local headman takes the chair of course; and, subject to the authority of the majority present, conducts the proceedings.

But to no such meeting is his presence, either in person or by deputy, in such sort essential, as to render invalid any proceedings at which a majority of the persons entitled to vote are present. They are free, if they think fit, to elect any other person president.

3. *Beneficent-mediation Function.* In the exercise of this function, for prevention of litigation, on application made to him, the local headman, in so far as he sees good, will apply his good offices to the reconciliation of *family differences* within his territory.

Of family differences, or say *disagreements*, examples the following:

1. Differences between *husband* and *wife*.

2. Differences between *parent* and *child*.

3. Differences between *brother* and *brother*, *sister* and *sister*, or *brother* and *sister*, inhabiting the same house, and without a common parent.

4. Differences between any two other *near relatives*, inhabiting the same household: especially if without the near vicinity of any common superordinate in the order of genealogy.

5. Differences between *employer* and *helper*, in any business, especially if inhabiting the same household.

In the case of husband and wife, and in other cases, where the parties are of different sexes, he will do well to call in, as his assistant, a person of the female sex, wife or widow, and past the age of child-bearing.

4. *Beneficent-information Function.* In the exercise of this function, on application made to him, the local headman affords useful information and advice, on various occasions, to the otherwise

helpless—in so far as the means in his power extend, and his
employable time admits. Of these occasions, examples are as
follows:

1. For subsistence the applicant has need of employment, and
though *able* to perform work, knows not where, or how to obtain
it. If unable to labour for subsistence his case belongs to the
indigence relief minister's subdepartment.

2. From the estate of a person lately deceased, or become
insolvent, in a distinct bis-subdistrict, or in a foreign country,
money is believed by the applicant to be due to him; for example,
on the ground of natural relationship or debt; his wish is to know
by what means, if any, he may take the best adapted course for the
obtaining of it.

3. On an account, to which he was not privy, by the decease of a
relative, money is become due to him from government, and his
wish is to know in what manner to make application and proof.

5. *Travelling-disputes-settling Function.* In the exercise of this
function, in subordination to the immediate judicatory, with the
advice and assistance of his registrar, the local headman employs his
endeavours in settling *travelling disputes*; thereby, in so far as on him
depends, giving execution and effect to the traveller's subcode.
Of travelling disputes, examples are the following:

1. Disputes between a traveller and a conductor of a public
vehicle, respecting the *quantum* to be paid.

2. So, respecting loss of, or damage to, traveller's effects.

3. So, respecting damage alleged by the conductor to have been
done to the vehicle, or the effects therein, or the beasts of draught,
by a passenger.

4. The like as between a traveller and an innkeeper.

5. Disputes respecting the accommodation afforded in the
vehicle, or the inn, as between traveller and traveller.

CHAPTER 19

Fallacies[1]

[Bentham's *Book of Fallacies* existed in outline as early as 1806. It was first published by Dumont in French in 1816 under the title of *Traite des sophismes politiques*, as a second part of his *Tactique des assemblées législatives*. Dumont rewrote several parts of it, omitted many of Bentham's references to British political and parliamentary life, and reclassified Bentham's list of fallacies in a way that seemed to him more satisfactory. In 1824, on Bentham's suggestion, Peregrine Bingham published a fuller and less inaccurate English edition. Bowring published the book in his collected works, Vol. II pp. 375–487; his version differs from Bingham's in several respects.

A look at the mss shows that they have been edited pretty drastically. In some cases nearly whole paragraphs have been cancelled; and in several others, they have been completely re-written. Deletions and insertions are not in Bentham's hand, and it is difficult to believe that they would all have been approved by him. While it would be desirable to produce the original ms. as Bentham wrote it, ignoring all the subsequent editorial deletions and insertions made by both Bingham and Bowring, this seems an impossible task, especially as the deletions in several cases make it impossible to read the original writing. Another difficulty posed by the mss. is that Bentham also wrote alternative versions of many of the fallacies at different times. I have ignored these alternative formulations and relied entirely on the final and complete version as corrected by his editor. In a book of this size, it would have been impossible to include the entire work. However, I have tried to include most of the fallacies that Bentham discussed and to give a faithful account of the way he expounded and exposed them.

Bentham was undecided as to how best to classify the fallacies. At times when he thought that they could be classified on the basis of the mental faculty to which they appeal, he classified them into those appealing to the understanding and those appealing to the affection, to which he later added the third category of those appealing to imagination. (Box 104, p. 57/8) At other times he thought they could be best classified on the basis of their source, and then he divided them into the fallacies employed by those in power (which he called fallacies of the *Ins*), those employed by opposition parties (fallacies of the *Outs*), those used or capable of being used by both (*either side* fallacies), and those employed by men rejecting the very institution of the government (anarchical fallacies) (*Ibid.*, pp. 48–9). Sometimes Bentham modified the second classification and dropped the fourth category altogether. (*Ibid.*, p. 57). Given this uncertainty in Bentham's mind, it was thought best not to classify fallacies but to present them in the order in which Bentham discussed them, giving in each case the Latin name that he gave to the mental faculty to which in his view the fallacy in question appealed.]

A. INTRODUCTION

1. *A fallacy, what.*

By the name of *fallacy*, it is common to designate any argument that is considered as having been employed, or topic suggested, for the purpose, or with a probability, of producing the effect of deception, of causing some erroneous opinion to be entertained by any person to whose mind such argument may have been presented.

2. *Fallacies, by Whom Treated of Heretofore.*

The earliest author extant, in whose works any mention is made on the subject of *fallacies*, is Aristotle; by whom, in the course or rather on the occasion of his treatise on logic, not only is this subject started, but a list of the species of argument to which this denomination is applicable, is undertaken to be given. Upon the principle of the exhaustive method at so early a period employed by that astonishing genius, and, in comparison of what it might and ought to have been, so little turned to account since, *two* is the number of parts into which the whole mass is distributed—fallacies in the diction, fallacies not in the diction; and thirteen (whereof in

the diction six, not in the diction seven) is the number of the
articles distributed between those two parts.[a]

As from Aristotle down to Locke, on the subject of the origination
of our ideas (deceptitious and undeceptitious included)—so from
Aristotle down to this present day, on the subject of the forms, of
which such ideas or combinations of ideas as are employable in
the character of instruments of deception, are susceptible—all is a
blank.

To do something in the way of filling up this blank, is the object of
the present work.

In speaking of Aristotle's collection of fallacies, as a stock to
which, from his time to the present, no addition has been made, all
that is meant is, that whatsoever arguments may have had deception
for their object, none besides those brought to view by Aristotle,
have been brought to view in that character and under that name:
for between the time of Aristotle and the present, treatises of the
art of oratory, or popular argumentation, have not been wanting in
various languages and in considerable number; nor can any of
these be found in which, by him who may wish to put a deceit
upon those to whom he has to address himself, instruction in no
small quantity may not be obtained.

What in these books of instruction is professed to be taught,
comes under this general description: viz. how—by means of words
aptly employed, to gain your point—to produce upon those with
whom you have to deal—those to whom you are to address
yourself, the impression, and, by means of the impression, the
disposition most favourable to your purpose, whatsoever be that
purpose.

As to the impression and disposition, the production of which

---

[a] Σοφισμα, whence our English word *sophism*, is the word
employed by Aristotle. The choice of the appellation is singular
enough: συφος is the word that was already in use for designating
a wise man. It was the same appellation that was commonly employed for the designation of the seven sages. Σοφιστής, whence
our *sophist*, being an impretative of Σοφος, was the word applied,
as it were in irony, to designate the tribe of wranglers, whose pre-
tension to the praise of wisdom had no better ground than an abuse
of words.

might happen to be desired—whether the impression were correct or deceptitious—whether the disposition were, with a view to the individual or community in question, salutary, indifferent, or pernicious—was a question that seemed not in any of these instances to have come across the author's mind. In the view taken by them of the subject, had any such question presented itself, it would have been put aside as foreign to the subject; exactly as, in a treatise on the art of war, a question concerning the justice of the war.

Dionysius of Halicarnassus, Cicero, and Quintilian, Isaac Voss, and, though last and in bulk least, yet not the least interesting, our own Gerard Hamilton (of whom more will be said), are of this stamp.

Between those earliest and these latest of the writers who have written on this subject and with this view, others in abundance might be inserted; but these are quite enough.

After so many ages past in teaching with equal complacency and indifference the art of true instruction and the art of deception—the art of producing good effects and the art of producing bad effects—the art of the honest man and the art of the knave—of promoting the purposes of the benefactor, and the purposes of the enemy of the human race; after so many ages during which, with a view to persuasion, disposition, action, no instructions have been endeavoured to be given but in the same strain of imperturbable impartiality, it seemed not too early, in the nineteenth century, to take up the subject on the ground of morality, and to invite common honesty for the first time to mount the bench, and take her seat as judge.

As to Aristotle's fallacies—unless his *petitio principii* and his *fallacia, non causa pro causa,* be considered as exceptions—upon examination so little danger would be found in them, that, had the philosopher left them unexposed to do their worst, the omission need not have hung very heavy upon his conscience: scarce in any instance will be discovered any the least danger of final deception —the utmost inconvenience they seem capable of producing seems confined to a slight sensation of embarrassment. And as to the embarrassment, the difficulty will be, not in pronouncing that the proposition in question is incapable of forming a just ground for the conclusion built upon it, but in finding words for the description of the weakness which is the cause of this incapacity—not in discovering the proposition to be absurd, but in giving an exact description of the form in which the absurdity presents itself.

3. *Relation of Fallacies to Vulgar Errors*

Error—*vulgar error*,[b] is an appellation given to an opinion which, being considered as false, is considered in itself only, and not with a view to any consequences, of any kind, of which it may happen to be productive.

It is termed *vulgar* with reference to the persons by whom it is supposed to be entertained: and this either in respect of their multitude, simply, or in respect of the lowness of the station occupied by them, or the greater part of them, in the scale of respectability, in the scale of intelligence.

Fallacy is an appellation applied not exclusively to an opinion or to propositions enunciative of supposed opinions, but to discourse in any shape considered as having a tendency, with or without design, to cause any erroneous opinion to be embraced, or even, through the medium of erroneous opinion or otherwise, to cause any pernicious course of action to be engaged or persevered in.

Thus, to believe that they who lived in early or old times were, because they lived in those times, wiser or better than those who live in later or modern times, is vulgar error: the employing that vulgar error in the endeavour to cause pernicious practices and institutions to be retained, is fallacy.

By those by whom the term *fallacy* has been employed—at any rate, by those by whom it was originally employed—deception has been considered not merely as a consequence more or less probable, but as a consequence the production of which was aimed at on the part at least of some of the utterers.

Σλεγχοι σοφιστων, arguments employed by the sophists, is the

---

[b] *Vulgar errors* is a denomination which, from the work written on this subject by a physician of name in the seventeenth century, has obtained a certain degree of celebrity.

Not the moral (of which the political is a department), but the physical, was the field of the errors which it was the object of Sir Thomas Browne to hunt out and bring to view: but of this restriction no intimation is given by the words of which the title of his work is composed.

denomination by which Aristotle has designated his devices, thirteen in number, to which his commentators, such of them who wrote in Latin, give the name of *fallaciae* (from *fallere* to deceive), from which our English word *fallacies*.

That in the use of these instruments, such as they are, deception was the object of the set of men mentioned by Aristotle under the name of sophists, is altogether out of doubt. On every occasion on which they are mentioned by him, this intention of deceiving is either directly asserted or assumed.

B. FALLACIES

1. *The Wisdom of our Ancestors; or Chinese Argument (ad verecundiam)*

Exposition: This argument consists in stating a supposed repugnancy between the proposed measure, and the opinions of men by whom the same country was inhabited in former times; these opinions collected either from express words of some writer living at the period of time in question, or from laws or institutions that were then in existence.

'*Our wise ancestors*'—'*The wisdom of our ancestors*'—'*The wisdom of ages*'—'*Venerable antiquity*'—'*Wisdom of old times*':

Such are the leading terms and phrases of those propositions, the object of which is to cause the alleged repugnance to be regarded as a sufficient reason for the rejection of the proposed measure.

Exposure: This fallacy affords one of the most striking of the numerous instances in which, under the conciliatory influence of *custom*—that is, of *prejudice*—persuasions the most repugnant to one another are capable of maintaining their ground in the same mind.

This fallacy, prevalent as it is in matters of law, is directly repugnant to a principle or maxim universally admitted in almost every other department of human intelligence, and which is the foundation of all useful knowledge and of all rational conduct.

'Experience is the mother of wisdom', is among the maxims handed down to the present and all future ages, by the wisdom, such as it has been, of past ages.

8*

No! says this fallacy, the true mother of wisdom is not *experience*, but *inexperience*.

An absurdity so glaring carries in itself its own refutation; and all that we can do is, to trace the causes which have contributed to give to this fallacy such an ascendency in matters of legislation.

As between individual and individual living at the same time and in the same situation, he who is old possesses, as such, more experience than he who is young; as between generation and generation, the reverse of this is true, if, as in ordinary language, a preceding generation be, with reference to a succeeding generation, called *old*, the *old* or preceding generation could not have had so much experience as the succeeding. With respect to such of the materials or sources of wisdom as have come under the cognisance of their own senses, the two are on a par; with respect to such of those materials and sources of wisdom as are derived from the reports of others, the later of the two possesses an indisputable advantage.

In giving the name of old or elder to the earlier generation of the two, the misrepresentation is not less gross, nor the falsity of it less incontestable, than if the name of *old man* or *old woman* were given to the infant in its cradle.

What, then, is the wisdom of the times called old? Is it the wisdom of grey hairs? No: it is the wisdom of the cradle.[c]

The learned and honourable gentlemen of Thibet do homage to superior wisdom—superiority raised to the degree of divinity—in the person of an infant lying and squalling in his cradle.

2. *No-Precedent Argument (ad verecundiam)*

Exposition: 'The proposition is of a novel and unprecedented com-

---

[c] No one will deny that preceding ages have produced men eminently distinguished by benevolence and genius; it is to them that we owe in succession all the advances which have hitherto been made in the career of human improvement: but as their talents could only be developed in proportion to the state of knowledge at the period in which they lived, and could only have been called into action with a view to then-existing circumstances, it is absurd to rely on their authority, at a period and under a state of things altogether different.

plexion: the present is surely the first time that any such thing was ever heard of in this house.'

Whatsoever may happen to be the *subject* introduced, above is a specimen of the infinite variety of forms in which the opposing *predicate* may be clothed.

To such an observation there could be no objection, if the object with which it were made was only to fix attention to a new or difficult subject: 'Deliberate well before you act, as you have no precedent to direct your course.'

Exposure: But in the character of an argument, as a ground for the rejection of the proposed measure, it is obviously a fallacy.

If the observation presents a conclusive objection against the particular measure proposed, so it would against any other that ever was proposed, including every measure that ever was adopted, and therein every institution that exists at present. If it proves that this ought not to be done, it proves that nothing else ought ever to have been done.

It may be urged that if the measure had been a fit one, it would have been brought upon the carpet before. But there are several obstacles, besides the inexpediency of a measure, which, for any length of time, may prevent its being brought forward:

1. If, though beyond dispute promotive of the interest of the many, there be anything in it that is adverse to the interests, the prejudices, or the humours of the ruling few, the wonder is, not that it should not have been brought forward before, but that it should be brought forward even now.

2. If in the complexion of it there be anything which it required a particular degree of ingenuity to contrive and adapt to the purpose, this would of itself be sufficient to account for the tardiness of its appearance.

3. *Self-assumed Authority (ad ignorantiam; ad verecundiam)*

Exposition: This fallacy presents itself in two shapes:

1. An avowal, made with a sort of mock modesty and caution by a person in exalted station, that he is incapable of forming a judgment on the question in debate, such incapacity being sometimes real, sometimes pretended; 2. open assertion, by a person so situated, of the purity of his motives and integrity of his life, and the

entire reliance which may consequently be reposed on all he says or does.

Exposure: 1. The first which may be called *the Fallacy of Browbeating Nescience* is commonly played off as follows: An evil or defect in our institutions is pointed out clearly, and a remedy proposed, to which no objection can be made; up starts a man high in office, and, instead of stating any specific objection, says, 'I am not prepared' to do so and so, 'I am not prepared to say,' etc. The meaning evidently intended to be conveyed is, 'If I, who am so dignified, and supposed to be so capable of forming a judgment, avow myself incompetent to do so, what presumption, what folly, must there be in the conclusion formed by any one else!' In truth, this is nothing else but an indirect way of browbeating—arrogance under a thin veil of modesty.

If you are not prepared to pass a judgment, you are not prepared to condemn, and ought not, therefore, to oppose; the utmost you are warranted in doing, if sincere, is to ask for a little time for consideration.

Supposing the unpreparedness real, the reasonable and practical inference is—say nothing, to take no part in the business.

2. The second of these two devices may be called the self-trumpeter's fallacy. I do not here allude to those occasional impulses of vanity which lead a man to display or overrate his pretensions to superior intelligence. Against the self-love of the man whose altar to himself is raised on this ground, rival altars, from every one of which he is sure of discouragement, raise themselves all around. But there are certain men in office, who in discharge of their functions arrogate to themselves a degree of probity which is to exclude all imputations and all inquiry; their assertions are to be deemed equivalent to proof; their virtues are guarantees for the faithful discharge of their duties; and the most implicit confidence is to be reposed in them on all occasions. If you expose any abuse, propose any reform, call for securities, inquiry, or measures to promote publicity, they set up a cry of surprise, amounting almost to indignation, as if their integrity were questioned, or their honour wounded. With all this, they dexterously mix up intimations that the most exalted patriotism, honour, and perhaps religion, are the only sources of all their actions.

Exposure: Such assertions must be classed among fallacies, because:
1. They are irrelevant to the subject in discussion; 2. the degree in
which the predominance of motives of the social or disinterested
cast is commonly asserted or insinuated, is, by the very nature of
man, rendered impossible; 3. the sort of testimony thus given
affords no legitimate reason for regarding the assertion in question
to be true. For it is no less completely in the power of the most
profligate than in that of the most virtuous of mankind; nor is it in a
less degree the interest of the profligate man to make such assertions.
Be they ever so completely false, not any the least danger of punishment does he see himself exposed to, at the hands either of the law
or of public opinion.

For ascribing to any one of these self-trumpeters the smallest
possible particle of that virtue which they are so loud in the pro-
fession of, there is no more rational cause, than for looking upon
this or that actor as a good man, because he acts well the part of
Othello, or bad, because he acts well the part of Iago.

4. On the contrary, the interest he has in trying what may be
done by these means, is more decided and exclusive than in the case
of the man of real probity and social feeling. The virtuous man,
being what he is, has that chance for being looked upon as such;
whereas the self-trumpeter in question, having no such ground of
reliance, beholds his only chance in the conjunct effects of his own
effrontery, and the imbecility of his hearers.

These assertions of authority, therefore, by men in office, who
would have us estimate their conduct by their character, and not
their character by their conduct, must be classed among political
fallacies. If there be any one maxim in politics more certain than
another, it is, that no possible degree of virtue in the governor can
render it expedient for the governed to dispense with good laws and
good institutions.[d]

---

[d] Madame de Stael says that in a conversation which she had at
Petersburgh with the Emperor of Russia, he expressed his desire to
better the condition of the peasantry, who are still in a state of
absolute slavery; upon which the female sentimentalist exclaimed,
'Sire, your character is a constitution for your country, and your
conscience is its guarantee.' His reply was, '*Quand cela serait, je ne
serais jamais qu'un accident heureux.*'—*Dix années d'Exit*, p. 313.

4. *Personality Laudative (ad amicitiam)*

Exposition: The argument indeed is generally confined to persons of this description, and is little else than an extension of the self-trumpeter's fallacy. In both of them authority derived from the virtues of talents of the persons lauded, is brought forward as superseding the necessity of all investigation.

'The measure proposed implies a distrust of the members of his Majesty's government; but so great is their integrity, so complete their disinterestedness, so uniformly do they prefer the public advantage to their own, that such a measure is altogether unnecessary: their disapproval is sufficient to warrant an opposition: precautions can only be requisite where danger is apprehended; here, the high character of the individuals in question is a sufficient guarantee against any ground of alarm.'

The panegyric goes on increasing in proportion to the dignity of the functionary thus panegyrised.

Subordinates in office are the very models of assiduity, attention, and fidelity to their trust; ministers, the perfection of probity and intelligence: and as for the highest magistrate in the state, no adulation is equal to describe the extent of his various merits.

Exposure: There can be no difficulty in exposing the fallacy of the argument attempted to be deduced from these panegyrics:

1. They have the common character of being irrelevant to the question under discussion. The measure must have something extraordinary in it, if a right judgment cannot be founded on its merits, without first estimating the character of the members of the government.

2. If the goodness of the measure be sufficiently established by direct arguments, the reception given to it by those who oppose it will form a better criterion for judging of their character, than their character (as inferred from the places which they occupy) for judging of the goodness or badness of the measure.

3. If this argument be good in any one case, it is equally good in every other; and the effect of it, if admitted, would be to give to the persons occupying for the time being the situation in question, an absolute and universal negative upon every measure not agreeable to their inclinations.

4. In every public trust, the legislator should, for the purpose of prevention, suppose the trustee disposed to break the trust in every imaginable way in which it would be possible for him to reap, from the breach of it, any personal advantage. This is the principle on which public institutions ought to be formed; and when it is applied to all men indiscriminately, it is injurious to none. The practical inference is, to oppose to such possible (and what will always be probable) breaches of trust every bar that can be opposed, consistently with the power requisite for the efficient and due discharge of the trust. Indeed, these arguments, drawn from the supposed virtues of men in power, are opposed to the first principles on which all laws proceed.

5. Such allegations of individual virtue are never supported by specific proof—are scarce ever susceptible of specific disproof; and specific disproof, if offered, could not be admitted, *viz.* in either House of Parliament. If attempted elsewhere, the punishment would fall, not on the unworthy trustee, but on him by whom the unworthiness had been proved.

5. *Personality Vituperative (ad Odium)*

Exposition: To this class belongs a cluster of fallacies so intimately connected with each other, that they may first be enumerated, and some observations be made upon them in the lump. By seeing their mutual relations to each other, by observing in what circumstances they agree, and in what they differ, a much more correct as well as complete view will be obtained of them, than if they were considered each of them by itself.

The fallacies that belong to this cluster may be denominated:

1. Imputation of bad design.
2. Imputation of bad character.
3. Imputation of bad motive.
4. Imputation of inconsistency.
5. Imputation of suspicious connexions—*Noscitur ex sociis.*
6. Imputation founded on identity of denomination—*Noscitur ex cognominibus.* Of the fallacies belonging to this class, the common character is the endeavour to draw aside attention from the *measure* to the *man*; and this in such sort as, from the supposed imperfection on the part of the man by whom a measure is supported or opposed,

to cause a correspondent imperfection to be imputed to the measure so supported, or excellence to the measure so opposed.

The argument in its various shapes amounts to this: In bringing forward or supporting the measure in question, the person in question entertains a bad design; therefore the measure is bad: he is a person of a bad character; therefore the measure is bad: he is actuated by a bad motive; therefore the measure is bad: he has fallen into inconsistencies; on a former occasion, he either opposed it, or made some observation not reconcilable with some observation which he has advanced on the present occasion; therefore the measure is bad: he is on a footing of intimacy with this or that person, who is a man of dangerous principles and designs, or has been seen more or less frequently in his company, or has professed, or is suspected of entertaining some opinion which the other has professed, or been suspected of entertaining; therefore the measure is bad: he bears a name that at a former period was borne by a set of men now no more, by whom bad principles were entertained, or bad things done; therefore the measure is bad.

Exposure: Various are the considerations which concur in demonstrating the futility of the fallacies comprehended in this class, and (not to speak of the improbity of the utterers) the weakness of those with whom they obtain currency—the weakness of the acceptors:

1. In the first place comes that general character of irrelevancy which belongs to these, in common with the several other articles that stand upon the list of fallacies.

2. In the next place comes the complete inconclusiveness. Whatsoever be their force as applied to a bad measure—to the worst measure that can be imagined, they would be found to apply with little less force to all good measures—to the best measures that can be imagined.

Among 658, or any such large number of persons taken at random, there will be persons of all characters. If the measure is a good one, will it become bad because it is supported by a bad man? If it is bad, will it become good because supported by a good man? If the measure be really inexpedient, why not at once show that it is so? Your producing these irrelevant and inconclusive arguments in lieu of direct ones, though not sufficient to prove that the measure you thus oppose is a good one, *contributes* to prove that you yourselves regard it as a good one.

6. *The Hobgoblin Argument, or, No Innovation! (ad metum)*

Exposition: The hobgoblin, the eventual appearance of which is denounced by this argument, is *anarchy*; which tremendous spectre has for its forerunner the monster *innovation*. The forms in which this monster may be denounced are as numerous and various as the sentences in which the word *innovation* can be placed.

'*Here it comes!*' exclaims the barbarous or unthinking servant in the hearing of the affrighted child, when, to rid herself of the burthen of attendance, such servant scruples not to employ an instrument of terror, the effects of which may continue during life. '*Here it comes!*' is the cry; and the hobgoblin is rendered but the more terrific by the suppression of its name.

Of a similar nature, and productive of similar effects, is the political device here exposed to view. As an instrument of deception, the device is generally accompanied by personalities of the vituperative kind: imputation of bad motives, bad designs, bad conduct and character, etc. are ordinarily cast on the authors and advocates of the obnoxious measure; whilst the term employed is such as to beg the question in dispute. Thus, in the present instance, *innovation* means a *bad* change; presenting to the mind, besides the idea of a *change*, the proposition, either that change in general is a bad thing, or at least that the sort of change in question is a bad change.

Exposure: Whatever reason it affords for looking upon the proposed measure, be it what it may, as about to be mischievous, it affords the same reason for entertaining the same opinion of everything that exists at present. To say all new things are bad, is as much to say all things are bad—or, at any event, at their commencement: for of all the old things ever seen or heard of, there is not one that was not once new. Whatever is now *establishment*, was once *innovation*.

He who on this ground condemns a proposed measure, condemns, in the same breath, whatsoever he would be most averse to be thought to disapprove: he condemns the Revolution, the Reformation, the assumption made by the House of Commons of a part in the penning of the laws in the reign of Henry VI, the institution of the House of Commons itself in the reign of Henry III: all these he bids us regard as sure forerunners of the monster anarchy, but particularly the birth and first efficient agency of the House of Commons—an innovation, in comparison of which all others, past or future, are for efficiency, and consequently mischievousness, but as grains of dust in the balance.

7. The Quietist, or 'No Complaint' (ad quietem)

Exposition: A new law or measure being proposed in the character of a remedy for some incontestable abuse or evil, an objection is frequently started, to the following effect: 'The measure is unnecessary; nobody complains of disorder in that shape in which it is the aim of your measure to propose a remedy to it: even when *no* cause of complaint has been found to exist, especially under governments which admit of complaints, men have in general not been slow to complain; much less where any just cause of complaint has existed.' The argument amounts to this: Nobody complains, therefore nobody suffers. It amounts to a *veto* on all measures of precaution or prevention, and goes to establish a maxim in legislation, directly opposed to the most ordinary prudence of common life; it enjoins us to build no parapets to a bridge till the number of accidents has raised an universal clamour.

Exposure: The argument would have more plausibility than it has, if there were any chance of complaints being attended to—if the silence of those who suffer did not arise from despair, occasioned by seeing the fruitlessness of former complaints. The expense and vexation of collecting and addressing complaints to parliament being great and certain, complaint will not commonly be made without adequate expectation of relief. But how can any such expectation be entertained by any one who is in the slightest degree without adequate expectation of relief. But how can any such expectation be entertained by any one who is in the slightest degree acquainted with the present constitution of parliament? Members who are independent of and irresponsible to the people, can have very few and very slight motives for attending to complaints, the redress of which would affect their own sinister interests. Again, how many complaints are repressed by the fear of attacking powerful individuals, and incurring resentments which may prove fatal to the complainant!

8. *Fallacy of False Consolation (ad quietem)*

Exposition: A measure having for its object the removal of some abuse, *i.e.* of some practice, the result of which is, on the part of the many, a mass of suffering more than equivalent to the harvest of enjoyment reaped from it by the few; being proposed, this argument consists in pointing to the general condition of the people in this or that other country, under the notion that in that other country, either in the particular respect in question, or upon the whole, the condition of the people is not so felicitous as, notwithstanding the abuse. It is in the country in and for which the measure of reform is proposed.

'What is the matter with you?' 'What would you have?' Look at the people there, and there: think how much better off *you* are than *they* are. Your prosperity and liberty are objects of envy to them; your institutions are the models which they endeavour to imitate.

When a particular suffering, produced as it appears by an assignable and assigned cause, has been pointed out as existing, a man, instead of attending to it himself, or inviting to it the attention of others, employs his exertions in the endeavour to engage other eyes to turn themselves to any other quarter in preference (he being of the number of those whose acknowledged duty it is to contribute their best endeavours to the affording to every affliction within their view, whatsoever relief may be capable of being afforded to it without preponderant inconvenience)—then, and then only, is it, that the endeavour becomes a just ground for censure, and the means thus employed present a title to be received upon the list of *fallacies*.

Exposure: The pravity as well as fallaciousness of this argument can scarcely be exhibited in a stronger or truer light than by the appellation here employed to characterise it.

1. Like all other fallacies upon this list, it is nothing to the purpose.

2. In his own case, no individual in his senses would accept it. Take any one of the orators by whom this argument is tendered, or of the sages on whom it passes for sterling: with an observation of the general wealth and prosperity of the country in his mouth, instead of a half-year's rent in his hand, let any one of his tenants propose to pay him thus in his own coin; will he accept it?

3. In a court of justice, in an action for damages—to learned ingenuity did ever any such device occur as that of pleading assets in the hand of a third person, or in the hands of the whole country, in bar to the demand? What the largest wholesale trade is to the smallest retail, such, and more in point of magnitude, is the relief commonly sought for at the hands of the legislator, to the relief commonly sought for at the hands of the judge. What the largest wholesale trade is to the smallest retail trade, such in point of magnitude, yea and more, is the injustice endeavoured at by this argument when employed in the seat of legislative power, in comparison of the injustice that would be committed by deciding in conformity to it in a court of justice.

Seriously and pointedly, in the character of a bar to any measure of relief—no, nor to the most trivial improvement, can it ever be employed. Suppose a bill brought in for converting an impassable road anywhere into a passable one, would any man stand up to oppose it who could find nothing better to urge against it than the multitude and goodness of the roads we have already? No: when in the character of a serious bar to the measure in hand, be that measure what it may, an argument so palpably inapplicable is employed, it can only be for the purpose of creating a diversion—of turning aside the minds of men from the subject really in hand, to a picture which by its beauty it is hoped, may engross the attention of the assembly, and make them forget for the moment for what purpose they came there.

9. *Procrastinator's Argument (ad socordiam)*
'Wait a little, this is not the time.'

Exposition: To this head belongs every form of words by which, speaking of a proposed measure of relief, an intimation is given, that the time, whatever it be, at which the proposal is made, is too early for the purpose; and given without any proof being offered of the truth of such intimation; such as, for instance, the want of requisite information, or the convenience of some preparatory measure.

Exposure: This is the sort of argument or observation which we so often see employed by those who, being in wish and endeavour hostile to a measure, are afraid or ashamed of being seen to be so.

They pretend, perhaps, to approve of the measure—they only differ as to the proper time of bringing it forward; but it may be matter of question whether, in any one instance, this observation has been applied to a measure by a man whose wish it was not, that it should remain excluded for ever.

A serious refutation would be ill bestowed upon so frivolous a pretence. The objection exists in the will, not in the judgment, of the objector. 'Is it lawful to do good on the sabbath day?' was the question put by Jesus to the official hypocrites. Which is the properest day to do good? Which is the properest day to remove a nuisance? Answer: The very first day that a man can be found to propose the removal of it; and whosoever opposes the removal of it on that day, will, if he dare, oppose the removal on every other.

The doubts and fears of the parliamentary procrastinator are the conscientious scruples of his prototype the Pharisee; and neither the answer nor the example of Jesus has succeeded in removing these scruples. To him, whatsoever is too soon today, be assured that tomorrow, if not too soon, it will be too late.

True it is, that, the measure being a measure of reform or improvement, an observation to this effect may be brought forward by a friend to the measure: and in this case, it is not an instrument of deception, but an expedient of unhappily necessary prudence.

Whatsoever it may be some centuries hence, hitherto the fault of the people has been, not groundless clamour against imaginary grievances, but insensibility to real ones; insensibility, not to the effect—the evil itself, for that, if it were possible, far from being a fault, would be a happiness—but to the cause—to the system or course of misrule which is the cause of it.

What, therefore may but too easily be—what hitherto ever has been—the fact, and that throughout a vast proportion of the field of legislation, is, that in regard to the grievances complained of, the time for bringing forward a measure of effectual relief is not yet come. Why? Because, though groaning under the effect, the people, by the artifice and hypocrisy of their oppressors having been prevented from entertaining any tolerably adequate conception of the cause, would at that time regard either with indifference or with suspicion the healing hand that should come forward with the only true and effectual remedy. Thus it is, for example, with that Pandora's box of grievances and misery, the contents of which are composed of the evils opposite to the ends of justice.

10. *Snail's-pace Argument (ad socordiam)*

'One thing at a time! Not too fast! Slow and sure!'

Exposition: The proposed measure being a measure of reform, requiring that for the completion of the beneficial work in question a number of operations be performed, capable, all or some of them, of being carried on at the same time, or successively without intervals, or at short intervals, the instrument of deception here in question consists in holding up to view the idea of graduality or slowness, as characteristic of the course which wisdom would dictate on the occasion in question. For more effectual recommendation of this course, to the epithet *gradual* are commonly added some such eulogistic epithets as *moderate* and *temperate*; whereby it is implied, that in proportion as the pace recommended by the word *gradual* is quickened, such increased pace will justly incur the censure expressed by the opposite epithets, immoderate, violent, precipitate, extravagant, outrageous.

Exposure: This is neither more nor less than a contrivance for making out of a mere word an excuse for leaving undone an indefinite multitude of things, which the arguer is convinced, and cannot forbear acknowledging, ought to be done.

Suppose half a dozen abuses, which equally and with equal promptitude stand in need of reform—this fallacy requires that without any reason that can be assigned, other than what is contained in the pronouncing or writing of the word *gradual*, all but one or two of them shall remain untouched.

Or, what is better, suppose that, to the effectual correction of some one of these abuses, six operations require to be performed—six operations, all of which must be done ere the correction can be effected—to save the reform from the reproach of being violent and intemperate, to secure to it the praise of graduality, moderation, and temperance, you insist, that of these half a dozen necessary operations, some one or some two only shall be talked of, and proposed to be done; one, by one bill to be introduced this session, if it be not too late (which you contrive it shall be); another, the next session;

which time being come, nothing more is to be said about the matter
—and there it ends.

For this abandonment, no one reason that will bear looking at can
be numbered up, in the instance of any one of the five measures
endeavoured to be laid upon the shelf; for if it could, that would be
the reason assigned for the relinquishment, and not this unmeaning
assemblage of three syllables.

Transfer the scene to domestic life, and suppose a man who, his
fortune not enabling him without running into debt to keep one
race-horse, has been for some time in the habit of keeping six: to
transfer to this private theatre the wisdom and the benefit of the
gradual system, what you would have to recommend to your friend
would be something of this sort: Spend the first year in considering
which of your six horses to give up; the next year, if you can satisfy
yourself which it shall be, give up some one of them: by this sacrifice,
the sincerity of your intention and your reputation for economy will
be established; which done, you need think no more about the
matter.

As all psychological ideas have their necessary root in physical
ones, one source of delusion in psychological arguments consists in
giving an improper extension to some metaphor which has been
made choice of.

11. *Question-Begging Appellatives (ad judicium)*

Exposition: *Petitio principii*, or begging the question, is a fallacy
very well known even to those who are not conversant with the
principles of logic. In answer to a given question, the party who
employs the fallacy contents himself by simply affirming the point in
debate. Why does opium occasion sleep? Because it is soporiferous.
Exposure: When you have a practice or measure to condemn, find
out some more general appellative within the import of which the
obnoxious practice or measure in question cannot be denied to be
included, and to which you or those whose interests and prejudices
you have espoused, have contrived to annex a certain degree of
unpopularity, in so much that the name of it has contracted a
dyslogistic quality—has become a bad name.

Take, for example, *improvement* and *innovation:* under its own
name to pass censure on any improvement might be too bold:

applied to such an object, any expressions of censure you could employ might lose their force; employing them, you would seem to be running on in the track of self-contradiction and nonsense.

But improvement means something new, and so does *innovation*. Happily for your purpose, *innovation* has contracted a bad sense; it means something which is new and bad at the same time. Improvement, it is true, in indicating something new, indicates something good at the same time; and therefore, if the thing in question be good as well as new, innovation is not a proper term for it. However as the idea of *novelty* was the only idea originally attached to the term innovation, and the only one which is directly expressed in the etymology of it, you may still venture to employ the word innovation, since no man can readily and immediately convict your appellation of being an improper one upon the face of it.

With the appellation thus chosen for the purpose of passing condemnation on the measure, he by whom it has been brought to view in the character of an improvement, is not (it is true) very likely to be well satisfied: but of this you could not have had any expectation. What you want is a pretence which your own partisans can lay hold of, for the purpose of deducing from it a colourable warrant for passing upon the improvement that censure which you are determined, and they, if not determined, are disposed and intend to pass on it.

Of this instrument of deception, the potency is most deplorable. It is but of late years that so much as the nature of it has in any way been laid before the public: and now that it has been laid before the public, the need there is of its being opposed with effect, and the extreme difficulty of opposing it with effect, are at the same time and in equal degree manifest.

12. *Allegorical Idols (ad imaginationem)*

Exposition: The use of this fallacy is the securing to persons in office, respect independent of good behaviour. It consists in substituting to their proper official denomination the name of some fictitious entity, to whom, by customary language, and thence opinion, the attribute of excellence has been attached.

Examples: 1. *Government*; for members of the governing body. 2. *The law*; for lawyers. 3. *The church*; for churchmen. The advantage is, the obtaining for them more respect than might be bestowed on the class under its proper name.

Exposure: 1. *Government.* In its proper sense, in which it designates the set of operations, it is true, and universally acknowledged, that everything valuable to man depends upon it: security against evil in all shapes, from external adversaries as well as domestic.

2. *Law:* execution of the *law*! By this it is that men receive whatsoever protection they receive against domestic adversaries and disturbers of their peace.

By *government—law—the law*—are therefore brought to view the naturalest and worthiest objects of respect and attachment within the sphere of a man's observance: and for conciseness and ornament (not to speak of deception) the corresponding fictitious entities are feigned, and represented as constantly occupied in the performance of the above-mentioned all-preserving operations.

As to the real persons so occupied, if they were presented in their proper character, whether collectively or individually, they would appear clothed in their real qualities, good and bad together. But, as presented by means of this contrivance, they are decked out in all their good and acceptable qualities, divested of all their bad and unacceptable ones. Under the name of the god Aesculapius, Alexander the imposter, his self-constituted high priest, received to his own use the homage and offerings addressed to his god. Acquired, as it is believed, comparatively within late years, this word *government* has obtained a latitude of import in a peculiar degree adapted to the sinister purpose here in question. From *abstract*, the signification has become, as the phrase is, *concrete*. From the system, in all its parts taken together, it has been employed to denote the whole assemblage of the individuals employed in the carrying on of the system—of the individuals who, for the time being, happen to be members of the official establishment, and of these more particularly, and even exclusively, such of them as are members of the administrative branch of that establishment. For the designation either of the branch of the system, or of the members that belong to it, the language had already furnished the word *administration.* But the word administration would not have suited the purpose of this fallacy: accordingly, by those who feel themselves to have an interest in the turning it to account, to the proper word administration, the too ample, and thence improper word *govern-ment*, has been, probably by a mixture of design and accident, commonly substituted.

This impropriety of speech being thus happily and successfully established, the fruits of it are gathered in every day. Point out an abuse—point to this or that individual deriving a profit from the abuse: up comes the cry, 'You are an enemy to government!' then, with a little news in advance, 'Your endeavour is to destroy govern-ment!' Thus you are a Jacobin, an anarchist, and so forth: and the greater the pains you take for causing government to fulfil, to the greatest perfection, the professed ends of its institution the greater the pains taken to persuade those who wish, or are content to be deceived, that you wish and endeavour to destroy it.

13. *Popular Corruption (ad superbiam)*

Exposition: The instrument of deception, of which the argument here in question is composed, may be thus expressed: The source of corruption is in the minds of the people; so rank and extensively seated is that corruption, that no political reform can ever have any effect in it.[e]

Exposure: This fallacy consists in giving to the word corruption, when applied to the people, a sense altogether indeterminate—a

---

[e] This was an argument brought forward against parliamentary reform by William Windham in the House of Commons, and by him insisted on with great emphasis. This man was among the disciples, imitators of, and co-operators with, Edmund Burke— that Edmund Burke with whom the subject many were the swinish multitudes—swinish in nature, and apt therefore to receive the treatment which is apt to be given to swine. In private life, that is, in their dealings with those who were immediately above them—at any rate, such of them as were of their own class—many of these men, many of these haters and calumniators of mankind at large, are not unamiable; but, seduced by that sinister interest which is possessed by them in common, they encourage in one another the anti-social affection in the case where it operates upon the most extensive scale. If, while thus encouraging himself in the hating and condemning the people, a man of this cast finds himself hated by them and, whatever it may happen to him to suffer from it, he has himself to thank for it.

sense in and by which all that is distinctly expressed is the disaffection of the speaker as towards the persons spoken of, imputing to them a bad moral character or cast of mind, but without any intimation given of the particular nature of it.

A circumstance that renders this fallacy in a peculiar degree insidious and dangerous is a sort of obscure reference made by it to certain religious notions—to the doctrine of original sin as delivered in the compendium of Church of England faith, termed the Thirty-nine Articles.

Into the doctrine, considered in a religious point of view, it is not necessary on this occasion to make an inquiry. The field here in question is the field of politics; and, applied to this field, the fallacy in question seeks to lay the axe to the root of all government. It applies not only to *this* but to all other remedies against that preponderance of self-regarding over social interest and affection, which is essential to man's existence, but which, for the creation and preservation of political society, and thence for his well-being in it, requires to be checked—checked by a force formed within itself. It goes to the exclusion of all laws, and in particular of all penal laws; for if, for remedy to what is amiss, nothing is to be attempted by arrangements which, such as those relative to the principle and mode of election as applied to rulers, bring with them no punishment—no infliction—how much less should the accomplishment of any such object be attempted by means so expensive and afflictive as those applied by penal laws!

Nearly akin to the cry of popular corruption is language commonly used to the following effect: 'Instead of reforming others—instead of reforming your betters, instead of reforming the state, the constitution, the church, everything that is most excellent—let each man reform himself—let him look at home; he will find there enough to do, and what is in his power, without looking abroad and aiming at what is out of his power,' etc., etc.

Language to this effect may at all times be heard from antireformists—always, as the tone of it manifests, accompanied with an air of triumph—the triumph of superior wisdom over shallow and presumptuous arrogance.

Certain it is, that if every man's time and labour is exclusively employed in the correcting of his own personal imperfections, no part of it will be employed in the endeavour to correct the imperfections and abuses which have place in the government; and thus the mass of those imperfections and abuses will go on, never diminishing, but perpetually increasing with the torments of those who suffer by them, and the comforts of those who profit by them: which is exactly what is wanted.

14. *Anti-Rational Fallacies (ad verecundiam)*

Exposition: When reason is found or supposed to be in opposition to a man's interests, his study will naturally be to render the faculty itself, and whatsoever issues from it, an object of hatred and content.

1. Sometimes a plan, the adoption of which would not suit the official person's interest, is without more ado pronounced a *speculative* one; and by this observation all need of rational and deliberate discussion—such as objection to the end of proposed, as not a fit one objection to the means employed, as not being fit means—is considered as being superseded.

To the word *speculative*, for further enforcement, are added or substituted, in a number more or less considerable, other terms, as nearly synonymous to it and to one another, as it is usual for words called *synonymous* to be; *viz.* theoretical, visionary, chemical, romantic, utopian.

2. Sometimes a distinction is taken, and thereupon a concession made. The plan is good in theory, but it would be bad in practice; *i.e.* its being good in theory does not hinder its being bad in practice.

3. Sometimes, as if in consequence of a further progress made in the art of irrationality, the plan is pronounced to be too good to be practicable; and its being so good as it is, is thus represented as the very cause of its being bad in practice.

4. In short, such is the perfection at which this art is at length arrived that the very circumstance of a plan's being susceptible of the appellation of a plan, has been gravely stated as a circumstance sufficient to warrant its being rejected; rejected, if not with hatred, at any rate with a sort of accompaniment which, to the million, is commonly felt still more galling—with contempt.

Exposure: What is altogether out of dispute is that many and many a measure has been proposed, to which this class of epithets, or some of them, would be justly applicable. But a man's conceptions must be woefully indistinct, or his vocabulary deplorably scanty if, be the bad measure what it may, he cannot contrive to give intimation of what, in his view, there is bad in it, without employing an epithet, the effect of which is to hold out, as an object of contempt, the very act of thinking—the operation of thought itself.

The fear of theory has to a certain extent its foundation in reason. There is a general propensity in those who adopt this or that theory to push it too far: *i.e.* to set up a general proposition which is not true until certain exceptions have been taken out of it—to set it up without any of those exceptions to pursue it without regard to the xceptions, and thence, *pro tanto*, in cases in which it is false, fallacious, repugnant to reason and utility.

The propensity thus to push theory too far is acknowledged to be almost universal.

But what is the just reference? Not that theoretical propositions, *i.e.* propositions of considerable extent, should from such their extent be concluded to be false *in toto*; but only that, in the particular case, inquiry should be made whether, supposing the proposition to be in the character of a general rule generally true, there may not be a case in which, to reduce it within the limits of truth, reason and utility, an exception ought to be taken out of it.

But from the mere circumstances of its being theoretical, by these enemies to knowledge its falsehood is inferred as if it were a necessary consequence—with as much reason as if, from a man's speaking, it were inferred as a necessary consequence, that what he speaks must be false.

One would think that in thinking there were something wicked or else unwise: everybody feels or fancies a necessity of disclaiming it: 'I am not given to speculation'—'I am no friend to theories'. Speculation, theory, what is it but thinking? Can a man disclaim speculation, can he disclaim theory, without disclaiming thought? If they do not mean thought, they mean nothing; for, unless it be a little more thought than ordinary, theory, speculation, mean nothing.

A plan proposes a wrong end, or, the end being right, proposes a wrong set of means. If this be what a man means, can he not say so? Would not what he says have somewhat more meaning, be a little more consistent with the principles of common sense, with common honesty, than saying of it that it is theoretical, that it is speculative?

C. OF THE MISCHIEF PRODUCIBLE BY FALLACIES

The first division that presents itself in relation to the mischief of a fallacy, may be expressed by the words specific and general.

Ths specific mischief of a fallacy consists in the tendency which it has to prevent or obstruct the introduction of this or that useful measure in particular.

The general mischief consists in that moral or intellectual depravation which produces habits of false reasoning and insincerity.

D. CAUSES OF THE UTTERANCE OF THESE FALLACIES

The causes of the utterance of these fallacies may, it should seem, be thus denominated and enumerated:

1. Sinister interest—self-conscious sinister interest.
2. Interest-begotten prejudice.[2]
3. Authority begotten prejudice.[3]
4. Self-defence, *i.e.* sense of the need of self-defence against counter-fallacies.[4]

E. USES OF THE PRECEDING EXPOSURE

But of these disquisitions concerning the state and character of the mind of those by whom these instruments of deception are employed, what, it may be asked, is the practical use?

The use is, the opposing such check as it may be in the power of reason to apply to the practice of employing these poisoned weapons. In proportion as the virtue of sincerity is an object of love and veneration, the opposite vice is held in abhorrence; the more generally and intimately the public in general are satisfied of the insincerity of him by whom the arguments in question are employed, in that same proportion will be the efficiency of the motive by the force of which a man is withheld from employing these arguments.

Suppose the deceptitious and pernicious tendency of these arguments, and thence the improbity of him who employs them, in such sort help up to view as to find the minds of men sufficiently sensible of it, and suppose, that in the public mind in general, virtue in the form of sincerity is an object of respect, vice in the opposite form an object of aversion and contempt, the practice of this species of improbity will become as rare as is the practice of any other species of improbity to which the restrictive action of the same moral power is in the habit of applying itself with the same force.

Now, the mere *utterance* of these base arguments is not the only, it is not so much as the principal, mischief in the case. It is the reception of them in the character of conclusive or influential arguments that constitutes the principal mischief, the only ultimate mischief. To the object of making men ashamed to utter them must therefore be added the ulterior object of making men ashamed to receive them: ashamed as often as they are observed to see or hear them, ashamed to be known to turn towards them any other aspect than that of aversion and contempt.

But if the practice of insincerity be a practice which a man ought to be ashamed of, so is the practice of giving encouragement to, of forbearing to oppose discouragement to, that vice; and to this same desirable and useful end does that man most contribute by whom the immorality of the practice is held up to view in the strongest and clearest colours.

Nor upon reflection will the result be found so hopeless as at first sight might be supposed. In the most numerous assembly that ever sat in either House, perhaps not a single individual could be found, by whom, in the company of a chaste and well-bred female, an obscene word was ever uttered. And if the frown of indignation were as sure to be drawn down upon the offender by an offence against this branch of the law of probity as by an offence against the law of delicacy, transgression would not be less effectually banished from both those great public theatres than it is already from the domestic circle.

If, of the fallacies in question, the tendency be really pernicious, whosoever he be, who by lawful and unexceptionable means of any kind shall have contributed to this effect, will thereby have rendered to his country and to mankind good service.

But whosoever he be who to the intellectual power adds the moderate portion of pecuniary power necessary, in his power it lies completely to render this good service.

In a printed report of the debates of the assembly in question, supposing any such instruments of deception discoverable, in each instance in which any such instrument is discoverable, let him at the bottom of the page by the help of the usual marks of reference give intimation of it: describing it, for instance, if it be of the number of those which are included in the present list, by the name by which it stands designated in this list, or by any more apt and clearly designative denomination that can be found for it.

For the suppression of this nuisance another very simple and different expedient is almost too obvious to need mentioning. Whatsoever be the theatre of debate a table of these instruments of deception being constructed, let it be kept hung up in view of the whole assembly, and the chairman may be authorised to indicate any delinquency committed by the utterance of any of these instruments of deception.[5]

The want of sufficient time for adequate discussion, when carried on orally in a numerous assembly, has in no inconsiderable extent been held out by experience in the character of a real and serious evil. To this evil, the fallacy table furnishes, to an indefinite extent, a powerful remedy.

In the course of time, when these imperfect sketches shall have received perfection and polish from some more skilful hand, so shall it be done unto him (nor is there need of inspiration for the prophecy), so shall it be done to him, who in the tabernacle of St Stephen's or in any other mansion, higher or lower, of similar design and use, shall be so far off his guard, as through craft or simplicity to let drop any of these irrelevant and at one time deceptitious arguments: and instead of, Order! Order! a voice shall be heard, followed, if need [be] by voices in scores, crying aloud, 'Stale! Stale! Fallacy of authority! Fallacy of distrust!' etc., etc.

The faculty which detection has of divesting deception of her power is attested by the poet:

Quaere peregrinum, vicinia rauca reclamat.

The period at which in the instance of the instruments of deception here in question this change shall have been acknowledged to have been completely effected will form an epoch in the history of civilisation.

CHAPTER 20

A Critical Examination of the Declaration of Rights[1]

[Bentham's preoccupation with what he was later to call anarchical fallacies goes at least as far back as 1776. Referring to the American Declaration of Independence he then wrote: 'This they "hold to be" a "truth self-evident". At the same time to secure these rights they are satisfied that government should be instituted. They see not . . . that nothing that was ever called Government ever was or ever could be exercised but at the expense of one or other of those rights, that . . . some one or other of those pretended inalienable rights is alienated . . . In those tenets they have outdone the extravagance of all former fanatics.' (Cited in Mary Mack, *Jeremy Bentham: An Odyssey of Ideas, 1748–1792*, Heinemann, 1962, p. 186.) Continuing to feel that 'the only effectual antidote against the fascinations of political enthusiasm' lay in a 'sober and accurate apprehension' of the import of fundamental words, Bentham later worked out a careful critique of the French declarations of rights. (Mss. UCL, Box 69, p. 62.) In his letter of 30th June 1801 he unsuccessfully offered his critique, entitled *Pestilential Nonsense Unmasked*, to Cobbett for publication, suggesting that if unsuitable for his purpose, he could pass it on to the editor of the *Anti-Jacobin* (Mss, Box 146, pp. 239–240.) Several years later in 1816 it was finally published by Dumont in French. In 1819 when the question of publishing it in English came up again, Bentham decided against it on the ground that he had changed his views on the subject. Professor Burns is right to wonder if this was Bentham's real reason and to suggest that, having turned radical, Bentham was perhaps anxious not to alienate radicals. See his essay in *Jeremy Bentham: Ten Critical Essays*, op cit.

Bentham's criticism of 'anarchical' or 'anarchy-preacher's' fallacies is contained in three different documents: first, his criticism of the *Declaration of the Rights of Man and the Citizen*

9

decreed by the French Constituent Assembly in 1791; second his criticism of the 1795 *Declaration of Rights and Duties of the Man and the Citizen*; and, finally, his criticism of the Declaration of Rights by Citizen Sieyes. Of the three the first is obviously the most interesting. As Bentham's criticism of the 1795 *Declaration* does not say anything not said by the other two, I have ignored it.]

Preliminary observations

The Declaration of Rights—I mean the paper published under that name by the French National Assembly in 1791—assumes for its subject-matter a field of disquisition as unbounded in point of extent as it is important in its nature. But the more ample the extent given to any proposition or string of propositions, the more difficult it is to keep the import of it confined without deviation within the bounds of truth and reason. If in the smallest corner of the field it ranges over, it fail of coinciding with the line of rigid rectitude, no sooner is the aberration pointed out, than (inasmuch as there is no medium between truth and falsehood) its pretensions to the appellation of a truism are gone, and whoever looks upon it must recognise it to be false and erroneous—and if, as here, political conduct be the theme, so far as the error extends and fails of being detected, pernicious.

In a work of such extreme importance with a view to practice, and which throughout keeps practice so closely and immediately and professedly in view, a single error may be attended with the most fatal consequences. The more extensive the propositions, the more consummate will be the knowledge, the more exquisite the skill indispensably requisite to confine them in all points within the pale of truth. The most consummate ability in the whole nation would not have been too much for the task—one may venture to say, it would not even have been equal to it. But that in the sanctioning of each proposition, the most consummate ability should happen to be vested in the heads of the sorry majority in whose hands the plenitude of power happened on that same occasion to be vested, is an event against which the chances are almost as infinity to one.

Here, then, is a radical and all-pervading error—the attempting to give to a work on such a subject the sanction of government;

especially of such a government—a government composed of members so numerous, so unequal in talents as well as discordant in inclinations and affections. Had it been the work of a single hand, and that a private one, and in that character given to the world, every good effect would have been produced by it that could be produced by it when published as the work of government, without any of the bad effects which in case of the smallest error must result from it when given as the work of governments.

The revolution, which threw the government into the hands of the penners and adopters of this declaration, having been the effect of insurrection, the grand object is evidently to justify the cause. But by justifying it, they invite it: in justifying past insurrection, they plant and cultivate a propensity to perpetual insurrection in time future. They sow the seeds of anarchy broadcast: in justifying the demolition of existing authorities, they undermine all future ones, their own consequently in the number. Shallow and reckless vanity! They initiate in their conduct the author of that fabled law, according to which the assassination of the prince upon the throne gave to the assassin a title to succeed him. 'People, behold your rights! Let upon[2] a single article of them be violated, insurrection is not your right only, but the most sacred of your duties.' Such is the constant language, for such is the professed object, of this source and model of all laws—this self-consecrated oracle of all nations.

The more abstract—that is, the more extensive the proposition is, the more liable [is it] to involve a fallacy. Of fallacies, one of the most natural modifications is that which is called begging the question—the abuse of making the abstract proposition resorted to for proof, a cover[3] for introducing, in the company of other propositions that are nothing to the purpose, the very proposition which is admitted to stand in need of proof.

Is the provision in question fit in point of expediency [to be] passed into a law for the government of the French nation? That, *mutatis mutandis*, would have been the question put in England. That is the proper question to have been put in relation to each provision proposed to enter into the composition of the body of French laws.

Instead of that, as often as the utility of a provision appeared (by reason of the wideness of its extent, for instance) of a doubtful nature, the way taken to clear the doubt was to assert it to be a provision fit to be made law for all men—for all Frenchmen—and for all Englishmen, for example, into the bargain. This medium of proof was the more alluring, inasmuch as to the advantage of removing opposition, was added the pleasure, the sort of titillation so exquisite to the nerve of vanity in a French heart—the satisfaction, to use a homely, but not the less apposite proverb, of teaching grandmothers to suck eggs. Hark! ye citizens of the other side of the water! Can you tell us what rights you have yet belonging to you? No, that you can't. It's we that understand rights: not our own only, but yours into the bargain; while you, poor simple souls! know nothing about the matter.

Hasty generalisation, the great stumbling-block of intellectual vanity!—hasty generalisation, the rock that even genius itself is so apt to split upon!—hasty generalisation, the bane of prudence and of science!

In the British Houses of Parliament, more especially in the most efficient house for business, there prevails a well-known jealousy of, and repugnance to, the voting of abstract propositions. This jealousy is not less general than reasonable. A jealousy of abstract propositions is an aversion to whatever is beside the purpose—an aversion to impertinence.

The great enemies of public peace are the selfish and dissocial passions: necessary as they are, the one to the very existence of each individual, the other to his security. On the part of these affections, a deficiency in point of strength is never to be apprehended: all that is to be apprehended in respect of them, is to be apprehended on the side of their excess. Society is held together only by the sacrifices that men can be induced to make of the gratifications they demand: to obtain these sacrifices is the great difficulty, the great task of government. What has been the object, the perpetual and palpable object, of this declaration of pretended rights? To add as much force as possible to these passions, already but too strong, to burst all the ties that hold them in, to say to the selfish passions, there—everywhere—is your prey!—to the angry passions, there—everywhere—is your enemy.

Such is the morality of this celebrated manifesto, rendered

famous by the same qualities that gave celebrity to the incendiary of the Ephesian temple.

The logic of it is of a piece with its morality: a perpetual vein of nonsense flowing from a perpetual abuse of words, words having a variety of meanings where words with single meanings were equally at hand; the same words used in a variety of meanings in the same page; words used in meanings not their own where proper words were equally at hand; words and propositions of the most unbounded signification turned loose without any of those exceptions or modifications which are so necessary on every occasion to reduce their import within the compass, not only of right reason, but even of the design in hand, of whatever nature it may be; the same inaccuracy, the same inattention in the penning of this cluster of truths on which the fate of nations was to hang, as if it had been an oriental tale, or an allegory for a magazine: stale epigrams, instead of necessary distinctions; figurative expressions preferred to simple ones; sentimental conceits, as trite as they are unmeaning, preferred to apt and precise expressions; frippery ornament preferred to the majestic simplicity of good sense, and the acts of the senate loaded and disfigured by the tinsel of the playhouse.

In a play or a novel, an improper word is but a word: and the impropriety, whether noticed or not, is attended with no consequences. In a body of laws, especially of laws given as constitutional and fundamental ones, an improper word may be a national calamity: and civil war may be the consequence of it. Out of one foolish word may start a thousand daggers.

Imputations like these may be styled general and declamatory, and rightly so, if they stood alone: but they will be justified even to satiety by the details that follow. Scarce an article which in rummaging it will not be found a true Pandora's box.

In running over the several articles, I shall on the occasion of each article point out, in the first place, the errors it contains in theory; and then, in the second place, the mischiefs it is pregnant with in practice.

The criticism is verbal: true, but what else can it be? Words— words without a meaning, or with a meaning too flatly false to be maintained by anybody, are the stuff it is made of. Look to the letter, you find nonsense; look beyond the letter, you find nothing.

ARTICLE I

Men (all men) are born and remain free, and equal in respect of rights. Social distinctions cannot be founded, but upon common utility.

In this article are contained two distinct sentences grammatically speaking. The first is full of error, the other of ambiguity.

In the first are contained four distinguishable propositions, all of them false—all of them notoriously and undeniably false:

1. That all men are born free.
2. That all men remain free.
3. That all men are born equal in rights.
4. That all men remain (*i.e.* remain for ever, for the proposition is indefinite and unlimited) equal in rights.

All men are born free? All men remain free? No, not a single man: not a single man that ever was, or is, or will be. All men, on the contrary, are born in subjection, and the most absolute subjection— the subjection of a helpless child to the parents on whom he depends every moment for his existence. In this subjection every man is born, in this subjection he continues for years, for a great number of years, and the existence of the individual and of the species depends upon his so doing.

What is the state of things to which the supposed existence of these supposed rights is meant to bear reference? A state of things prior to the existence of government, or a state of things subsequent to the existence of government? If to a state of things prior to the existence of government, what would the existence of such rights as these be to the purpose, even if it were true, in any country where there is such a thing as government? If to a state of things subsequent to the formation of government, if in a country where there is a government, in what single instance, in the instance of what single government, is it true? Setting aside the case of parents and child, let any man name that single government under which any such equality exists, in which any such equality is recognised.

All men born free? Absurd and miserable nonsense! When the great complaint, a complaint made perhaps by the very same people at the same time, is that so many men are born slaves. Oh! but when we acknowledge them to be born slaves, we refer to the laws in being; which laws being void, as being contrary to those laws of nature which are the efficient causes of those rights of man that we are declaring, the men in question are free in one sense, though slaves in another; slaves, and free, at the same time: free in respect of the laws of nature, slaves in respect of the pretended human laws, which, though called laws, are no laws at all, as being contrary to the laws of nature. For such is the difference, the great and perpetual difference, betwixt the good subject, the rational censor of the laws, and the anarchist—between the moderate man and the man of violence. The rational censor, acknowledging the existence of the law he disapproves, proposes the repeal of it: the anarchist, setting up his will and fancy for a law before which all mankind are called upon to bow down at the first word—the anarchist, trampling on truth and decency, denies the validity of the law in question, denies the existence of it in the character of a law, summoning all mankind to rise up in a mass, and resist the execution of it.

Whatever is, is—was the maxim of Descartes, who looked upon it as so certain as well as so instructive a truth, that everything else which goes by the name of knowledge might be deduced from it. The philosophical vortex-maker who, however mistaken in his philosophy and his logic, was harmless enough at least, the manufacturer of identical propositions and celestial vortices—little thought how soon a part of his own countrymen, fraught with pretensions as empty as his own, and as mischievous as his were innocent, would contest with him even this his favourite and fundamental maxim, by which everything else was to be brought to light. Whatever is, is not—is the maxim of the anarchist, as often as anything comes across him in the shape of a law which he happens not to like.

Cruel is the judge, says Lord Bacon, who, in order to enable himself to torture men, applies torture to the laws. Still more cruel is the anarchist, who, for the purpose of effecting the subversion of the laws themselves, as well as the massacre of the legislators, tortures not only the words of the law, but the very vitals of the language.

All men are born equal in rights. The rights of the heir of the most indigent family equal to the rights of the heir of the most wealthy. In what case is this true? I say nothing of hereditary dignities and powers. Inequalities such as these being proscribed under and by the French government in France, are consequently proscribed by that government under every other government, and consequently have no existence anywhere. For the total subjection of every other government to French government is a fundamental principle in the law of universal independence—the French law. Yet neither was this true at the time of issuing this Declaration of Rights, nor was it meant to be so afterwards. The 13th article, which we shall come to in its place, proceeds on the contrary supposition. For considering its other attributes, inconsistency could not be wanting to the list. It can scarcely [be] more hostile to all other laws than it is at variance with itself.

All men (i.e. all human creatures of both sexes) remain equal in rights. All men, meaning doubtless all human creatures. The apprentice, then, is equal in rights to his master; he has as much liberty with relation to the master, as the master has with relation to him; he has as much right to command and punish the master as the master has to command and punish him, he is as much owner and master of the master's house, as the master himself. The case is the same as between ward on the death of a father and guardian. So again as between wife and husband. The madman has as good a right to confine anybody else as anybody else has to confine him. The idiot has as much right to govern everybody as anybody can have to govern him. The physician and the nurse, when called in by the next friends of a sick man seized with a delirium have no more right to prevent his throwing himself out of the window, than he has to throw them out of it. All this is plainly and incontestably included in this article of the Declaration of Rights: in the very words of it, and in the meaning—if it have any meaning. Was this the meaning of the authors of it? Or did they mean to admit this explanation as to some of the instances, and to explain the article away as to the rest? Not being idiots, nor lunatics, nor under a delirium, they would explain it away with regard to the madman, and the man under a delirium. Considering that a child may become an orphan as soon as it has seen the light, and that in that case, if not subject to government, it must perish, they would explain it away, I think, and contradict themselves, in the case of guardian and ward.

In the case of master and apprentice, I would not take upon me to decide. It may have been their meaning to proscribe that relation altogether. At least, this may have been the case, as soon as the repugnancy between that institution and this oracle was pointed out. For the professed object and destination of it is to be the standard of truth and falsehood, of right and wrong, in everything that relates to government. But to this standard, and to this article of it, the subjection of the apprentice to the master is flatly and diametrically repugnant. If it do not proscribe this inequality, it proscribes none: if it does not so this mischief, it does nothing.

So, again, in the case of husband and wife. Amongst the other abuses which the oracle was meant to put an end to, may, for aught I can pretend to say, have been the institution of marriage. For what is the subjection of a small and limited number of years, in comparison of the subjection of a whole life? Yet without subjection and inequality, no such institution can by any possibility take place; for of two contradictory wills, both cannot take place at the same time.

I have the same doubts with regard to the case of master and hired servant. Better a man should starve than hire himself; better half the species starve, than hire itself out to service. For where is the compatibility between liberty and servitude, for how can liberty and servitude subsist in the same person? What good citizen is there, that would hesitate to die for liberty? And, as to those who are not good citizens, what matters is whether they live or starve? Besides that every men who lives under this constitution being equal in rights, equal in all sorts of rights, is equal in respect to rights of property. No man, therefore, can be in any danger of starving: no man can have so much as that motive, weak and inadequate as it is, for letting himself out to service.

Sentence 2. Social distinctions can not be founded but upon common utility. This proposition has two or three meanings. According to one of them, the proposition is notoriously false: according to another, it is in contradiction to the four propositions that preceded it in the same sentence.

What is meant by social distinctions? What is meant by can? What is meant by founded?

What is meant by social distinctions? Distinctions not respecting equality? Then these are nothing to the purpose. Distinctions in

respect of equality? Then, consistently with the preceding propositions in this same article, they can have no existence: not existing,
they cannot be founded upon anything. The distinctions above
exemplified, are they in the number of the social distinctions here
intended? Not one of them (as we have been seeing), but has
subjection—not one of them, but has inequality for its very essence.

What is meant by can not be founded but upon common utility?
Is it meant to speak of what is established, or of what *ought to be
established*? Does it mean that no social distinctions but those
which it approves of as having the foundation in question, *are*
established anywhere, or simply that none such ought to be
established anywhere? Or that, if the establishment or maintenance
of such dispositions by the laws is attempted anywhere, such laws
ought to be treated as void, and the attempt to execute them to be
resisted? For such is the venom that lurks under such words as can
and can not when set up as a check upon the laws. They contain
all these three so perfectly distinct and widely different meanings.
In the first, the proposition they are inserted into refers to practice,
and makes an appeal to observation—to the observation of other men
in regard to a matter of fact: in the second, it is an appeal to the
approving faculty of others in regard to the same matter of fact;
in the third, it is no appeal to anything or to anybody, but a violent
attempt upon liberty of speech and action on the part of others by
the terrors of anarchical despotism, rising up in opposition to the
laws. It is an attempt to lift the dagger of the assassin against all
individuals who presume to hold an opinion different from that of
the orator or the writer, and against all governments who presume
to support any such individuals in any such presumption. In the
first of these imports, the proposition is perfectly harmless: but
it is commonly so untrue, so glaringly untrue, so palpably untrue,
even to drivelling, that it must be plain to everybody it can never
have been the meaning that was intended.

In the second or these imports the proposition may be true or
not, as it may happen, and at any rate is equally innocent: but it is
such as will not answer the purpose; for an opinion that leaves
others at liberty to be of a contrary one will never answer the purpose
of the passions: and if this had been the meaning intended, not this
ambiguous phraseology, but a clear and simple one presenting

this meaning and no other would have been employed. The third, which may not improperly be termed the ruffian-like or threatening import is the meaning intended to be presented to the weak and timid, while the two innocent ones, of which one may even be reasonable, are held up before it as a veil to blind the eyes of the discerning reader, and screen from him the mischief that lurks beneath.

Can and can not, when thus applied, can and can not when used instead of ought and ought not; can and can not, when applied to the binding force and effect of laws—not of the acts of individuals, nor yet of the acts of subordinate authority, but of the acts of the supreme government itself, are the disguised cant of the assassin: after them there is nothing but do it, betwixt the preparation for murder and the attempt. They resemble that instrument which in outward appearance is but an ordinary staff, but which within that simple and innocent semblance conceals a dagger. These are the words that speak daggers, if daggers can be spoken: they speak daggers, and there remains nothing but to use them.

Look where I will, I see but too many laws, the alteration or abolition of which would in my poor judgment be a public blessing. I can conceive some, to put extreme and scarcely exampled cases, to which I might be inclined to oppose resistance, with a prospect of support such as promised to be effectual. But to talk of what the law, the supreme legislature of the country, acknowledged as such, can not do! To talk of a void law as you would of a void order or a void judgment! The very act of bringing such words into conjunction is either the vilest of nonsense, or the worst of treasons: treason, not against one branch of the sovereignty, but against the whole: treason, not against this or that government, but against all governments.

ARTICLE II

The end in view of every political association is the preservation of the natural and imprescriptible rights of man. These rights are liberty, prosperity, security, and resistance to oppression.

Sentence 1. The end in view of every political association is the preservation of the natural and imprescriptible rights of man.

More confusion—more nonsense, and the nonsense, as usual, dangerous nonsense. The words can scarcely be said to have a meaning: but if they have, or rather if they had a meaning, these would be the propositions either asserted or implied:

1. That there are such things as rights anterior to the establishment of governments: for *natural*, as applied to rights, if it meant anything, is meant to stand in opposition to legal; to such rights as are acknowledged to owe their existence to government, and are consequently posterior in their date to the establishment of government.

2. That these rights can not be abrogated by government: for can not is implied in the form of the word imprescriptible, and the sense it wears when so applied, is the cut-throat sense above explained.

3. That the governments that exist derive their origin from formal associations or what are now called conventions: associations entered into by a partnership contract with all the members for partners, entered into at a day prefixed for a predetermined purpose, the formation of a new government where there was none before; for as to formal meetings holden under the control of an existing government, they are evidently out of question here. In which it seems again to be implied in the way of inference, though a necessary and an unavoidable inference, that all governments (that is, self-called governments, knots of persons exercising the powers of government) that have had any other origin than an association of the above description, are illegal, that is, no governments at all; resistance to them, and subversion of them, lawful and commendable; and so on.

Such are the notions implied in this first part of the article. How stands the truth of things? That there are no such things as natural rights, no such things as rights anterior to the establishment of government, no such things as natural rights opposed to, in contradistinction to, legal; that the expression is merely figurative; that when used, in the moment you attempt to give it a literal meaning it leads to error, and to that sort of error that leads to mischief, to the extremity of mischief.

We know what it is for men to live without government and, living without government, to live without rights; we know what it is for men to live without government, for we see instances of such a way of life in abundance. We see it in many savage nations, or rather races of mankind; for instance, among the savages of New South Wales, whose way of living is so well known to us: no habit of obedience, and thence no government; no government, and thence no laws; no laws, and thence nor any such things as rights, no security, no property: liberty, as against regular control, the control of laws and government, perfect; but as against all irregular control, the mandates of stronger individuals, none. In this state, at a time earlier than the commencement of history—in this same state, judging from analogy, we, the inhabitants of the part of the globe we call Europe, were; no government, consequently no rights: no rights, consequently no property; no legal security, no legal liberty: security not more than belongs to beasts—forecast and sense of insecurity keener—consequently in point of happiness below the level of the brutal race.

In proportion to the want of happiness resulting from the want of rights, a reason [exists] for wishing that there were such things as rights. But reasons for wishing there were such things as rights, are not rights; a reason for wishing that a certain right were established, is not that right; want is not supply; hunger is not bread.

That which has no existence cannot be destroyed; that which cannot be destroyed cannot require anything to preserve it from being destroyed. Natural rights is simple nonsense: natural and imprescriptible rights, rhetorical nonsense, nonsense upon stilts. But this rhetorical nonsense ends in the old strain of mischievous nonsense; for immediately a loss of these pretended natural rights is given, and those are so expressed as to present to view legal rights. And of these rights, whatever they are, there is not, it seems, any one of which any government can, in the cut-throat sense of the word *can* upon any occasion whatever, abrogate the smallest particle.

So much for terrorist language. What is the language of reason and plain sense upon this same subject? That in proportion as it is right and proper, *i.e.* advantageous to the society in question, that this or that right, a right to this or that effect, should be established and maintained, in that same proportion it is wrong that it should be abrogated; but that as there is no right which ought not to be maintained so long as it is upon the whole advantageous to the society that it should be maintained, so there is no right which, when the abolition of it is advantageous to society, should not be abolished. To know whether it would be more for the advantage of society that this or that right should be maintained or abolished, the time at which the question about maintaining or abolishing is proposed must be given, and the circumstances under which it is proposed to maintain or abolish it; the right itself must be specifically described, not jumbled with an undistinguishable heap of others under any such vague general terms as property, liberty, and the like.

One thing in the midst of all this confusion is but too plain. They know not what they are talking of under the name of natural rights, and yet they would have them imprescriptible, proof against all the power of the laws, pregnant with occasions summoning the members of the community to rise up in resistance against the laws. What, then, was their object in declaring the existence of imprescriptible rights, and without specifying a single one by any such mark as it could be known by? This and no other—to excite and keep up a spirit of resistance to all laws, a spirit of insurrection against all governments, against the governments of all other nations instantly, against the government of their own nation, against the government they themselves were pretending to establish, even that is as soon as their own reign should be at an end. In us is the perfection of virtue and wisdom: in all mankind besides, the extremity of wickedness and folly. Our will shall consequently reign without control, and for ever: reign now we are living— reign after we are dead. All nations, all future ages, shall be, for they are predestined to be, our slaves. Future governments will not have honesty enough to be trusted with the determination of what rights shall be maintained, what abrogated—what laws kept in force, what repealed. Future subjects (I should say future citizens, for French government does not admit of subjects) will not have wit enough to be trusted with the choice whether to submit to the determination of the government of their time or to resist it; governments, citizens, all to the end of time, all must be kept in chains.

Such are their maxims, such their premises; for it is by such premises only that the doctrine of imprescriptible rights and unrepealable laws can be supported.

What is the true source of these imprescriptible rights, these unrepealable laws? Power turned blind by looking from its own height: self-conceipt and tyranny exalted into insanity. No man was to have any other man for a servant, yet all men were forever to be their slaves. Making laws on pretence of declaring them; giving for laws anything that came uppermost, and these unrepealable ones, on pretence of finding them ready made. Made by what? Not by a god—they allow of none; but by their goddess, Nature.

The origination of governments from a contract is a pure fiction, or in other words, a falsehood. It never has been known to be true in any instance; the allegation of it does mischief by involving the subject in error and confusion, and is neither necessary nor useful to any one good purpose whatsoever.

All governments that we have any account of have been gradually established by habit, after having been formed by force; unless in the instance of governments formed by individuals that have been emancipated, or emancipated themselves, from governments already formed, the governments under which they were born—a rare case, and from which nothing follows with regard to the rest. What signifies it how governments are formed? Is it the less proper, the less conducive to the happiness of society, that the happiness of society should be the one object kept in view by the members of the government in all their measures? Is it less the interest of men to be happy, less to be wished that they may be so, less the moral duty of their governors to make them so, as far as they can, at Mogadore than at Philadelphia?

Whence is it but government that contracts derive their binding force? Contracts came from government, not government from contracts. It is to the habit of enforcing contracts, and seeing them enforced, that governments are chiefly indebted for whatever disposition they have to observe them.

Sentence 2. These rights (these imprescriptible as well as natural rights,) are liberty, property, security, and resistance to oppression.

Observe the extent of these pretended rights, each of them belonging to every man, and all of them without bounds. Unbounded liberty; that is, amongst other things, the liberty of doing or not doing on every occasion whatever each man pleases; unbounded property; that is, the right of doing with everything around him (with every thing at least, if not with every person), whatever he pleases; communicating that right to anybody, and withholding it from anybody he pleases; unbounded security; that is, security for such his liberty, for such his property, and for his person, against every defalcation that can be called for on any account in respect of any of them; unbounded resistance to oppression; that is, unbounded exercise of the faculty of guarding himself against whatever unpleasant circumstance may present itself to his imagination or his passions under that name. Nature, say some of the interpreters of the pretended law of nature, gave to each man a right to everything; which is, in effect, but another way of saying, nature has given no such right to anybody; for in regard to most rights, it is as true that what is every man's right is no man's right, as that what is every man's business is no man's business. Nature gave, gave to every man, a right to everything. Be it so, and hence the necessity of human government and human laws to give to every man his own right, without which no right whatsoever would amount to anything. Nature gave every man a right to everything before the existence of laws, and in default of laws. This nominal universality and real nonentity of right, set up provisionally by nature in default of laws, the French oracle lays hold of, and perpetuates it under the law and in spite of laws. These anarchical rights that nature had set out with, democratic art attempts to rivet down and declares them indefeasible.

Unbounded liberty—I must still say unbounded liberty; for though the next article but one returns to the charge, and gives such a definition of liberty as seems intended to set bounds to it, yet in effect the limitation amounts to nothing; and when, as here, no warning is given of any exception in the texture of the general rule, every exception which turns up is not a confirmation but a contradiction of the rule: liberty, without any pre-announced or intelligible bounds; and as to the other rights, they remain unbounded to the end: rights of man composed of a system of contradictions and impossibilities.

In vain would it be said, that though no bounds are here assigned to any of these rights, yet it is to be understood as taken for granted, and tacitly admitted and assumed that they are to have bounds; *viz.* such bounds as it is understood will be set them by the laws. Vain, I say, would be this apology; for the supposition would be contradictory to the express declaration of the article itself, and would defeat the very object which the whole declaration has in view. It would be self-contradictory, because these rights are, in the same breath in which their existence is declared, declared to be imprescriptible; and imprescriptible, or, as we in England should say, indefeasible, means nothing unless it exclude the interference of the laws.

It would be not only inconsistent with itself, but inconsistent with the declared and sole object of the declaration, if it did not exclude the interference of the laws. It is against the laws themselves, and the laws only, that this declaration is levelled. It is for the hands of the legislator and all legislators, and none but legislators, that the shackles it provides are intended; it is against the apprehended encroachments of legislators that the rights in question, the liberty and property, and so forth, are intended to be made secure; it is to such encroachments, and damages, and dangers, that whatever security it professes to give has respect. Precious security for unbounded rights against legislators, if the extent of those rights in every direction were purposely left to depend upon the will and pleasure of those very legislators!

Nonsensical or nugatory, and in both cases mischievous: such is the alternative.

So much for all these pretended indefeasible rights in the lump: their inconsistency with each other, as well as the inconsistency of them in the character of indefeasible rights with the existence of government and all peaceable society, will appear still more plainly when we examine them one by one.

1. Liberty, then, is imprescriptible, incapable of being taken away, out of the power of any government ever to take away: liberty, that is, every branch of liberty, every individual exercise of liberty; for no line is drawn—no distinction—no exception made. What these instructors as well as governors of mankind appear not to know is that all rights are made at the expense of liberty—all laws by which rights are created or confirmed; no right without a correspondent obligation. Liberty, as against the

coercion of the law, may, it is true, be given by the simple removal
of the obligation by which that coercion was applied, by the simple
repeal of the coercing law. But as against the coercion applicable
by individual to individual, no liberty can be given to one man
but in proportion as it is taken from another. All coercive laws,
therefore (that is, all laws but constitutional laws, and laws repealing
or modifying coercive laws,) and in particular all laws creative of
liberty are, as far as they go, abrogative of liberty. Not here and
there a law only, not this or that possible law, but almost all laws,
are therefore repugnant to these natural and imprescriptible rights:
consequently null and void, calling for resistance and insurrection,
and so on, as before.

2. Second species of natural and imprescriptible right: rights of
property. Laws creative of those rights are still struck by the same
anathema. How is property given? By restraining liberty; that is, by
taking it away so far as is necessary for the purpose. How is your
house made yours? By my being debarred from the liberty of
entering it without your leave.

Proprietary[4] rights are in the number of the natural and imprescriptible rights of man—of the rights which a man is not
indebted for to the laws, and which cannot be taken from him by
the laws. Men, that is, every man (for a general expression given
without exception is a universal one) has a right to property, to
proprietary rights, and which cannot be taken away from him by
the laws. To proprietary rights—good; but in relation to what
subject? for as to proprietary rights—without a subject to which
they are referable—without a subject in or in relation to which
they can be exercised—they will hardly be of much value, will
hardly be worth taking care of with so much solemnity. In vain
would all the laws in the world have ascertained that I have a right
to something. If this be all they have done for me, if there be no
specific subject in relation to which my proprietary rights are
established, I must either take what I want without right, or
starve. As there is no such subject specified with relation to each
man, or to any man (indeed how could there be?) the necessary
inference (taking the passage literally) is that every man has all
manner of proprietary rights with relation to every subject of
property without exception: in a word, that every man has a right to

every thing. Accordingly *nature dedit unicingua*: there the proposition is left as indefinite with regard to the designation of the subject of property as with regard to the designation of the owners.

It will probably be acknowledged that according to this construction, the clause in question is equally ruinous and absurd: and hence the inference may be that this was not the construction, this was not the meaning in view. But by the same rule every possible construction which the words employed can admit of might be proved not to have been the meaning in view: nor is this clause a whit more absurd or ruinous than all that goes before it and a great deal of what comes after it. And, in short, if this be not the meaning of it, what is? Give it a sense, give it any sense whatever, it is mischievous; to save it from that imputation, there is but one course to take, which is to acknowledge it to be nonsense.

Thus much would be clear, if anything were clear in it, that according to this clause, whatever proprietary rights, whatever property a man once has, no matter how, being imprescriptible, can never be taken away from him by any law: or of what use or meaning is the clause? So that the moment it is acknowledged in relation to any article, that that article is my property, no matter how or whence it became so, that moment it is acknowledged that it can never be taken away from me; therefore, for example, all laws and all judgments, whereby anything is taken away from me without my free consent, all taxes, for example, and all fines, are void, and, as such, call for resistance and insurrection, and so forth, as before.

3. Security. Security stands third in the list of these natural and imprescriptible rights which laws did not give, and which laws are not in any degree to be suffered to take away. Under the head of security, liberty might have been included, so likewise property: since security for liberty, or the enjoyment of liberty, may be spoken of as a branch of security; security for property, or the enjoyment of proprietary rights, as another. Security for person is the branch that seems here to have been understood; security for each man's person as against all those hurtful or disagreeable impressions (exclusive of those which consist in the mere disturbance of the enjoyment of liberty,) by which a man is affected in his person; which have a man's person for their subject: loss of

life, loss of limbs, loss of the use of limbs, wounds, bruises, and the like. All laws are null and void, then, which on any account or in any manner seek to expose the person of any man to any risk, which appoint capital or other corporal punishment, which expose a man to personal hazard in the service of the military power against foreign enemies, or in that of the judicial power against delinquents: all laws which, to preserve the country from pestilence, authorise the immediate execution of a suspected person, in the event of his transgressing certain bounds.

4. Resistance to oppression. Fourth and last in the list of natural and imprescriptible rights, resistance to oppression—meaning, I suppose, the right to resist oppression. What is oppression? Power misapplied to the prejudice of some individual. What is it that a man has in view when he speaks of oppression? Some exertion of power which he looks upon as misapplied to the prejudice of some individual, to the producing on the part of such individual some suffering to which (whether as forbidden by the laws or otherwise) we conceive he ought not to have been subjected. But against everything that can come under the name of oppression, provision has been already made, in the manner we have seen, by the recognition of the three preceding rights; since no oppression can fall upon a man which is not an infringement of his rights in relation to liberty, rights in relation to property, or rights in relation to security, as above described. Where, then, is the difference? To what purpose this fourth clause after the three first? To this purpose: the mischief they seek to prevent, the rights they seek to establish, are the same; the difference lies in the nature of the remedy endeavoured to be applied. To prevent the mischief in question, the endeavour of the three former clauses is to tie the hand of the legislator and his subordinates, by the fear of nullity and the remote apprehension of general resistance and insurrection. The aim of this fourth clause is to raise the hand of the individual concerned to prevent the apprehended infraction of his rights at the moment when he looks upon it as about to take place.

Whenever you are about to be oppressed, you have a right to resist oppression: whenever you conceive yourself to be oppressed, conceive yourself to have a right to make resistance, and act accordingly. In proportion as a law of any kind, any act of power, supreme or subordinate, legislative, administrative, or judicial, is unpleasant to a man, especially if, in consideration of such its unpleasantness, his opinion is, that such act of power ought not to have been exercised, he of course looks upon it as oppression. As often as anything of this sort happens to a man, to inflame his passions, this article, for fear his passions should not be sufficiently inflamed of themselves, sets itself to work to fan the flame, and urges him to resistance. Submit not to any decree or other act of power of the justice of which you are not yourself perfectly convinced. If a constable calls upon you to serve in the militia, shoot the constable and not the enemy; if the commander of a press-gang trouble you, push him into the sea; if a bailiff, throw him out of the window. If a judge sentences you to be imprisoned or put to death, have a dagger ready, and take a stroke first at the judge.

ARTICLE IV[5]

Liberty consists in being able to do that which is not hurtful to another, and therefore the exercise of the natural rights of each man has no other bounds than those which insure to the other members of the society the enjoyment of the same rights. These bounds cannot be determined but by law.

In this article, three propositions are included:

Proposition 1. Liberty consists in being able to do that which is not hurtful to another. What, in that, and nothing else? Is not the liberty of doing mischief liberty? If not, what is it? and what word is there for it in the language, or in any language by which it can be spoken of? How childish, how repugnant to the ends of language, is this perversion of language! To attempt to confine a word in common and perpetual use, to an import to which nobody ever confined it before, or will continue to confine it! And so I am never to know whether I am at liberty or not to do or to omit doing one act, till I see whether or no there is anybody that may be hurt by it— till I see the whole extent of all its consequences? Liberty! What liberty? As against what power? As against coercion from what source? As against coercion issuing from the law? Then to know whether the law has left me at liberty in any respect in relation to any act, I am to consult not the words of the law, but my own conception of what would be the consequences of the act. If among these consequences there be a single one by which anybody would be hurt, then, whatever the law says to me about it, I am not at liberty to do it. I am an officer of justice, appointed to superintend the execution of punishments ordered by justice. If an officer of justice is ordered to cause a thief to be whipped, to know whether he is at liberty to cause the sentence to be executed, he must know whether whipping would hurt the thief: if it would, then the officer is not at liberty to whip the thief, to inflict the punishment which it is his duty to inflict.

Proposition 2. And so the exercise of the natural rights of each man has no other bounds than those which insure to the other members of the society the enjoyment of those same rights. Has no other bounds? Where is it that it has no other bounds? In what nation? Under what government? If under any government, then the state of legislation under that government is in a state of absolute perfection. If there be no such government, then, by a confession necessarily implied, there is no nation upon earth in which this definition is conformable to the truth.

Proposition 3. These bounds cannot be determined but by the law. More contradiction, more confusion. What then? This liberty, this right, which is one of four rights that existed before laws, and will exist in spite of all that laws can do, owes all the boundaries it has, all the extent it has, to the laws. Till you know what the laws say to it, you do not know what there is of it, nor what account to give of it: and yet it existed, and that in full force and vigour, before there were any such things as laws; and so will continue to exist, and that for ever, in spite of anything which laws can do to it. Still the same inaptitude of expressions, still the same confusion of that which it is supposed is, with that which it is conceived *ought to be*.

What says plain truth upon this subject? What is the sense most approaching to this nonsense?

The liberty which the law ought to allow of, and leave in existence, leave uncoerced, unremoved, is the liberty which concerns those acts only by which, if exercised, no damage would be done to the community upon the whole; that is, either no damage at all or none but what promises to be compensated by at least equal benefit.

Accordingly, the exercise of the rights allowed to and conferred upon each individual ought to have no other bounds set to it by the law than those which are necessary to enable it to maintain every other individual in the possession and exercise of such rights as the regard due to the interests or greatest possible happiness of the whole community taken together admit of his being allowed. The marking out of these bounds ought not to be left to anybody but the legislator acting as such, to anybody but him or them who are acknowledged to be in possession of the sovereign power: that is, it [ought] not to be left to the occasional and arbitrary declaration of any individual, whatever share he may possess of subordinate authority.

The word *autrui*—another is so loose, making no distinction between the community and individuals, as, according to the most natural construction, to deprive succeeding legislators of all power of repressing, by punishment or otherwise, any acts by which no individual sufferers are to be found; and to deprive them beyond a doubt of all power of affording protection to any man, woman, or child, against his or her own weakness, ignorance, or imprudence....[6]

ARTICLE V

The law has no right to forbid any other actions than such as are hurtful to society. Whatever is not forbidden by the law cannot be hindered; nor can any individual be compelled to do that which the law does not command.

Sentence 1. The law has no right (*n'a le droit*) to forbid any other actions than such as are hurtful to society. The law has no right (*n'a le droit*, not *ne peut pas*). This, for once, is free from ambiguity. Here the mask of ambiguity is thrown off. The avowed object of this clause is to preach constant insurrection, to raise up every man in arms against every law which he happens not to approve of. For, take any such action you will, if the law has no right to forbid it, a law forbidding it is null and void, and the attempt to execute it an oppression, and resistance to such attempt, and insurrection in support of such resistance, legal, justifiable, and commendable.

To have said that no law ought to forbid any act that is not of a nature prejudicial to society would have answered every good purpose, but would not have answered the purpose which is intended to be answered here.

A government which should fulfil the expectations here held out would be a government of absolute perfection. The instance of a government fulfilling these expectations never has taken place, nor till men are angels ever can take place. Against every government which fails in any degree of fulfilling these expectations, then, it is the professed object of this manifesto to excite insurrection: here, as elsewhere, it is therefore its direct object to excite insurrection at all times against every government whatsoever.

Sentence 2. Whatever is not forbidden by the law cannot be hindered, nor can any individual be compelled to do what the law does not command.

The effect of this law, for want of the requisite exceptions or explanations, is to annihilate, for the time being and for ever, all powers of command: all power the exercise of which consists in the issuing and inforcing obedience to particular and occasional commands; domestic power, power of the police, judicial power, military power, power of superior officers, in the line of civil administration over their subordinates. If I say to my son, do not mount that horse which you are not strong enough to manage; if I say to my daughter, do not go to that pond where there is a young man abathing; they may set me at defiance, bidding me show them where there is anything about mounting unruly horses, or going where there are young man abathing, in the laws. By the same clause they may each of them justify themselves in turning their back upon the lesson I have given them; while my apprentice refuses to do the work I have given him; and my wife, instead of providing the dinner I had desired her to provide for ourselves and family, tells me she thinks fit to go and dine[7] with another man whose company is more to her taste. In the existing order of things, under any other government than that which was here to be organised, whatever is commanded or forbidden in virtue of a power which the law allows of and recognises, is virtually and in effect commanded and forbidden by the law itself, since, by the support it gives to the persons in question in the exercise of their respective authorities, it shows itself to have adopted those commands and considered them as its own before they are issued, and, whatever may be the purport of them, so long as they are confined within the limits which it has marked out. But all these existing governments, being fundamentally repugnant to the rights of man, are null and void, and incapable of filling up this or any other gap in the texture of the new code. Besides, this right of not being hindered from doing anything which the law itself has not forbidden, nor compelled to do anything which it has not itself commanded, is an article of natural, unalienable, sacred, and imprescriptible rights over which political laws have no sort of power; so that the attempt to fill up the gap, and to establish any such power of commanding or forbidding what is not already commanded and forbidden by the law, would be an act of usurpation, and all such powers so attempted to be established, null and void. And how can any such powers subsist in a society of which all the members are free and equal in point of rights?

Admit, however, that room is given for the creation of the powers in question by the spirit, though not by the letter, of this clause. What follows? That in proportion as it is harmless, it is insignificant, and incapable of answering its intended purpose. This purpose is to protect individuals against oppressions, to which they might be subjected by other individuals possessed of powers created by the law, in the exercise or pretended exercise of those powers. But if these powers are left to the determination of succeeding and, according to the doctrine of this code, inferior legislatures, and may be of any nature and to any extent which these legislatures may think fit to give them, what does the protection here given amount to, especially as against such future legislatures, for whose hands all the restraints which it is the object of this declaration to provide are intended? Mischievous or nugatory—still the old alternative.

The employment of the improper word *can*, instead of the proper word *shall*, is not unworthy of observation. *Shall* is the language of the legislator who knows what he is about and aims at nothing more. Can, when properly employed in a book of law, is the language of the private commentator or expositor, drawing inferences from the text of the law, from the acts of the legislator, or what is made to pass for and instead of the acts of the legislator, the practice of the courts of justice.[8]

'*Every man is sole proprietor of his own person, and this property is inalienable.*'[9]

More nonsense, more mischievous nonsense, tendencies of the most mischievous kind wrapped up under the cover of a silly epigram: as if a man were one thing, the person of the same man another thing; as if a man kept his person when he happened to have one, as he does his watch, in one of his pockets. While the sentence means nothing, it is as true as other nonsense: give it a meaning, any meaning whatsoever that the words are capable of bearing, according to any import ever given to them, and it is false. If by the property in question, it is meant to include all the uses that can be made of the proprietary subject, the proposition is not self-contradictory and nonsensical: it is only a *nugatory* proposition of the identical kind.

If each individual is the only individual that is to be allowed to make any use whatsoever of the faculties of all kinds, active and passive, mental and corporal, of that individual, and this be meant by being the proprietor of the person of an individual, then true it is that the person of each individual can have but one proprietor. But if the case be, in any instance, that while the individual himself, and he alone, is permitted to make use to certain purposes of the faculties of that individual for a certain time, some other, any other, is permitted to make use of the faculties of the same individual to other purposes for the same time, then the proposition, that no individual can have a property in the person of another individual, is false; the proposition that no man shall be suffered to have any property in the person of another would be a mischievous one, and mischievous to a degree of madness.

In what manner is the legal relation of the husband to the wife constituted, but by giving him a right for a certain time, to the use of certain faculties of hers, by giving him, in so far, a property in her person? And so on with respect to the legal relations of the father to the child under age, and of the master to the apprentice or other servant, whatever be the nature of the service.

[The present tense] is, is absurdly put for [the future] shall be. Injustice, and of the most cruel kind, lurks under this absurdity. The effect of the one [that is, shall be] would only be [to] cut up domestic power, and thence domestic society, for the future: the effect of no one is, is to cut it up at the *instant*, and, by necessary inference, as to the past, and to put every *past* exercise of such power upon the footing of a crime; in a word, to have the retroactive effect disclaimed by the constitution of 1795. If no individual has at this present time any property, however limited, in the person of any other individual, it must be in virtue of some cause which has prevented his ever having had any such property in any past period of time: it must be, in a word, in virtue of some such cause as this, *viz.* its being contrary to the eternal as well as inalienable and natural rights of man to possess any such property. If it is a crime in a man now to send his servant on an errand with a bundle on his back, to dip his ailing infant in a cold bath, or to exercise the rights supposed to be given him by marriage on his wife, it must have always been a crime, and a crime of equal dye, punishable at the mercy of such judges as Citizen Sieyes.

To make the matter worse, the mischief greater, the absurdity more profound, this property, such as it is, whatever it be—all the property that any individual has in his own person—is to be considered as inalienable. No individual is to be suffered to give any other individual a right to make use of his person, his faculties, his services, in any shape. No man shall let himself out to service; no man shall put himself or his son out to serve as an apprentice; no man shall appoint a guardian to his child; no woman shall engage herself to a man in marriage.

Will it be said that there is no such thing as alienation for a time? Or will it be said in justification of the Citizen, that the Citizen did not know what he was talking about, and that though he spoke of alienation in general, alienation for all manner of terms, the only sort of alienation he really meant to interdict, in respect of the property in question, was alienation during life? And that the meaning of the Citizen was not absolutely to forbid marriage, that he meant to allow of marriage for limited terms of years, and meant only to prohibit marriage in the case of its being for life?

But supposing even this to have been the purpose, and tha purpose ever so good an [*sic!*] one, the provision is still a futile one and inadequate to that purpose. To what purpose forbid an alienation for *life*, if you admit of it for years, without restricting it to such a number of years as shall ensure it against possessing a duratio n co-extensive with at least the longest *ordinary* term of life? No such limitation has the citizen vouchsafed to give; possibly as not finding it altogether easy to put any such limitation in years and figures into the mouth of Queen Nature, whose prime minister Citizen Sieyes, like so many other citizens, has been pleased to make himself.[10]

[The article][11] seems to be levelled against negro slavery. But I do not see what purpose it is capable of answering in that view. Does it mean to announce what *has been* the state of the law hitherto, or what *shall be* the state of the law in future? In the first case, its truth is questionable, and true or false, it is of no use. In the latter sense, does it mean to declare that no person shall have the right of exacting personal services of any other, or producing physical impressions on his passive faculties, without his consent? It reprobates . . .[12] the rights that may have been purchased to the professional services of the medical assistant, the barber, the nurse, the carrier, etc., and all powers of punishment. Does it declare that no such powers shall exist without limitation? It does not so much as provide against negro slavery, even where the conditions on which it is established are most indefensible; for nowhere has the power of the master over the slave subsisted without limitations.

Does this article mean to set at perfect liberty and all at once the negro slaves in St Domingo? For to St Domingo this declaration of rights must extend, since the deputation from St Domingo has been admitted. This would be not more irreconcilable with every idea of justice with regard to the interest of the present masters than with every idea of prudence with regard to the interest of the slaves themselves.

Practical Inferences

. . . What, then, shall we say of that system of government of which the professed object is to call upon the untaught and unlettered multitude (whose existence depends upon their devoting their whole time to the acquisition of the means of supporting it) to occupy themselves without ceasing upon all questions of government (legislation and administration included) without exception, important and trivial—the most general and the most particular, but more especially upon the most important and most general, that is, in other words, the most scientific—those that require the greatest measures of science to qualify a man for deciding upon, and in respect of which any want of science and skill happen to be attended with the most fatal consequences?

What should we have said if, with a view of collecting the surest grounds for the decision of the great question of the existence or non-existence of phlogiston the French Academy of Sciences (if its members had remained unmurdered) had referred such questions to the Primary Assemblies?

If a string of general propositions, put together with the design that seems to have given birth to this performance—propositions of the most general and extensive import, embracing the whole field of legislation—were capable of being so worded and put together as to be of use, it could only be on the condition of their being deduced in the way of abridgment from an already formed and existing assemblage of less general propositions included under them, the assemblage of propositions, constituting the tenor of the body of the laws. But for these more general propositions to have been abstracted from that body of particular ones, that body must have been already in existence. The general and introductory part, though placed first, must have been constructed last; though first in the order of communication, it should have been last in the order of composition. For the framing of the propositions which were to be included, time, knowledge, genius, temper, patience, everything was wanting. Yet the system of propositions[13] that were to include them, it was determined to have at any rate. Of time a small quantity indeed might be made to serve, upon the single and very simple condition of not bestowing a single thought upon the propositions which they were to include: and as to knowledge, genius, temper, and patience, the place of all these trivial requisites was abundantly supplied by effrontery and self-conceit. The business, instead of being performed in the way of *abridgement*, was performed in the way of *anticipation*—by a loose conjecture of what the particular propositions in question, were they to be found, might amount to.

What I mean to attack is not the subject or citizen of this or that country, not this or that citizen, not Citizen Sieyes or citizen anybody else, but all *ante*-legal and *anti*-legal rights of man, all declarations of such rights. What I mean to attack is not the execution of such a design in this or that instance, but the design itself.

It is not that they have failed in their execution of the design by using the same word promiscuously in two or three senses, contradictory and incompatible senses, but in undertaking to execute a design which could not be executed at all without this abuse of words, without using the same word at the same time in a multitude of such incompatible and contradictory senses. Let a man distinguish the senses, let him allot and allot invariably a separate word for each, he will find the impossibility of making up any such declaration of rights all, without running into such nonsense as must stop the hand even of the maddest of the mad.

Ex uno, disce omnes—from this declaration of rights, learn what all other declarations of rights, of rights asserted as against government in general, must ever be—the rights of anarchy—the order of chaos.

It is right I should continue to possess the coat I have upon my back, and so on with regard to everything else I look upon as my property, at least till I choose to part with it.

It is right I should be at liberty to do as I please; I should be better if I might be permitted to add, whether other people were pleased with what it pleased me to do or not. But as that is hopeless, I must be content with such a portion of liberty, though it is the least I can be content with, as consists in the liberty of doing as I please, subject to the exception of not doing harm to other people.

It is right I should be secure against all sorts of harm.

It is right I should be upon a par with everybody else—upon a par at least; and if I can contrive to get a peep over other people's heads, where will be the harm in it?

But if all this is right now, at what time was it ever otherwise? It is then naturally right. And at what future time will it be otherwise? It is then unalterably right for everlasting.

As it is right I should possess all these blessings, I have a right to all of them.

But if I have a right to the coat on my back, I have a right to knock any man down who attempts to rob me of it; else what signifies my having a right to it?

For the same reason, if I have a right to be secure against all sorts of harm, I have a right to knock any man down who attempts to harm me.

For the same reason, if I have a right to do whatever I please, subject only to the exception of not doing mischief to other people, it follows that, subject only to that exception, I have a right to knock any man down who attempts to prevent my doing anything that I please to do, in any instance to prevent my doing as I please.

For the same reason, if I have a right to be upon a par with every-body else in every respect, it follows that should any man take upon him to raise his house higher than mine, rather than it should continue so, I have a right to pull it down about his ears, and to knock him down if he attempts to hinder me.

Thus easy, thus natural, under the guidance of the selfish and anti-social passions, thus insensible is the transition from the language of utility and peace to the language of mischief. Transition, did I say? What transition? From right to right? The propositions are identical; there is no transition in the case. Certainly, as far as words go, scarcely any: no more than if you were to trust your horse with a man for a week or so, and he were to return it blind and lame: it was your horse you trusted to him; it is your horse you have received again: what you had trusted to him, you have received.

It is in England, rather than in France, that the discovery of the rights of man ought naturally to have taken its rise: it is we, we English, that have the better right to it. It is the English language that the transition is more natural than perhaps in most others: at any rate, more so than in the French. It is in English, and not in French, that we may change the sense without changing the word, and like Don Quixote on the enchanted horse, travel as far as the moon, and farther, without ever getting off the saddle. One and the same word, right; right, that most enchanting of words is sufficient for operating the fascination. The word is ours, that magic word which, by its single unassisted powers, completes the fascination. In its adjective shape, it is as innocent as a dove: it breathes nothing but morality and peace. It is the shape that, passing in at the heart, it gets possession of the understanding; it then assumes its substantive shape, and joining itself to a band of suitable associates, plants the banner of insurrection, anarchy, and lawless violence.

It is right that men should be as near upon a par with one another in every respect as they can be made, consistently with general security: here we have it in its adjective form, synonymous with desirable, proper, becoming, consonant to general utility, and the like. I have a right to put myself upon a par with everybody in every respect: here we have it in its substantive sense, forming with the other words a phrase equivalent to this—wherever I find a man who will not let me put myself on a par with him in every respect, it is right, and proper, and becoming, that I should knock him down, if I have a mind to do so, and if that will not do, knock him on the head, and so forth.

The French language is fortunate enough not to possess this mischievous abundance. But a Frenchman will not be kept back from his purpose by a want of words; the want of an adjective composed of the same letters as the substantive right is no loss to him. Is, has been, ought to be, shall be, can; all are put for one another; all are pressed into the service; all made to answer the same purposes. By this inebriating compound, we have seen all the elements of the understanding confounded, every fibre of the heart inflamed, the lips prepared for every folly, and the band for every crime.

Our right to this precious discovery, such as it is, of the rights of man, must, I repeat it, have been prior to that of the French. It has been seen how peculiarly rich we are in materials for making it. Right, the substantive right, is the child of law; and when once brought into the world, what more natural than for poets, for rhetoricians, for all dealers in moral and intellectual poisons, to give the child a spurious parentage to lay it at nature's door and set it up in opposition with the real author of its birth. (Impregnated by the breath of these magicians there comes a bastard brood of monsters 'gorgons and chimeras dire'.)[14] I will prove its parentage. It shall be seen how from *real* laws come *real* rights; and thence it will be seen how from *imaginary* laws come imaginary ones. And thus it is, that from *legal rights*, the offspring of law, and friends of peace, come *anti-legal* rights, the mortal enemies of law, the subverters of government, and the assassins of security.

Will this antidote to French poisons have its effect? Will this preservative for the understanding and the heart, against the fascination of sounds, find lips to take it? This, in point of speedy or immediate efficacy at least, is certainly too much to hope for. Alas! how dependent are opinions upon sound! What Hercules shall break the chains by which opinions are enslaved by sounds? By what force of words shall associations between words and ideas be dissolved, associations to which every book and every conversation give added strength? By what authority shall this original vice in the structure of the language be corrected? [How] shall a word which has taken root in the vitals of the language be expelled? By what drastic force shall a word in continual use be deprived of half its signification, an article of necessary use to the body politic be purged of half its properties? The language of plain and strong sense is difficult to learn; the language of smooth nonsense easy and familiar. The one requires a force of attention capable of stemming the tide of usage and example; the other requires nothing but to swim with it.

It is for education to do what can be done; and in education lies, though unhappily the slowest, the surest as well as earliest resource. The recognition of the nothingness of the laws of nature and of the rights of man that have been grounded on them, is a branch of knowledge of as much importance to an Englishman, though a negative one, as the most perfect acquaintance that can be formed with the existing laws of England.

It must be so: Shakespeare, whose plays were filling English hearts with rapture, while the Drama of France was not superior to that of Caffraria; Shakespeare, who had a key to all the passions and to all the stores of language could never have let slip an instrument of delusion of such superior texture. No: it is not possible that the rights of man—the natural, pre-adamitical, ante-legal, and anti-legal rights of man—should have been unknown to Shakespeare. How could the Macbeths, the Jaffiers, the Iagos, do without them? They present a cloak for every conspiracy; they hold out a mask to every crime; they are every villain's armoury, every spendthrift's treasury.

But if the English were the first to bring the rights of man into the closet from the stage, it is to the stage and the closet that they have confined them. It was reserved to France, to France in her days of degradation and degeneration—in those days, in comparison of which the worst of her days of fancied tyranny were halcyon ones—to turn debates into tragedies, and the senate into a stage.

The mask is now taken off, and the following are the marks by which the anarchist may be recognised.

Asserting rights of any kind, acknowledging them at the same time not to be recognised by government. Using, instead of *ought* and *ought not*, the words *is* or *is not*, *can* or *can not*.

In former times, in the times of Grotius and Puffendorf, these expressions were little more than improprieties in language, prejudicial to the growth of knowledge; at present, since the French Declaration of Rights has adopted them, and the French Revolution displayed their import by a practical comment, the use of them is already a *moral* crime, and not undeserving of being constituted a legal crime, hostile to the public peace.

CHAPTER 21

[*Nature of Political Argument*][1]

The greatest happiness of the greatest number requires that those Reasons[2] be such throughout as shall show the conduciveness of the several arrangements to the all-comprehensive and only defensible end thus expressed. *Rationale indicates conduciveness to happiness.*

Except in so far as they do this, whatsoever portions of discourse are given under the name of reasons do what is nothing to the purpose: the name of reasons is not with any use or propriety applicable to them. Any thing that has no influence on happiness, on what ground can it be said to have any claim to man's regard? And, on what ground, in the eyes of a common guardian, can any one man's happiness be shown to have any stronger or less strong claim to regard than any others? If, on the ground of delinquency, in the name of punishment, it be right that any man should be rendered unhappy, it is not that this happiness has less claim to regard than another man's, but that it is necessary to the greatest happiness of the greatest number, that a portion of the happiness of that one be sacrificed.

Reasons, indicative of this conduciveness, are reasons derived from the principle known by the name of the principle of utility: more expressively say the greatest-happiness principle. To exhibit these reasons is to draw up the account between law and happiness: to apply arithmetical calculations to the elements of happiness. Political arithmetic—a name that has by some been given to political economy—is an application, though but a particular and far short of an all-comprehensive one, of arithmetic and its calculations, to happiness and its elements.

To convey a sufficiently clear, correct and comprehensive conception of what is meant by reason when derived from the principle of utility, and applied to law, a few words of explanation seem indispensable. . . . [3]

Till the principle of utility, as explained by the phrase *the greatest happiness of the greatest number* is on each occasion, if not explicitly, implicitly referred to as the source of all reasoning, and arithmetic, as above, employed in making application of it, every thing that, in the field of legislation, calls itself *reasoning* or *argument* will—say who can in what large proportion—be a compound of nonsense and falsehood; both ingredients having misrule for their effect, after having, in no small proportion, had it for their object. In words opposite to one another in character, but all of them indeterminate in quantity, may be seen the ordinary instruments of debate: the weapons with which the warfare of tongues and pens is, in a vast proportion, carried on. In penal law, *justice* and *humanity*; in finance, *economy* and *liberality*; in judicial procedure, *strictness* and *liberality of construction*; in constitutional law, *liberty* and *licentiousness*. It is with trash such as this, that corruptionists feed their dupes, teaching them, at the same time, to feed one another with it, as well as themselves. It is with one part of it in their mouths that the holders of power pass for wise, and the hunters after it for eloquent. Thus cheap is the rate, at which, in any quantity, each combatant finds matter of laud for those of his own side of the question (not forgetting himself) and matter of vituperation for his antagonists. It is by nonsense in this shape that the war, made upon the *principle of utility* by *ipsedixitism* and *sentimentalism*, with or without rhyme, is carried on.

In the titles, with which the several sections of this paper are headed, it may be observed as a singularity, that the words *the greatest happiness of the greatest number* occupy the first place. The use of them is to serve as a momento, that, whatever be the subject of consideration—in so far as it belongs to the field of government— matters be so ordered, as that the only defensible end of government shall never be out of sight.

To this instructive phrase, substitute any of those unmeaning terms, to which, under the lash of perpetually-accusing conscience, the enemies of good government are, at every turn, constrained to have recourse. Substitute, for example, the word *legitimacy*, or the word *order*, and say—*maintenance of legitimacy* requires, or *maintenance of order* requires, that the state be provided with an *all-comprehensive*—with a *rationalised* code of law—that, in the *rationale*, the several reasons, or sets of reasons, be contiguously attached to the several arrangements to which they apply, and so forth. The substitution made, see then, ask yourself, what *guide*, what *check*, is furnished by the nonsense thus substituted to useful sense? Why then is *legitimacy* any where the word? Because, owing to intellectual blindness and weakness, absolute monarchy is still *established* by law in so many more countries than any better form of government is. Why is *order* the word? Because, while the best government can no more exist without *order* in some shape or other than the worst, the worst *order* is as much *order* as the best. In the worst government, *order* of some sort is *established*. Does it follow that it must be *good*, because it is *established*? Must everything be good that is established? What is thus said of the body politic, apply it thus to the body natural. Take a man in whose head or stomach the *gout* is *established*: take a man in whose bladder a *stone* is *established*. Established as it is, does the gout, does the stone, contribute any thing to his happiness?

Good is pleasure or exemption from pain: or a cause or instrument of either, considered in so far as it is a cause or instrument of either.

Evil is pain or loss of pleasure; or a cause or instrument of either; considered in so far as it is a cause or instrument of either.

Happiness is the sum of pleasures, deduction made or not made of the sum of pains.

Government is in each community the aggregate of the acts of power exercised therein, by persons in whom the existence of a right to exercise political power is generally recognised. Every act of power, in the exercise of which *evil* as above is employed, is itself an evil: and, with small exceptions, no otherwise than by such acts, can the business of government be carried on. No otherwise than through the instrumentality of punishment can even such parcels of the matter of *good* as are employed in the way of reward, be in any comparatively considerable proportion, got into the hands by which they are applied.

To warrant the employment of *evil*, whether in the character of punishment or in any other character, two points require to be made out: 1. that, by means of it, *good* to a preponderant amount will be produced; 2. that, at any less expense of *evil*, *good* in so great a proportion can not be produced.

In every *rationale*, both these points ought to be constantly kept in view; in the rationale hereby offered, they will be constantly kept in view.

No otherwise than by reference to the *greatest happiness* principle, can epithets such as *good* and *evil*, or *good* and *bad*, be expressive of any quality in the *act* or other *object* to which they are applied: say an act of an individual: say an act of government: a *law*, a *measure* of government, a *system* of government, a *form* of government. But for this reference, all they designate is—the *state of mind* on the part of him in whose discourse they are employed.

When, and in proportion as, this standard is employed as the standard of reference, then for the first time, and thenceforward for ever, will the import of those same perpetually employed and primarily important adjuncts, considered as indicative of qualities belonging to the objects they are applied to, be determinate.

CHAPTER 22

[*Summary of Basic Principles*]

A general political catechism: containing a bird's eye view of the field of law and government in which government as it is is contrasted throughout with government as it ought to be.[1]

Q.[2] What is the best form of government?

A.   That which is most conducive to the proper end of government.

Q.   What is the proper end of government?

A.   The greatest happiness of the greatest number.

Q.   What is the form of government most conducive to that end?

A.   Pure democracy.

Q.   How many pure and simple forms of government are there?

A.   Three: namely pure monarchy, pure aristocracy and pure democracy.

Q.   What is the circumstance by which these three forms are distinguished from one another?

A.   Number: monarchy being the government of one; aristocracy, that of the few; democracy, that of the many.

Q.   How many fixed forms of government may there be?

A.   As many that are capable of being made by the mixture of those three simple forms.

Q.   How many forms of government are there to which the term monarchy is commonly applied?

A.   Two: namely pure monarchy and mixed monarchy.

Q.   What is the most common sort of mixed monarchy?

A.   That in which the power of the monarch is more or less checked and lessened by portions of power possessed by aristocratical bodies or democratical bodies or both.

Q.   What is the form of government in Great Britain and Ireland?

Q.[3] What is the actual end actually pursued by man in general?

A.   His own greatest happiness.

Q.   What is the actual end of government under a democracy?

A. The greatest happiness of the greatest number.

Q. What is the actual end of government under every other form of government?

A. The greatest happiness of those among whom the powers of government are shared.

Q. Under the English monarchy who are those among whom the powers of government are shared?

A. The king and those under his command, the House of Lords and the House of Commons.

Q. What are the means by which under a democracy the possessors of the powers of government pursue their ends and support themselves?

A. A free consent of the people or the subject many as signified by their representatives, whom they have freely chosen as such.

Q. What are the means by which, in a pure monarchy, those who possess the powers of government pursue their ends and support themselves?

A. Force (military force) and intimidation.

Q. What are the means by which in the English monarchy, the possessors of the powers of government pursue their ends and support themselves?

A. Force (military force), intimidation, corruption and deceit (delusion).

Q. [4][What is][5] the form most conducive to the proper end of government?

A. Democracy—pure representative democracy.

Q. What is the form least conducive, and most adverse, to that only proper end?

A. Pure monarchy.

Q. Amongst mixed governments, what are the forms which are most conducive, and least adverse, to that same proper end?

A. Those in which the mixture has most of pure representative democracy, and least of pure monarchy in it.

Q. What are the causes by which pure monarchy is rendered thus adverse to the proper end of government?

A. Its vices.

Q. What are those vices?

A. They are all collected in that one all-comprehensive view which constitutes its essence—*viz.* despotism. The uncontrollableness of its power, whereby the despot, adding to the inclination the power of making a constant sacrifice of the happiness of all other members of the community to his own individual happiness, does accordingly, on all occasions, make that sacrifice.

Q. What are the vices by which mixed monarchy is rendered, in the next degree, least conducive to that same proper end?

A. They consist of, or are constituted by, the means by which the monarch and those under his command and influence, are enabled, and, in a manner, necessitated to employ, in pursuit of their several particular ends—*viz.* force, intimidation, corruption, and deceit as above.

Q. Considering that, to pure monarchy, there belong but those two vices, *viz.* force and intimidation, *i.e.* the employing of the instruments so denominated as means, how is it that mixed monarchy which, in addition to those two vices, has two others, *viz.* corruption and deceit, is not, in a still higher degree, more adverse to the proper end of government than monarchy is?

Q.[6]What are the advantages of monarchy as compared with representative democracy?

A. None.

Q. How comes it then to have place?

A. By its being established as such, almost all men are born under it, all men are used to it, few men are used to anything else: till of late years nobody ever dispraised it, everybody praised it, nobody saw anything better, nobody knew of anything better, few had heard of anything better: men are reconciled to mixed monarchy in England by the same causes by which they were reconciled to pure monarchy in Morocco, Turkey and Industan. No state of things so bad, but that acquiescence under it may be produced by ignorance of better, in a word, by habit, by authority, and by the instruments of corruption and delusion by which it became surrounded and with which it became equipped.

Q. By what causes was it originally established?

A. First by necessity, then by force and intimidation.

Q. How by necessity?

A. In the early stages of society all men were at war with one another: warring like brutes for the means of subsistence and sexual intercourse; united by chance in bands associated for that purpose. But no band could on any occasion act in concert without submitting and paying obedience, on that occasion at least, to the orders of a leader. As the occasions of war multiplied the habit of obedience, obsequiousness, strengthened; as wars multiplied, war or expectation of war became permanent and perpetual: and thus chieftainship became monarchy.

Q. Monarchy being thus established, how came it to be hereditary?

A. It was hereditary first in males, then at last in females. Among males first in the children of the last monarchy, then failing them in others of his kindred according as they were mixed akin to his. Among his children first to one in entirety, then in some instances where the country was large enough in shares; when in entirety at first in the eldest son, then incidentally as circumstances give occasion to choice in this or that other of the sons.

Q. What is delusion?

A. Producing in the mind of the person in question such conceptions or opinions as are erroneous, and to the person in question or any others, pernicious.[7]

Q. What are the instruments by which delusion operates?

A. Discourse and other signs having the effect of discourse.

Q. What are the modes in which delusion operates by discourse?

A. Assertion and insinuation.

Q. On occasions such as the present and for purposes such as the present, what are the discourses by which delusion operates?

Q.[8] On occasions such as the present and for purposes such as the present, what are the signs which, not being the signs of which discourse is composed, contribute to the production of the same effect as that which is produced by the signs of which discourse is composed?

Q.[9] Then it was not by any experience or supposition of its advantages that it was established or has been continued: meaning its advantages to the many by whose obsequiousness the power belonging to it is constituted.

A. No. It was first established: and therein as now can be found under its bad effects, and a look out for something [to] better its advantages, or what might be made to appear as such, were looked for by men who saw their interest in it.[10]

Q. What are the advantages of aristocracy?

A. As compared with representative democracy, to the subject many none.

Q. How came aristocracy to have place?

A. The causes and manners have been different according as the aristocracy meant is that which is subordinate or that which is supreme.

Q. What is meant by a subordinate aristocracy?

A. An aristocracy within, and subordinate to, a monarchy.

Q. How came a subordinate aristocracy to be established?

A. As a monarchy came to be established.

Q. What is meant by the distributive branch of law?

A. That by which distribution is made of the benefits and burdens of political society.

Q. Has it not more commonly been termed the Civil Branch of Law?

A. Yes.

Q. Why then do you not prefer the calling it by that name?

A. Because it is so uncharacteristic and inadequate to the purpose of indicating what is meant.

Q. How so?

A. By the same persons this same word is employed to designate that which is not the constitutional branch, that which is not the military, that which is not the ecclesiastical, and that which has been adopted from the Law of Ancient Rome under the Emperors.

Q. Why are any burdens included in the distribution made of the benefits?

A. Because without distributing burdens no benefits can be distributed. With the exception of those by which burdens already imposed are taken off, no law can without the creation of a burden be established. By every command a corresponding burden is imposed on him to whom it is directed.

Q. What are the benefits which this branch of law is occupied in the distribution of?

A. They may all of them be designated under one or other of four heads: subsistence, abundance, security and equality.

Q. What then are the proper objects or ends in view of the distributive branch of law?

A. The causing the greatest number possible of the community to be at all times possessed of these several benefits, each of them in the most perfect degree possible.

Q. Is not subsistence included in abundance?

A. Yes.

Q. Then why make a separate object of it, consider it stated as a separate object?

A. Because subsistence may be possessed by many by whom abundance neither is nor can be possessed.

Q. Is not subsistence included in security for person? And in security against physical calamity?

A. Yes, but in speaking of subsistence, time present is alone considered; in speaking of security for person, time present and an indefinite length of time besides: in so far as subsistence is the object directly in view, one set of legal arrangements is provided; in so far as security for person is the object directly in view, another and a different set.

Q. What are the arrangements of which subsistence is the direct object?

A. Those which belong to the art and science called political economy and which depend more upon the distributive than the penal branch of law.

Q. What are the arrangements of which security of person is the direct object?

A. In so far as the security is against foreign hostility, those by which the military force is raised, organised and kept up; in so far as it is against internal punishable delinquency, those which belong to the penal branch of law; in so far as it is against abuse of official power and private influence, those which belong to the constitutional branch of law; in so far as it is against physical calamity and annoyance, those which belong to the system of police: a system which is carried into effect partly by the distributive, partly by the penal branch of law.

Q. *For* what is security desirable?

A. For persons, for reputation, for property, for condition in life,

Q. *Against* what is security desirable?

A. Against foreign hostility, against internal punishable delinquency, against abuse of official power and private opulence, against physical calamity and annoyance.

Q. What are the actual ends of this branch of law?

A. Distributing among the rulers as large a portion as possible of the benefits, among the subject many as large a portion as possible of the burdens.

Q. How does this apply to the more particular or immediately subordinate benefits just mentioned?

A. The object is to confer on themselves in the greatest possible quantity the benefits or blessings of abundance and security.

Q. You do not mention subsistence; how does this apply to subsistence?

A. Subsistence is necessarily included in abundance. They cannot in any degree be possessed of abundance without being possessed of subsistence.

Q. Is not equality among the benefits which they endeavour to confer [to which], their endeavours are directed?

A. No, it is the object of terror and aversion. It is directly repugnant to that which has already been mentioned as comprehending the whole object of their endeavours, namely administering and of the greatest quantity possible to the benefits of society, to the subject many the burdens.

Q. What is here meant by equality?

A. Not absolute equality, only such an approach towards equality as is generally desirable.

Q. Why not absolute equality?

A. Because that would be destruction of security, abundance and subsistence. By being deprived of all security for their property, those who had abundance would be deprived of their abundance, and those who had only subsistence would be deprived of that subsistence.

Q. How is it that by the production of absolute equality, in other words, by giving to every person an equal portion to property, all such security would be destroyed?

A. Property itself would be destroyed: and all inducement to produce more would be destroyed along with it.

Q. How is it the property itself would be destroyed?

A. In this as in every civilised country and indeed in every country without exception, the distribution which at this or any other given time differs more or less widely from an equal one. To render it equal would be necessary that an entire new division of it should be made: that the whole should be put together into one mass and that then that mass should be divided into exactly equal parts: namely on each given day into as many equal parts as on that day the community contained members. But of this whole mass of property a large portion is so circumstanced that by division, especially such minute division, the whole value of it would be destroyed. The whole value and thereby its capacity of contributing to abundance. But the number of members of which the community is composed will every day be different; therefore every day throughout the whole country a fresh division will be to be made, and more such destruction of property effected. All this while the time of all the members of the community would be completely occupied with this division, some in endeavouring to make it, others in endeavouring to prevent or modify it. In the meantime all will perish one after the other: the sick and infirm for want of attendance, all for want of subsistence.

Q. By what is the penal distinguished from the distributive branch of law?[11]

Q. What is the proper end of penal law?

A. Punishment, wheresoever it falls, is a burden. The use of it is to secure to the people in the greatest quantity the benefits of political society with as small a portion as possible of the burdens by a mode[12] of which they are produced.

Q. What is the parallel case by the contemplation of which the means employed on this occasion may be kept in due subordination and subservience to that exclusively proper [end]?

A. Medical practice.

Q.[13] What are the actual ends of penal law?

A. The proper end and some others which are improper ends.

Q. What are these improper ends?

A. 1. Promotion of the narrow and sinister interest which constitutes the actual and improper end of the distributive branch of law. 2. Gratification of vengeance. 3. Gratification of antipathy.

Q. What is vengeance?

A. The gratification of a desire of producing suffrance [to] the person in question that desire being produced by the supposition of an injury received from that same person.

Q. What is antipathy in the case in which if produced the desire to produce suffrance in the person who is the object of it?

A. It is a desire unaccompanied with any such supposition just mentioned.

Q. What are the most common and extensively operating causes of antipathy?

A. Differences in opinion and differences in taste.

Q. What are the most common subjects of such differences in opinion as are apt to be productive of antipathy?

A. Religion and government.

Q. What are those instruments of delusion that operate by discourse?

A. They are of two sorts: 1. falsehoods; 2. fallacies.

Q. What on this occasion is meant by falsehoods in contradistinction to fallacies?

A. Discourses, having, for their object or effect, the producing delusion and thence erroneous judgment, by assertions, directly contrary to the truth of things.

Q. What, on this occasion, is meant by fallacies?

A. Discourses, having, for their object and effect, the producing erroneous judgment, and thence pernicious conduct, without being directly contrary to the truth of things.

Q. What are the falsehoods of most extensive application commonly employed for the production of delusion in this case?

A. They are the falsehoods which, by means of qualities on endowments ascribed to the several branches of which the sovereign and absolute power of the government is composed, would, if really possessed by all of them, have the effect of causing to be pursued the proper end of government, and not the improper ends actually pursued.

Q. What are those branches of the sovereign's power?

A. There are three: *viz.* 1. the monarch, 2. the body called the House of Lords, the Lord's House or the Upper House of Parliament, 3. the House of Commons, Common's House or Lower House of Parliament.

Q. What are the qualities or endowments above referred to?

A. They are the qualities and endowments of which appropriate aptitude with reference to the exercise of the branch of power in question, is composed.

Q. What, in the case of each such branch, are those qualities and endowments?

A. They are, with reference to each such branch: 1. appropriate probity; 2. appropriate intellectual aptitude; 3. appropriate active talent.

Q. What, in the instance of those several branches of power, are the assertions to which, on the present occasion, the character of falsehood is to be ascribed?

A. The assertions by which those qualities or endowments are ascribed to the occupants of the three branches of supreme power above spoken of.

Q. How does it appear that falsity is justly imputable to the assertion by which appropriate probity is ascribed to the monarch?

A. Under appropriate probity, in this case, are included the disposition to contribute, to his utmost, to the accomplishment of the proper end of political society or government—the greatest happiness of the greatest number as before mentioned, in preference to the pursuit of his own or any other particular interest, and the practice of acting in conformity to such disposition.

Q. What are the portions of discourse by which this quality or endowment, in its two above-mentioned branches, is commonly ascribed to the individual, whoever he be, by which that situation is occupied?

A. The attributives most excellent, most gracious, and other phrases in infinite number, to that or the like effect.

Q. How does it appear that, to these assertions, falsehood is justly imputable?

A. From two considerations: *viz.* 1. as it is not consistent with the nature of man in any situation that in the general tenor of his life, he should be occupied in the promotion of any other interest in preference to his own particular interest any further than as he feels himself laid, by external causes, under the necessity of giving such preference and because, in that situation, no man is laid under such necessity by any such external causes; 2. because, in that situation, a man has much less inducement to give such preference than in any other; in other words, in that situation it is much easier than in any other for a man to promote his own interests at the expense of every other, or, at any rate, to give effect to his own will to the exclusion, and at the expense, of every other.

That, whereas although men will in the respect above-mentioned, so far agree as to give each man preference to his own will at the expense of every other, yet, in different individuals in that situation as in every other, different degrees of regard for the universal interest will have place, the highest degree of regard is, on all occasions, by these several phrases, attributed indiscriminately to every individual by whom that situation is filled.

Q. How does it appear that falsity is justly imputable to the assertions by which appropriate probity is ascribed to the House of Lords, that is to say, on each occasion on which it acts, to every one, or, in case of dissension, to the major part at least of its members?

A. On the same consideration by which this appears in the case of the monarch as just mentioned.

Q. What are the two classes into which the mass of falsehoods thus employed may be divided so as to leave no remainder?

A. Two: namely the unavowed and the avowed.

Q. What are the unavowed?

A. Those which stand upon the same footing as falsehoods in general: namely such as are uttered under the expectation of their being taken for truth.

Q. What are the avowed?

A. They are those which by lawyers are called fictions of law: they are not uttered under any such expectation and that of their being taken for truth. On this subject see further under the head of fictions.

Q. In the case where discourses are falsehoods and capable of being shown to be such by appropriate proofs, what are the two classes in which the aggregate of such proofs is capable of being divided without a remainder?

A. Two, extrinsic and intrinsic.

Q. What are the extrinsic?

A. Such as are not contained in the body of the discourse itself, but are derived from other courses.

Q. What are the intrinsic?

A. Inconsistencies.

Q. What are the principal inconsistencies involved in the falsehoods by which the character or frame of mind of the monarch are customarily misrepresented?

A. First, inconsistency between the character given of him, that it is to say, of all monarchs without exception in general terms, and the particular or individual practices in which he is continually spoken of as being engaged.

Q. Give an instance of the character commonly attributed to him in general terms.

A. Most excellent, most sacred, most religious, most gracious.

Q. What are the discourses which to the above are chargeable with being inconsistent?[14]

Q. What are the circumstances by which fictions stand distinguished from ordinary falsehoods?

A. Two, the one following from the other: namely the circumstance of their being avowed to be falsehoods and the sentiment of contempt expressed by those who employ them as to those who are called upon and forced to see them acted upon as if they were truths.

Q. What are the purposes for which they have been employed?

A. The support of misrule in all its shapes.

Q. How does it appear that falsity is justly imputable to the assertion by which appropriate probity is ascribed to the House of Commons?

A. By the same consideration by which this is made appears in the two before mentioned, cases of the monarch and the House of Lords.

Q. In this cases are there no external causes by the operation of which a man is effectually laid under the necessity of giving to the universal interest the preference as against his own particular interest?

A. No, there is but one such cause by which he could be laid under the general necessity of giving desirable and legitimate preference: that is that on each occasion the majority of the

House should be composed of men subject to the operation if the only causes by which such necessity issues, according to the nature of men be produced, namely the being elected and at all times promptly removable by a majority of those of whose interest the individual interest is composed.

Q. What is corruption in government?

A. Any state of things by which individual interest is put in a state of effectual opposition to the universal interest in such sort that by yielding to the seductions of the individual interest he contributes to the sacrifice of the universal interest.

Q. To effect the purpose of political corruption is it necessary in any case that there should be a corruption?

A. No.

Q. What in this case is meant by corruption?

A. Corruption may be said to have place wherever matters are so ordered as that doing mischief to the public, a man is enabled to reap a net profit to himself in any shape: in other words, wherever it is so ordered that by a violation of his duty a man is enabled to promote and promotes accordingly his own interests.

Q. By whom is corruption capable of being practised?

A. By anyone, from the highest to the lowest.

Q. On whom is corruption capable of being practised?

A. On anyone, from the highest to the lowest.

Q. When and where corruption has place, to what and whom is it to be imputed?

A. To the system and to some person or persons who act under it.

Q. To whom do we mean to impute it, when we impute it to the system?

A. To those whoever they are by whom the system whatever it is was brought into the state in which in this respect it is.

Q. Wherein, then, lies a distinction between the two cases?

A. In this: *viz.* that in one case the source of the corruption is permanent; in the other occasionally and transiently.

Q. In the case of a corrupt transaction, how many parties must there be in it?

A. In general there are two but in some cases the two parts may be acted by one and the same person. This will be the case wherever the two powers are united in one hand: *viz.* the power of giving the profit or source of profit, or of receiving it.

Q. What are the situations by which the two powers are thus placed in one hand?

A. They abound throughout the whole system: and with these varieties that in some instances the power of receiving requires the concurrence of several hands for the exercise of it, while the power of conferring requires but one hand for the exercise of it; in others the case is reversed; in others again no more than one hand is requisite for the exercise of it; in others again hands more than one are requisite for the exercise of both powers.

The great functionaries—those on whose conduct the fate of the whole people continually depends—are by their situation in one or other of those four ways at the same time, and by the same act, corrupters and corrupted. Go through the several situations and show how each man is at once a giver and receiver of the wages of corruption.

[*Greatest Happiness of the Greatest Number*]¹

[These passages are excerpted from Bentham's unpublished article on Utilitarianism that he wrote to help James Mill in his famous controversy with Macaulay. Very little of it, however, was used in the *Westminster Review* article in 1829, and in *Deontology*. The article is largely a history and defence of the principle of utility, and contains a few interesting remarks on justice and virtue. They add nothing new, however, to the manuscript material included above in chapter 6.]

Greatest happiness *of the greatest number*. Some years have now elapsed since, upon a closer scrutiny, reason, altogether incontestable, was found for discarding this appendage. On the surface, additional clearness and correctness given to the idea: at bottom, the opposite qualities. Be the community in question what it may, divide it into two unequal parts, call one of them the majority, the other minority, layout of the account the feelings of the minority, include in the account no feelings but those of the majority, the result you will find is that of this operation, that to the aggregate stock of the happiness of the community, loss not profit is the result of the operation. Of this proposition the truth will be the more palpable, the greater the ratio of the number of the minority to that of the majority: in other words, the less difference between the two unequal parts: and suppose the condivident part equal, the quantity of the error [evil?] will then be at its maximum.

Number of the majority, suppose 2001; number of the minority, 2000. Suppose in the first place the stock of happiness in such sort divided that by every one of the 4001, an equal portion of happiness shall be possessed. Take now from every one of the 2000 his share of happiness, and divide it anyhow among the 2001: instead of augmentation, vast is the diminution you will find to be the result. The feelings of the minority being by the supposition laid entirely out of the account (for such in the enlarged form is the import of the propositions), the vacuum thus left may, instead of remaining a *vacuum*, be filled with unhappiness, positive suffering, magnitude, intensity and duration taken together, the greatest which it is in the power of human nature to endure.

Take from your 2000 and give to your 2001 all the happiness you find your 2000 in possession of: insert in the room of the happiness you have taken out, unhappiness in as large a quantity as the receptacle will contain: to the aggregate amount of the happiness possessed by the 4001 taken together will the result be net profit? on the contrary, the whole profit will have given place to loss. How so? because so it is that such is the nature of the receptacle, the quantity of unhappiness it is capable of containing during any given portion of time is greater than the quantity of happiness.

At the outset place your 4001 in a state of equal perfect equality in respect of the means or say instruments of happiness—and in particular power and opulence: every one of them in a state of equal liberty—every one independent of every other: every one of them possessing an equal portion of money and money's worth: in this state it is that you find them. Taking in hand now your 2000 reduce them to a state of slavery, and no matter in what proportions of the slaves thus constituted divide the whole number with such their property among your 2001: the operation performed, of the happiness of the whole number 4001, will an augmentation be the result? The question answers itself.

Were it otherwise, note now the practical application that would be to be made of it in the British Isles. In Great Britain take the whole body of the Roman Catholics, make slaves of them and divide them in any proportion, them and their progeny, among the whole body of the Protestants. In Ireland take the whole body of the Protestants and divide them in like manner among the whole body of the Roman Catholics.

APPENDIX B

[*On James Mill*]¹

Written on reading Mills article *Government* as reprinted from supplement to *Encyclopaedia Britannica* P. 21.

After the position the object of which is to place all females under the absolute dominion of all males comes:

Exclusion of all under 25, 30 or even 40 years of age. Reason for the exclusion none. Reasons against it:

1. Youth is the source of virtue. Thus it diminishes moral aptitude.

2. Youth is the source of activity. Thus it diminishes active aptitude.

3. Debarring youth of all hope of a participation of power in this shape, it deprives them proportionably of the inducement to engage in any course of study in the use of fitting them for that situation: it thus diminishes intellectual aptitude. Thus is its tendency to diminish appropriate aptitude in every one of its shapes.

4. No one age is proposed at which, for any special reason, the line shall be drawn between those who are excluded and those who are admitted. Some say 25, some 30. One says 40: some one else may say 50: the age of Nestor, whatever it was, might be preferred by some: and here would be, if not a reason, the shadow of one.

For fixing the time at which a person is to be admitted to the management of his private concerns, a line could not fail [to] be drawn in the law of any country.

Barring special reason to the contrary, this then should be the line by which admissibility into official situations should be determined.

Now for admitting into the situation in question persons at an age earlier than those at which they are admitted to the management of their own private concerns, there exist two reasons, and those as it should seem, either of them of itself is conclusive.

1. One is that in the situation in question, the power is but fractional: no individual being capable of himself to give exercise to it in any one instance: in no shape can the functionary do mischief without having a majority of the whole number to join with him in it.

2. The other is—that with this same fraction of a power he cannot be invested without having been the object of choice to the majority of[2] the free voters. Those in favour of a man of the age in question, what but the opinion of extraordinary aptitude should be capable of inciting such a multitude of votes? Those to whom the individual is known, either from observation or at least report, say he is more apt than any other person. Our exclusionist, to whom the individual is altogether unknown insists upon it, that without any evil results, he may be set aside on the ground of his being utterly unapt. Which is most likely to be in the right?

One observations here, though drawn from private history, is too important to be omitted.

Continually under his eye while perusing this article our exclusionist had before him a youth who at the age of 18 was beyond all doubt fitter for a situation of the sort in question, by appropriate aptitude in every shape, in the legislative assembly of his country than a vast majority of those by whom it is filled: a son to whom, by the instruction given him by his father without any coadjutor whatsoever, this extraordinary aptitude had been given: and by whom at that same age, no inconsiderable part was acted in the disposal of the lot of a hundred million of human beings.

Nor very easy will it be to find here positions pregnant with greater evil, or more likely to become productive of that evil than the two which are included in the compass of this one page, preceeded and succeeded as it is with so many excellent and unexceptionable ones.

In the . . . [3] situation in question, a selfish and tyrannical husband, how eagerly will he be apt to catch at it, and make out of it a pretence for aggravating the already universally existing tyranny of the male sex over the female.

A selfish and severe father, how eagerly will he be apt to catch at it, and make out of it a pretence for converting into puppets, the wires of which are in his hands, the minds as well as bodies of his children of both sexes!

[*On Locke*]¹

In thus holding up to view *property*, that being the appellation employed by him, though the *matter of wealth* would have been the more determinate and better defined one, in thus holding up to view in connection with '*injustice*'—the opposite to justice—Locke showed that on that occasion he had missed sight of so many other valuable subject matters of possession, namely, power, reputation, condition in life in so far as beneficent, not forgetting exemption from *pain* in all the several shapes in which either body or mind is the seat of it (a possession for which unfortunately language has not been found to furnish any shorter name), possessions giving security to which is among the functions and cares of justice: so many subject-matters of *maleficence* on the part of individuals, of inhibition and punishment at the hands of government, and, to the extent of such inhibition (termed also prohibition) of delinquency on the part of individuals.

Sad, unguarded, unfelicitous was in truth that ill-considered definition—that attempt to lay with such loose materials the foundation of human happiness, in so far at least as resting upon justice. Sad the triumph which by a deserving and uncandid antagonist might on that occasion have been reaped over that honest, candid and in every respect amiable mind. Property the only thing entitled to be the object of care to government. Possessors of property accordingly the only persons entitled to be objects of that same care! The possessors of property the only persons entitled to be represented in and by a representative body forming part and parcel of the sovereign authority! The poor in a body, a community which the rich in a body are entitled to make slaves of and for ever treat as such. Corporal slavery, a state of things still worse perhaps than individual slavery, a state of things the production and maintenance of which is a proper object of government. Meridian of the West Indies, the meridian for which the principles of this supposed champion of liberty and good government! ... [2]

The case is that, in the mind of this philosopher, to whom, after all, the debt owed by mankind is so indisputable, real and extensive—expansion had not at that time at least, gone beyond *aristocracy*, the opulent, the ruling, the influential few: the people, the purely subject many, had not as yet fallen within the sphere of his observation—arrived at the apparent magnitude, necessary to the being numbered among the objects of his case.

That in respect of expansion such was the state of his mind—that in respect of objects belonging to the art and science of morals, politics, and thence legislation included, is a proposition the truth of which is rendered but too accountable in and by his constitution of one of the Carolinas: a performance which from that day to this has never been spoken of in any other character than that of a failure.

He is accordingly the properest of all Gods which, within the sphere of politics, can be found for the idolatry of the Whigs, for the worshipping of the matchless and all perfect constitution, for the glorious revolution of 1688.

APPENDIX D

[*Social Contract*]¹

36. As to the Original Contract, . . . a few pages, perhaps, may not be ill bestowed in endeavouring to come to a precise notion about its reality and use. The stress laid on it formerly, and still, perhaps, by some, is such as renders it an object not undeserving of attention. I was in hopes, however, till I observed the notice taken of it by our Author² that this chimera has been effectually demolished by Mr Hume.ᵃ I think we hear not so much of it now as

---

ᵃ In the third volume of his Treatise of Human Nature. . . . For my own part, I well remember, no sooner had I read that part of the work which touches on this subject, than I felt as if scales had fallen from my eyes. I then, for the first time, learned to call the cause of the people the cause of Virtue.

Perhaps a short sketch of the wanderings of a raw but well-intentioned mind, in its researches after moral truth, may, on this occasion, be not unuseful: for the history of one mind is the history of many. . . .

Conversing with Lawyers, I found them full of the virtues of their Original Contract, as a recipe of sovereign efficacy for reconciling the accidental necessity of resistance with the general duty of submission. This drug of theirs they administered to me to calm my scruples. But my unpractised stomach revolted against their opiate. I bid them open to me that page of history in which the solemnisation of this important contract was recorded. They shrunk from this challenge; nor could they, when thus pressed, do otherwise than our Author has done, confess the whole to be a fiction. This, methought, looked ill. It seemed to me the acknowledgement of a bad cause, the bringing a fiction to support it. 'To prove fiction, indeed,' said I, 'there is need of fiction; but it is the characteristic of truth to need no proof but truth. Have you then really any such privilege as that of coining facts? You are spending argument to no purpose. Indulge yourselves in the licence of supposing that to be true which is not, and as well may you suppose that proposition itself to be true, which you wish to prove, as that other whereby

formerly. The indestructible prerogatives of mankind have no need to be supported upon the sandy foundation of a fiction.

37. With respect to this, and other fictions, there was once a time, perhaps, when they had their use. With instruments of this temper, I will not deny but that some political work may have been done, and that useful work, which, under the then circumstances of things, could hardly have been done with any other. But the season of fiction is now over: insomuch, that what formerly might have been tolerated and countenanced under that name, would, if now attempted to be set on foot, be censured and stigmatised under the harsher appellations of *encroachment* or *imposture*. To attempt to introduce any *new* one, would be *now* a crime: for which reason there is much danger, without any use, in vaunting and propagating such as have been introduced already. In point of *political discernment*, the universal spread of learning has raised mankind in a manner to a level with each other, in comparison of what they have been in any former time: nor is any man now so far elevated above his fellows, as that he should be indulged in the dangerous licence of cheating them for their good.

38. As to the fiction now before us, in the character of an *argumentum ad hominem*, coming when it did, and managed as it was, it succeeded to admiration.

That compacts, by whomsoever entered into, *ought* to be kept; that men are *bound* by compacts, are propositions which men, without knowing or inquiring why, were disposed universally to accede to. The observance of promises they had been accustomed to see pretty constantly enforced. They had been accustomed to see kings, as well as others, behave themselves as if bound by them. This proposition, then, 'that men are bound by *compacts*'; and this other, 'that, if one party performs not his part, the other is released

---

you hope to prove it.' Thus continued I, unsatisfying and unsatisfied, till I learnt to see that *utility* was the test and measure of all virtue; of loyalty as much as any: and that the obligation to minister to general happiness was an obligation paramount to and inclusive of every other. Having thus got the instruction I stood in need of, I sat down to make my profit of it. I bid adieu to the original contract: and I left it to those to amuse themselves with this rattle, who could think they needed it.

from his', being propositions which no man disputed, were propositions which no man had any call to prove. In theory they were assumed for axioms: and in practice they were observed as rules.[b] If, on any occasion, it was thought proper to make a show of proving them, it was rather for form's sake than for any thing else; and that, rather in the way of momento or instruction to acquiescing auditors, than in the way of proof against opponents. On such an occasion the common-place retinue of phrases was at hand; *Justice, Right Reason* required it; the *Law of Nature* commanded it, and so forth: all which are but so many ways of intimating that a man is firmly persuaded of the truth of this or that moral proposition, though he either thinks he *need not*, or finds he *can't*, tell *why*. Men were too obviously and too generally interested in the observance of these rules, to entertain doubts concerning the force of any arguments they saw employed in their support. It is an old observation, how Interest smooths the road to Faith.

39. A compact, then, it was said, was made by the king and people: the terms of it were to this effect. The people, on their part, promised to the king a *general obedience*. The king, on his part, promised to *govern* the people in such a *particular* manner always, as should be *subservient* to their happiness. I insist not on the words: I undertake only for the sense; as far as an imaginary engagement, so loosely and so variously worded by those who have imagined it, is capable of any decided signification. Assuming, then, as a general rule, that promises, when made, ought to be observed; and, as a point of fact, that a promise to this effect in particular had been made by the party in question, men were more ready to deem themselves qualified to judge when it was such a promise was *broken*, than to decide directly and avowedly on the delicate question, when it was that a king acted so far in *opposition* to the happiness of his people, that it were better no longer to obey him.

40. It is manifest, on a very little consideration, that nothing was gained by this manoeuvre after all: no difficulty removed by it.

---

[b] A *compact* or *contract* (for the two words, on this occasion at least, are used in the same sense) may, I think, be defined, [as] a pair of promises, by two persons reciprocally given, the one promise in consideration of the other.

It was still necessary, and that as much as ever, that the question men studied to avoid should be determined, in order to determine the question they thought to substitute in its room. It was still necessary to determine, whether the king in question had, or had not, acted so far in *opposition* to the happiness of his people, that it were better no longer to obey him; in order to determine, whether the promise he was supposed to have made, had or had not been broken. For what was the supposed purport of this promise? It was no other than what has just been mentioned.

41. Let it be said, that part at least of this promise was to govern in *subservience to Law*: that hereby a more precise rule was laid down for his conduct, by means of this supposal of a promise, than that other loose and general rule to govern in subservence to the *happiness of his people*: and that, by this means, it is the letter of the *Law* that forms the tenor of the rule.

Now true it is, that the governing in opposition to Law, is *one* way of governing in opposition to the happiness of the people: the natural effect of such a contempt of the Law being, if not actually to destroy, at least to threaten with destruction, all those rights and privileges that are founded on it: rights and privileges on the enjoyment of which that happiness depends. But still it is not this that can be safely taken for the entire purport of the promise here in question: and that for several reasons. *First*, because the most mischievous, and under certain constitutions the most feasible, method of governing in opposition to the happiness of the people, is, by setting the Law itself in opposition to their happiness. *Secondly*, because it is a case very conceivable, that a king may, to a great degree, impair the happiness of his people without violating the letter of any single Law. *Thirdly*, because extraordinary occasions may now and then occur, in which the happiness of the people may be better promoted by acting, for the moment, in *opposition* to the Law, than in *subservience* to it. *Fourthly*, because it is not any single violation of the Law, as such, that can properly be taken for a breach of his part of the contract, so as to be understood to have released the people from the obligation of performing theirs. For, to quit the fiction, and resume the language of plain truth, it is scarce ever any single violation of the Law that, by being *submitted to*, can produce so much mischief as shall surpass the probable mischief of *resisting* it. If every single instance whatever of such a violation were to be deemed an entire dissolution of the contract, a man who reflects at all would scarce find any where, I believe, under the sun, that government which he could allow to subsist for twenty years together. It is plain, therefore, that to pass any sound decision upon the question which the inventors of this fiction substituted instead of the true one, the latter was still necessary to be decided. All they gained by their contrivance was the convenience of deciding it obliquely, as it were, and by a side wind—that is, in a crude and hasty way, without any direct and steady examination.

42. But, after all, for what *reason* is it, that men *ought* to keep their promises? The moment any intelligible reason is given, it is this: that it is for the *advantage* of society they should keep them; and if they do not, that as far as *punishment* will go, they should be *made* to keep them. It is for the advantage of the whole number that the promises of each individual should be kept: and, rather than they should not be kept, that such individuals as fail to keep them should be punished. If it be asked, how this appears? the answer is at hand: such is the benefit to gain, and mischief to avoid, by keeping them, as much more than compensates the mischief of so much punishment as is requisite to oblige men to it. Whether the dependence of *benefit* and *mischief* (that is, of *pleasure* and *pain*) upon men's conduct in this behalf, be as here stated, is a question of *fact*, to be decided, in the same manner that all other questions of fact are to be decided, by *testimony*, *observation*, and *experience*.[c]

43. This, then, and no other, being the *reason* why men should be made to keep their promises, *viz.* that is for the advantage of society that they should, is a reason that may as well be given at

---

[c] The importance which the observance of promises is of to the happiness of society, is placed in a very striking and satisfactory point of view, in a little apologue of Montesquieu, entitled, *The History of the Troglodytes*. The Troglodytes are a people who pay no regard to promises. By the natural consequences of this disposition, they fall from one scene of misery into another; and are at last exterminated. The same Philosopher, in his *Spirit of Laws*, copying and refining upon the current jargon, feigns a law for this and other purposes, after defining a Law to be a *relation*. How much more instructive on this head is the fable of the Troglodytes, than the pseudo-metaphysical sophistry of the *Esprit des Loix*!

once why kings, on the one hand, in governing, should in general keep within established Laws, and (to speak universally) abstain from all such measures as tend to the unhappiness of their subjects: and, on the other hand, why subjects should obey kings as long as they so conduct themselves, and no longer; why they should obey, in short, *so long as the probable mischiefs of obedience are less than the probable mischiefs of resistance*: why, in a word, taking the whole body together, it is their *duty* to obey just so long as it is their *interest*, and no longer. This being the case, what need of saying of the one, that *he* promised so to *govern*; of the other, that they promised so to *obey*, when the fact is otherwise?

44. True it is, that, in this country, according to ancient forms, some sort of vague promise of *good government* is made by kings at the ceremony of their coronation: and let the acclamations, perhaps given, perhaps not given, by chance persons out of the surrounding multitude, be construed into a promise of *obedience* on the part of the *whole* multitude: that whole multitude itself a small drop collected together by chance out of the ocean of the state: and let the two promises thus made be deemed to have formed a perfect *compact*: not that either of them is declared to be the *consideration* of the other.

45. Make the most of this concession: one experiment there is, by which every reflecting man may satisfy himself, I think beyond a doubt that it is the consideration of *utility*, and no other, that, secretly, perhaps, but unavoidably, has governed his judgment upon all these matters. The experiment is easy and decisive. It is but to reverse, in supposition, in the first place, the import of the *particular* promise thus feigned; in the next place, the effect in point of *utility* of the observance of promises *in general*. Suppose the king to promise that he would govern his subjects *not* according to Law; *not* in the view to promote their happiness: would this be binding upon *him*? Suppose the people to promise they would obey him *at all events*, let him govern as he will; let him govern to their destruction: would this be binding upon *them*? Suppose the constant and universal effect of an observance of promises were to produce *mischief*, would it *then* be men's *duty* to observe them? would it *then* be *right* to make Laws, and apply punishment to *oblige* men to observe them?

46. 'No,' (it may perhaps be replied); 'but for this reason: among promises, some there are that, as every one allows, are void: now these you have been supposing, are unquestionably of the number. A promise that is in itself *void*, cannot, it is true, create any obligation: But allow the promise to be *valid*, and it is the promise itself that creates the obligation, and nothing else.' The fallacy of this argument it is easy to perceive. For what is it, then, that the promise depends on for its *validity*? What is it that being *present* makes its *valid*? What is it that being *wanting* makes it *void*? To acknowledge that any *one* promise may be void, is to acknowledge that if any *other* is *binding*, it is not merely because it is a promise. That circumstance, then, whatever it be, on which the validity of a promise depends; that circumstance, I say, and not the promise itself, must, it is plain, be the cause of the obligation which a promise is apt in general to carry with it.

47. But farther. Allow, for argument's sake, what we have disproved: allow that the obligation of a promise is independent of every other: allow that a promise is binding *propria vi*: Binding, then, on whom? On him certainly who makes it. Admits this: for what reason is the same individual promise to be binding on those who *never* made it? The king, *fifty years ago*, promised my *great-grandfather* to govern him according to Law: my great-grandfather, *fifty years ago*, promised the king to obey him according to Law. The king, *just now*, promised my *neighbour* to govern him according to Law: my neighbour, *just now*, promised the king to obey him according to Law. Be it so: what are these promises, all or any of them, to *me*? To make answer to this question, some other principle, it is manifest, must be resorted to, than that of the *intrinsic* obligation of promises upon those who make them.

48. Now this *other* principle that still recurs upon us, what other can it be than the *principle of* utility?[d] The principle which furnishes

---

[d] To this denomination, has of late been added, or substituted, the *greatest-happiness* or *greatest-felicity* principle: this for shortness, instead of saying at length, *that principle* which states the greatest happiness of all those whose interest is in question, as being the right and proper, and only right and proper and universally desirable, *end* of human action: of human action in every situation; and,

us with that *reason*, which alone depends not upon any higher reason, but which is itself the sole and all-sufficient reason for every point of practice whatsoever.

---

in particular, in that of a functionary, or set of functionaries, exercising the powers of Government. The word *utility* does not so clearly point to the ideas of *pleasure* and *pain* as the words *happiness* and *felicity* do: nor does it lead us to the consideration of the *number* of the interests affected: so the *number*, as being the circumstance which contributes, in the largest proportion, to the formation of the standard here in question—the *standard of right and wrong*, by which alone the propriety of human conduct, in every situation, can with propriety be tried.

This want of a sufficiently manifest connexion between the ideas of *happiness* and *pleasure* on the one hand, and the idea of *utility* on the other, I have every now and then found operating, and with but too much efficiency, as a bar to the acceptance that might otherwise have been given, to this principle.

For further elucidation of the principle of *utility*, or say *greatest-happiness principle*, it may be some satisfaction to the reader, to see a note, inserted in a second edition, now printing, of a later work of the Author's, entitled, *An Introduction to the Principles of Morals and Legislation*. In Chapter I, subjoined to paragraph 13, is a note in these words: 'The principle of utility' (I have heard it said) 'is a dangerous principle: it is dangerous on certain occasions to consult it.' This is as much as to say—what? that it is not consonant to utility, to consult utility; in short, that it is *not* consulting it, to consult it. [I have omitted the rest of the footnote. It is polemical and of no interest. Ed.]

APPENDIX E

[*Perfection and Its Limits*][1]

The perfection of the law will be at its *acme* and the condition of mankind as far as depends upon the law will be at its *optimum* when the following signs are visible: when palpable injuries are unknown except by means of the laws by which they stand prohibited; when no acts to which man's nature is prone are included in the catalogue of offences that do not deserve to be so, when the rights and duties of the various classes of subjects are so well defined by the civil code that there are no longer any controversies in which the question turns upon the point of law; when the code of procedure is so formed that the few controversies which arise purely out of the matter of fact are terminated without any unnecessary expense or delay; when the courts of justice are seldom filled, though always open without intermission; where the military forces of nations being broken down by mutual stipulations not by mutual impotence, the burden of taxes is render'd imperceptible; when trade is so far free that no branch which might be carried on by many is confined to few, nor any branch pinched by pressure of taxes into a smaller compass than it would otherwise assume; when for the encouragement of such branches of industry as require positive encouragement,[2] positive encouragement is given; and liberty, perfect liberty to such as require nothing more. When the constitutional law is settled on such a footing and the rights, powers and duties of the servants of the public are so distributed and circumscribed, and the dispositions of the people to submission and to resistance so tempered and adjusted, that the prosperity resulting from the preceding circumstances is fixed;[3] lastly when the law, which is the rule of men's actions, is concise, intelligible, unambiguous and in the hands of every man. But to what does all this felicity amount: only to the absence of a certain quantity of evil: to the absence of a part of the various mass of evil to which human nature is now subject. That the accession of felicity would be great and the prospect comfortable is not to be denied: but still there is nothing in it that is mysterious and unknown: nothing but what the imagination of man at the present period is perfectly competent to conceive. Fire will burn, frost pinch, thirst parch, hunger gripe as heretofore: toil even as now must be the prelude to subsistence: that the few may be wealthy, the many must be poor; all must be tantalised more or less with the prospect of joys or supposed joys, which they are out of hope of tasting, and how much lighter so ever coercion may sit than it does now, coercion must still be felt, that all may be secure.

NOTES

PREFACE

1 Thanks to the Bentham committee, set up in 1959 under the chairmanship of Lord Cohen and ably guided since 1961 by Professor J. H. Burns, nearly all of Bentham's mss. should be generally available during the next few years.

INTRODUCTION

1 Mss, UCL, Box 169, p. 79. Bentham's dream is reprinted in David Baumgardt, *Bentham and the Ethics of Today*, Princeton University Press, 1952, Appendix I. In his account of his dream Bentham remarks, 'The world is persuaded not without some ground of reason that all reformers and system-mongers are mad. . . . My madness has not yet, as far as I can perceive myself, gone beyond a dream'. Although generally reliable, Baumgardt occasionally mistranscribes the manuscripts.

2 In addition to the well-known general discussions by Sidgwick, G. E. Moore, Rashdall and Broad, and the specifically Bentham-centred discussions by Mill, Halévy and Baumgardt, for good recent accounts see John Plamenatz, *The English Utilitarians*, Blackwell, 1958; A. J. Ayer, The Principle of Utility, in G. W. Keeton and G. Schwarzenberger ed. *Jeremy Bentham and the Law*, Stevens and Son, 1948; Mary P. Mack, *Jeremy Bentham: An Odyssey of Ideas, 1748–1792*, Heinemann, 1962; and David Lyons, 'Was Bentham an Utilitarian?' in *Royal Institute of Philosophy Lectures*, 1972.

3 It is surprising that Bentham's theory of sovereignty has received little attention from legal and political philosophers. A few exceptions are: H. L. A. Hart, 'Bentham on Sovereignty', *The Irish Jurist*, Winter 1967 (reprinted in Bhikhu Parekh, ed., *Jeremy Bentham: Ten Critical Essays*, Frank Cass, 1973); C. W. Everett's Introduction to Bentham's *A Comment on the Commentaries*, Oxford University Press, 1928; and James

Bryce, *Studies in History and Jurisprudence*, Oxford University Press, 1901. F. C. Montague's Introduction to his edition of *A Fragment on Government* and D. J. Manning, *The Mind of Jeremy Bentham*, Longmans, 1968 also contain a few brief remarks on Bentham's views on sovereignty.

4 *An Introduction to the Principles of Morals and Legislation*, ch.. 1, para. 1.

5 For the following four paragraphs I have relied on my 'Bentham's Justification of the Principle of Utility' in *Jeremy Bentham: Ten Critical Essays*, op. cit.

6 *The Works of Jeremy Bentham*, ed. John Bowring, Edinburgh, 1859, Vol. VIII, p. 280.

7 *Deontology*, Vol. 1. p. 165.

8 There is, of course, the big question whether an essentially egoistic creature can be expected to promote others' happiness. This is discussed later in the section on Bentham's theory of government.

9 *Principles*, p. 2, where in both paragraphs 2 and 3 it is clearly stated that the party whose interest is in question may be a private individual or the community as a whole.

10 It is worth observing that Priestley had in fact never used the phrase. It first appeared in the anonymous English translation of Beccaria's *Dei delitti e delle Pence*. The phrase, although inspired by Beccaria, was in fact first used by his translator.

11 *Principles*, ch. I, para 3, and ch. XVII, Para 20.

12 Mss, Box 15, pp. 20 and 57. It was this long disappearance of the formula that probably misled Bowring into saying that Bentham used it for the first time in 1822. Bentham had already used it 1776.

13 See Appendix A in this volume. Of the attempts made by several of Bentham's disciples to show that the greatest happiness of the greatest number formula is *not* self-contradictory, the most notable are those by Bowring, Mss, Box 14, p. 452, and Perronet Thompson, *Exercises*, 1842, Vol. I, pp. 135–6.

14 *Principles*, ch. I, para. 13, fn. 1. (Added in 1822.)

15 *Works*, Vol. I, p. 263. Although Bentham repeats this definition of political society at a number of places, he is not entirely happy with it, particularly with the term habit. Habit in his

view refers to past and not to future actions, whereas it is the willingness to continue to obey the sovereign in the future that seems to him to be the hall mark of a political society. In *Of Laws in General*, ed. H. L. A. Hart, Athlone Press, London, 1971, p. 18, he therefore defines political society in terms of 'disposition' to obey the sovereign and drops the term habit altogether. Sometimes he defines it in terms of both habit and disposition (Vol. I, p. 290). At other times, he argues that habit is the 'cause' of disposition (Vol. III, p. 219; also Vol. II, p. 521). At one place, Bentham rejects this view and says that 'strictly speaking, habit, being but a fictitious entity, and not really anything distinct from the acts or perceptions by which it is said to be formed, cannot be the cause of anything' (Vol. I p. 57). For Bentham's analysis of the nature of habit, see ibid, p. 37.

16 Bentham's concern to distinguish between political society and independent political society, and his view that only the latter needs a sovereign, are evident in *A Fragment on Government*, ch. I, paras. 22–5. The most accessible edition of *Fragment*, with a scholarly introduction, is *A Fragment on Government and An Introduction to the Principles of Morals and Legislation*, ed. Wilfrid Harrison, Basil Blackwell, 1960. John Austin criticises Bentham for 'forgetting to notice' that one of the essential negative characteristics of a political society is that its superior 'must not be habitually obedient to any other certain individual or body'. *The Province of Jurisprudence Determined*, ed. H. L. A. Hart, Weidenfeld and Nicolson, 1965, p. 212. Austin's criticism would be justified if Bentham was defining an *independent* political society. But he was not. He was defining political society, independent or otherwise. Bentham agrees with Austin that the superior must not obey anyone outside his society if his is to be an independent political society.

17 This question worried John Austin as well. See *Province of Jurisprudence*, op. cit., p. 203 f.

18 *Fragment*, ch. I, para. 19. Austin takes the opposite view that such a society is a natural society, because there is no general habit of obeying a common superior and therefore no law 'which can be called the law of that given society' (*Province of Jurisprudence*, op. cit. p. 209).

19 Mss, UCL, Box 69, p. 50.

20 *Ibid.*

21 'It was dread of evil, not the hope of good, that first cemented societies together.' He thinks that although fear may not be a predominant motive in all men, it is certainly so among 'the untutored many'. *Principles*, ch. XVI, para 17, fn. It is interesting to observe how Bentham relies on the history of language to offer him a clue to the political practices of the remote past. *Ibid.*

22 Vol. III, p. 219.

23 *Fragment*, ch. IV, para 20 f.

24 *Of Laws*, p. 20.

25 *Fragment*, ch. IV, para 34.

26 *Principles*, ch. XVI, para 17, fn.

27 *Ibid.*, p. 289.

28 *Of Laws*, p. 69.

29 *Jeremy Bentham: Ten Critical Essays*, op. cit.

30 *Of Laws*, p. 69.

31 *Fragment*, ch. IV, para 36.

32 *Ibid.*

33 P. 32f, infra.

34 *Fragment*, ch. IV. Austin took the opposite view that a sovereign cannot be a subject of rights. Every right, he argued, presupposes three parties: a party on whom it is conferred, a party on whom the corresponding obligation is imposed, and the sovereign who makes a law conferring the one and imposing the other. No such third party is available in the case of the sovereign. To say that a sovereign has a right is to say that a man can confer a right on himself, and that in Austin's view is absurd.

35 *Of Laws*, p. 18.

36 *Fragment*, ch. IV, paras 23 ff.

37 *Of Laws*, 64 ff; also p. 18.

38 *Ibid.*

39 *Ibid.*, p. 70.

40 *Fragment*, ch. IV, para 23, fn. 1.

41 *Ibid.*, para 26.

42 *Of Laws*, p. 18.

43 *Ibid.*, p. 67.

44 *Ibid.*, p. 16.

45 *Ibid.*, p. 65.

46 By interest Bentham means whatever conduces to happiness.

47 'By a service may be meant any such act whereby one man contributes to the pleasure of another'. Mss. UCL, Box 69, Folder 169, p. 1.

48 *Works*, Vol. III, p. 179.

49 It is worth observing that Bentham describes the wife's services as services of 'the purely passive faculty', of 'the inert human body'. *Ibid.*

50 Sympathy, Bentham believes, is natural to man. Man in his view is so constituted that it is difficult for him to see suffering without 'uneasiness' and without wanting to do something about it. Mss, UCL, Box 14, pp 202–3.

51 *Works*, Vol. VIII, p. 247.

52 *Works*, Vol. III, p. 184.

53 *Ibid.*, p. 220.

54 *Ibid.*, p. 221.

55 'By a condition in life understand an incorporeal subject: matter of possession by the possession of which . . . a person is subjected to a cluster of obligations and is put into the possession of a cluster of rights'. Mss, UCL, Box 30, p. 144.

56 *Works*, Vol. III, p. 211.

57 *Works*, Vol. II, p. 269.

58 *Works*, Vol. IX, p. 13.

59 *Ibid.*

60 *Works*, Vol. III, p. 339.

61 *Works*, Vol. I, p. 148.

62 *Works*, Vol. I, p. 340.

63 *Ibid.*

64 *Ibid.*, p. 331.

65 *Works*, Vol. III, p. 159.

66 *Ibid.*, p. 160.

67 *Ibid.*, p. 161.

68 *Works*, Vol. IX, p. 14.

69 *Ibid.*, p. 81; also Vol. III, p. 230.

70 *Works*, Vol. IX, p. 16.

71 For a critique of Bentham's theory of equality, see my 'Bentham's Theory of Equality', *Political Studies*, Dec., 1970.

72 For a detailed discussion of these see my Introduction in *Jeremy Bentham: Ten Critical Essays*, op. cit.

73 *Works*, Vol. I, p. 562.

74 One of the basic tasks of education is to instil 'a constant habit of applauding or condemning actions according to their general utility'. This involves cultivating 'attachments' and 'affections' to the nation and subordinating 'family affections . . . to national ones'. Mss. UCL, Box 15, p. 96.

75 Appendix C in this volume.

CHAPTER I

1 Mss., UCL, Box 102, pp. 7–31 and 78–9.

CHAPTER 2

1 Mss., UCL, Box 101, pp. 201–2 and 217–24. Written in 1814 and 1826.

2 The following three paragraphs are dated October 1813 and were written at different times. I have followed the order of the mss. in inserting them here.

CHAPTER 3

1 Mss., UCL, Box 101, pp. 406–14. Written in July 1816.

2 As the preceding paragraph disturbs the continuity of exposition, it has been omitted.

CHAPTER 4

1 *From A Table of the Springs of Action*, published by Bentham in 1815.

CHAPTER 5

1 From *An Introduction to the Principles of Morals and Legislation* first published in 1789 (although printed 13 November 1780) and then in 1823. The 1789 edition contains lists of 'Errata' and 'Corrections and Additions'. Since the book was printed in 1780, the text was not corrected, and the list of corrections was appended to the book. In his copy of the book, now in the

British Museum, Bentham also made several other small changes. They are largely either terminological or designed to give references to people whose views Bentham criticises in Chapter II of the *Introduction*. The 1823 edition overlooked many of these corrections and changes. Even Bowring who incorporated many of them overlooked or ignored some in Vol. I of his Collected Works. The best edition of *Introduction* is that by J. H. Burns and H. L. A. Hart. The editors have provided a scholarly introduction and helpful comparative references.

2 This is slightly misleading since it was not included in the text itself but in the list of 'Corrections and Additions' at the end of the book.

3 Bentham inserted a long footnote here in 1822. It has been omitted.

4 The rest of the footnote, consisting of six fairly long paragraphs, has been omitted.

5 The words 'and that a sufficient one' were not in the 1789 edition but were proposed in Bentham's list of 'corrections and additions'. They were not included in the 1823 edition. Bowring inserted them in Vol. I of his Works.

6 The names of philosophers holding the views criticised by Bentham were inserted by him in his copy of the 1789 edition. They were not included in the 1823 edition, but Bowring included them. I have followed Burns and Hart, *op. cit.*, in putting them in bracket.

7 The 1789 edition read 'of such actions of those individuals'. In the list of errata Bentham proposed deletion of 'of those individuals'. Both 1823 edition and Bowring accepted this but mysteriously turned 'such actions' into 'those actions'. See Burns and Hart, *op. cit.*, p. 28, fol. 2.

CHAPTER 6

1 Mss., UCL, Box 14, pp. 281–5. Written March 1827.

2 Mss., UCL, Box 14, pp. 266–7. Written November–December 1819.

3 Mss., UCL, Box 14. Written September 1795. The ms. is entitled 'virtue—what'.

4 I am not sure if this is a correct reading of the ms.

5 Mss., UCL, Box 14, pp. 94–6. Written September 1814.

6 I am not sure if this is a correct reading of the ms.

7 Mss., UCL, Box 14, p. 227. Written April 1819.

8 Mss., UCL, Box 14, pp. 219–22. Written February 1819.

9 A few words have been omitted as they appear rather muddled.

10 The ms. is slightly damaged; this could be either 'great' or 'greatest'. The latter is more plausible.

11 Mss., UCL, Box 14, pp. 97–9. Written September 1814.

12 Two short sentences at the top of page 98 have been omitted.

13 The next sentence simply repeats what has been said here and is therefore omitted.

14 The bracketed part of the sentence is in the margin and Bentham does not indicate where it is to be inserted. This seems to be its proper place.

15 Mss., UCL, Box 106, pp. 397–401. Written July 1829. The full title of the ms. reads: 'On the supposed love of Justice—occasioned by an article in the *Scotsman* of Sunday, 5 July 1829.'

16 Mss., UCL, Box 15, pp. 65–6. Written July 1816.

17 A sentence in the margin reads: 'It is that sort of opposition which howsoever social it may be when under control in its effects and tendency, belongs of itself to a different class'. It is not clear where Bentham wanted to insert it.

18 The ms. reads 'it', but it should clearly be 'in'.

19 Mss., UCL, Box 14, pp. 38–9. Written August 1814.

20 Ths next few words do not seem to make any sense. The ms. is difficult to read.

21 Mss., UCL, Box 14, pp. 256–63. Written October 1819.

22 Mss., UCL, Box 14, p. 264. Written December 1819.

23 Mss., UCL, Box 14, pp. 251–2. Written August 1819. Bentham attempts to show here that morally vanity is better than pride and could be called a virtue.

24 Mss., UCL, Box 14, p. 243. Written August 1819.

CHAPTER 7

1 Mss., UCL, Box 27, 29–30. (Written in 1778.)

2 Sections 12 to 14 are cancelled by Bentham.

3 A sentence has been omitted here. It repeats the point already made.

4 Mss., UCL, Box 27, pp. 32–40. (Written around 1778.) A small part of this ms. was published by E. Halevy in his *La formation du radicalisme philosophique*, tome I, 1901, pp. 398 ff. It was not, however, included in the English translation by Mary Morris in 1928. David Baumgardt published it as an appendix IV to his *Bentham & the Ethics of To-day* (Princeton University Press, 1952). Although Baumgardt transcribed the ms. fairly accurately, he unwisely interspersed the text with marginal remarks and with notes.

5 The phrase in the bracket is in the margin and there is no indication where Bentham wished to insert it. This seems to be its most appropriate place.

6 Bentham has a few words in the margin which he wished to insert here. But since they do not fit into the context they have been omitted.

7 Bentham does not indicate where the following footnote belongs, but this seems to be its proper place. 'To speak more accurately, as the number expressive of its intensity multiplied by the number expressive of its duration.'

8 There are two footnotes in the mss. which have been omitted. They are of no real interest.

9 The words from 'leaving' to 'magnitude' are in the margin and Bentham does not indicate where they are to be inserted. They seem to me to belong here.

CHAPTER 8

1 From *A Fragment on Government*, published by Bentham in 1773.
2 The preceding nine paragraphs have been omitted.

CHAPTER 9

1 Mss., UCL, Box 25, pp. 10–15. Written May 1786.

CHAPTER 10

1 Mss., UCL, Box 69, pp. 70–5. Written 1776.
2 See note (c) to para. 14.
3 Bentham has mistakenly numbered two paragraphs 25. To avoid confusion, I have marked them 25(i) and 25(ii).
4 I am not sure if this is a correct reading of the ms.

5 Although I have followed the ms. in leaving this paragraph here, clearly it does not belong here. The empty bracket before it in the ms. also indicates that Bentham meant it as a footnote in some other place. It is best seen as a footnote to para. 32.

6 There is no entry under para. 40.

7 Some remarks in the margin have been omitted.

8 Two sentences have been omitted here as they do not seem to make any sense in the context.

CHAPTER II

1 Mss., UCL, Box 88b, pp. 229–37. This and the following two chapters were first published in the *Limits of Jurisprudence Defined*, ed. Charles Warren Everett (Columbia University Press, 1945). They are also published in *Of Laws in General*, ed. H. L. A. Hart (University of London, Athlone Press, 1970). As will be seen in the notes, Everett mistranscribed and omitted a number of key words and phrases, and even Hart's otherwise excellent edition is not free from some of these blemishes.

2 That is, a law.

3 Everett and Hart read this as 'may perhaps'.

4 Everett and Hart read this phrase as 'may not be disposed to obey. . . .'

5 Everett and Hart read this as 'any'.

6 Everett and Hart read this as 'would'.

7 Bentham's page reference is to the edition published in 1789.

8 Everett reads this as 'but'.

9 Everett and Hart read this as 'laying'.

10 In the ms. a relevant sentence in the margin reads: 'To deny it is as much as to say that it is God Almighty indeed that keeps up the race of elephants, but it is somebody else that keeps up the race of mites.' Although Bentham has crossed it out, Everett chooses to retain it.

11 A rather long sentence follows here in the ms. Although Bentham has crossed it out, Everett retains it.

12 Everett reads this as 'issue'.

13 I have omitted a very long footnote.

14 Everett and Hart transcribe this phrase as 'because on the part of the sovereign a mandate. . . .'

15. Everett reads this as 'issue'.
16 Everett reads this as 'come'.
17 Everett reads this as 'ensue'.

CHAPTER 12

1 Mss., UCL, Box 88b, pp. 280–90.
2 Both Everett and Hart omit the words 'to be'.
3 Everett and Hart read 'being' as 'are', but this seems a mistake.
4 I have omitted a long footnote.
5 Both Everett and Hart read this word as 'certain'.
6 Both Everett and Hart omit 'and'.
7 Both Everett and Hart insert the word 'person' after 'one', but that seems a mistake.

CHAPTER 13

1 Mss., UCL, Box 88a, pp. 120–32. Written in 1780. I have omitted the first two paras. The mss. are entitled *Exposition*. Bentham explained in a footnote to Paragraph 25 of Ch. 16 of *An Introduction to Principles of Morals and Legislation* that, although he had there defined the idea of trust in terms of power and right, he had not defined and analysed these concepts themselves. He remarked that he had in fact prepared an 'exposition' of them, but felt that it was 'too voluminous and minute' to be included in the *Introduction*. In this chapter Bentham offers a systematic account of power, right and other related concepts, and, in so doing, explains the nature and function of law.
2 Everett & Hart omit the words 'in which'.
3 Everett reads it as 'one' but that seems wrong.
4 Both Everett & Hart omit 'of'.
5 Both Everett & Hart omit 'not'.
6 Everett omits 'its'.
7 Both Everett and Hart read as 'act' in the singular.
8 The alternative formulation in the ms. reads: 'As to this case it may be proper to observe that. . . .'
9 Both Everett & Hart end the sentence here and begin a new sentence with 'under any. . . .'. This changes the meaning.
10 Hart follows Everett in reading this as 'would'.
11 Everett and Hart omit the word 'in'.

12 Both Everett and Hart miss out this word.

13 Hart follows Everett in reading this word as 'that'.

14 Everett and Hart read 'fixing' as 'placing'.

15 Everett and Hart omit this word.

16 Everett and Hart read 'which' as 'that'.

17 Everett and Hart read 'objects' as 'object' in the singular.

18 Everett and Hart read the phrase 'in such a situation as to prevent. . . . ' as 'in any situation which prevent. . . . '

19 Everett and Hart read 'his' as 'the'.

20 Everett and Hart omit the word 'there'.

21 Everett and Hart omit this word.

22 Both Everett and Hart read this as 'for', which seems a mistake.

23 I follow Everett and Hart in reading this as 'latter' but doubt if this is a correct reading.

24 Both Everett and Hart omit 'of'.

25 Both Everett and Hart add the article 'a' before moral, which is not to be found in the ms.

26 Everett reads it as 'the', which seems wrong.

27 This entire phrase 'in favour of the person in question' is omitted by both Everett and Hart.

28 Both Everett and Hart omit 'of'.

29 Everett omits 'of'.

30 There is a gap in the mss. and I have followed Everett and Hart supplying this word as the most appropriate in the context.

31 Both Everett and Hart use the word 'order' in place of 'power'.

32 Both Everett and Hart read this as 'faculty' in the singular.

33 Everett reads this as 'law'.

34 Both Everett and Hart omit this word.

35 Both Everett and Hart use the term 'primary' instead of 'clear', but this seems a mistake. The alternative formulation reads 'precise'.

36 Both Everett and Hart read 'every' as 'any'.

37 Both Everett and Hart read 'a' as 'the'.

38 Everett and Hart interject the word 'cometh' after man.

39 Everett and Hart read this as 'do'.

40 Everett interjects 'or' after law.

41 Everett and Hart omit 'is'.

42 Both Everett and Hart omit the word 'in'.

43 Both Everett and Hart read this as 'nature' in the singular. Although the singular is more appropriate Bentham clearly uses the plural.

44 Both Everett and Hart read the 'former' as 'that person', which seems to be a mistake.

45 Everett and Hart read 'the' as 'that'.

46 Everett and Hart read 'this' as 'these'.

47 Everett and Hart read 'your' as 'my'.

48 Everett and Hart read 'a sort of indirect power' as 'sort of a indirect power'.

49 Although the ms. clearly reads 'you', I have followed Everett and Hart in changing it to 'me'.

50 Everett and Hart omit the words 'the last of'.

51 Bentham seems to use 'together' and 'in conjunction' as alternative formulations. Everett and Hart are therefore probably wrong to use both together.

CHAPTER 14

1 From the *Leading Principles of a Constitutional Code For Any State*, first published in *The Pamphleteer*, No. 44, 1823. Except for a few passages towards the end of Section I, I have included the complete text.

CHAPTER 15

1 Bentham argues that the general community can be looked upon as constituting a tribunal constantly judging the activities of its public officers. Every member of the community is an officer of this tribunal, a judge, and public opinion is the verdict passed by the tribunal.

CHAPTER 17

1 This is intended to ensure that voters should have several equally good candidates to choose from.

2 As this would vary from community to community, Bentham does not specify the number of years.

3 The legislation minister is the custodian of the Pannomion, the codified body of laws, and guides the legislature on legal matters.

4 It is worth observing that Bentham is in favour of popular militia in both the army and the navy. To distinguish them

from the mercenary or 'stipendiary' forces, Bentham calls them 'radical forces. He hopes that the navy in a 'pure republic' would largely consist of ships freely donated by public-spirited citizens.

4 His job is to take preventive measures against natural and human calamities like earthquake, drought, contagious disease and collapse of old buildings.

5 In addition to inspecting educational institutions, the education minister presides at all public examinations designed to select civil servants and ministers.

6 He manages government-owned land and buildings.

CHAPTER 18

1 Mss., UCL, Box 42b, pp. 656–727 and 826–40. Written 1823–4.

CHAPTER 19

1 Mss., UCL, Box 103(a) and (b), pp. 1–527.

2 What Bentham means is that when truth is not in man's interest, that is, when it is a source of pain to him, he will be inclined not to pursue it and will be led to accept pleasing but false ideas and beliefs. For a full discussion, see Bowring, Vol. II, pp. 477–8.

3 What Bentham means is that it is impossible to examine the grounds of all one's opinions, and therefore people accept many of them on others' authority. Usually, however, what happens is that sinister interests generate convenient opinions and beliefs which, through constant repetition and general acceptance, acquire an air of authority. For a full discussion, see *ibid.* pp. 478–9.

4 For an interesting discussion of whether deception is permitted in the cause of reform and progress, see *ibid.* p. 479–80.

5 Bowring omits the last two sentences.

CHAPTER 20

1 Mss., UCL, Box 146, pp. 61–232.

2 'Upon' should clearly be 'even'.

3 Bowring reads this as 'lever'.

4 There is a slight repetition in the ms. and I have omitted a couple of words.

5 Bentham's discussion of Article III has been omitted.

6 The following few lines in the ms. deal with classification of

offences, but, as they are irrelevant in the context, I have omitted them. Bowring omits them as well.

7 Bowring omits the following few words and ends the sentence with ' . . . dine elsewhere'. Perhaps his puritanical sense did not allow a woman to dine out with another man.

8 Bentham's discussion of remaining articles has been omitted.

9 These passages are excerpted from Bentham's criticisms of Sieye's *Declaration of Rights*.

10 Bentham's discussion of this article ends here. He also, however, comments on it later. What he says there is included below.

11 I have omitted a redundant sentence.

12 I have omitted a few words that only repeat the examples given earlier.

13 I have omitted a couple of words here, as they do not make any sense in the context.

14 This sentence is in the margin, but Bentham does not indicate where it is to be inserted. This seems to be its proper place.

CHAPTER 21

1 From *Codification Proposal Addressed by Jeremy Bentham to All Nations Professing Liberal Opinions*, published by Bentham in 1822.

2 That is, reasons that can be accepted as relevant in politics.

3 Bentham outlines here his familiar felicific calculus. As it has already been discussed earlier, I have omitted several paragraphs.

CHAPTER 22

1 Mss., UCL, Box 160, pp. 117–47. Written October 1820.

2 The page preceding this question is badly damaged and cannot be transcribed.

3 The answer to the preceding question is missing in the ms.

4 A page preceding this question is badly damaged and cannot be transcribed.

5 A small part of this page is damaged, and the words in the bracket are supplied by the editor.

6 The answer to the previous question is missing in the ms.

7 A question and an answer in the margin read: 'Q. What is delusion? A. Misrepresentation producing its intended effect: effectual misrepresentation'.

8 The answer to the previous question is missing in the ms.

9 The answer to the previous question is missing in the ms.

10 The entire sentence is illegible, and is transcribed here as accurately as the editor could.

11 There is no answer to this question in the ms. But Bentham has scribbled a few remarks that may have been intended as a basis for the answer. They are: 'The distributive law: benefit = good, burden = evil. Merited and deserved punishment.'

12 I am not sure if this is a correct rendering of the ms.

13 Bentham scribbles at the top of the page: 'The constitutional monarchy—instruments of delusion, 1. titles, 2. trappings.'

14 The anser to this question is missing in the ms.

APPENDIX A

1 Mss., UCL, Box 14, pp. 384-6. Written June 1829. As there are gaps in the copyist's version, I have also relied on Box 14, pp. 450–1.

APPENDIX B

1 Mss., UCL, Box 34, pp. 302–3. Written April 1824.

2 Ms. damaged. This part of the ms. is extremely difficult to read.

3 This word is undecipherable.

APPENDIX C

1 Mss., UCL, Box 14, pp. 392–3, and also pp. 432–3. Excerpted from Bentham's article on utilitarianism referred to earlier.

2 A sentence here is extremely difficult to read.

APPENDIX D

1 From *A Fragment on Government*, first published in 1776 and then in 1823. I have used the 1823 edition.

2 Blackstone.

3 I have omitted a few sentences that are largely polemical and autobiographical.

APPENDIX E

1 Mss., UCL, Box, 142, p. 200. Written in 1795.

2 The alternative formulation seems to read 'money, money'.

3 The alternative formulation reads: 'The happiness produced by the preceding causes is out of danger of a change'.